WEAPONS OF
WORLD WAR II

BY G. M. BARNES

Copyright © 2014 by Skyhorse Publishing

All rights reserved. No part of this book may be reproduced in any manner without the express written consent of the publisher, except in the case of brief excerpts in critical reviews or articles. All inquiries should be addressed to Skyhorse Publishing, 307 West 36th Street, 11th Floor, New York, NY 10018.

Skyhorse Publishing books may be purchased in bulk at special discounts for sales promotion, corporate gifts, fund-raising, or educational purposes. Special editions can also be created to specifications. For details, contact the Special Sales Department, Skyhorse Publishing, 307 West 36th Street, 11th Floor, New York, NY 10018 or info@skyhorsepublishing.com.

Skyhorse® and Skyhorse Publishing® are registered trademarks of Skyhorse Publishing, Inc.®, a Delaware corporation.

Visit our website at www.skyhorsepublishing.com.

10 9 8 7 6 5 4 3 2 1

Library of Congress Cataloging-in-Publication Data is available on file.

Cover design by Rose Storey
Cover photo credit Thinkstock

ISBN: 978-1-62914-394-1
Ebook ISBN: 978-1-63220-184-3
Printed in the United States

EDITOR'S NOTE

G. M. BARNES'
WEAPONS OF WORLD WAR II

by Dr. Jim Casada

The son of Frank and Selinda (LaCross) Barnes, Gladeon Marcus Barnes was born in Vermontville, Michigan, on June 15, 1887. After high school, Barnes enrolled in the engineering department at the University of Michigan. He graduated with high honors in 1910 and entered the Coast Artillery Corps, where he specialized in artillery and ordnance. After being made a lieutenant, Barnes was ordered to Sandy Hook, New Jersey, for duty as a proof officer, and from that point onward he progressed steadily through the ranks as an army career officer. Most of his professional life, from the time he was moved to Washington, D.C., at the level of captain, was devoted to research and development work with weaponry. Obviously, given the fact that he eventually rose to the rank of major general, he was a man of considerable ability and, as some of his achievements clearly show, towering intellect.

In 1939, a few years before America's entry into World War II, Barnes assumed the first of several top positions in the Office of the Chief of Ordnance, focusing particularly on research and development. The book being reprinted here is a direct offshoot of these efforts. Among the more noteworthy of his endeavors with the Ordnance Department was designing and developing the 60-ton Sherman tank with its 75-millimeter turret cannon. In 1951 Barnes would, at the request of the Office of the Chief of Ordnance's historical branch, write an overview history of Ordnance's activities during World War II, with particular emphasis on the tank. While apparently unpublished, this history is readily available on the Internet (http://worldoftanks .com/news/1812-chieftains-hatch-ordnance-dept-tank-development/). By the time of the completion of this report (June 12, 1951), Barnes was, as is indicated by his signing the document as "G. M. Barnes, Major General U.S.A. (Ret'd)," retired.

Another endeavor of surpassing importance in which Barnes was intimately involved was the ENIAC project at the University of Pennsylvania. ENIAC is the acronym for Electronic Numerical Integrator and Computer, a breakthrough in what Barnes described as "man's endless search for scientific truth." Barnes envisioned ENIAC as being a machine dedicated "to a career of scientific usefulness," although the "usefulness" he had in mind was work on equations connected with the development of a hydrogen bomb. For all his brilliance, not even Barnes would have grasped the fact that descendants of ENIAC would far transcend its original usage and limited thrust. Barnes also was instrumental in establishing White Sands, New Mexico, as a proving ground and the U.S. Army's missile testing range.

In the immediate post-war era, Barnes devoted considerable attention to researching and writing this book, his only major publication for public readership. The first edition, from the noted New York publisher D. Van Nostrand Company, appeared in 1947. This would apparently be the only edition during the author's lifetime, which is somewhat surprising given the interest in weaponry in the aftermath of World War II. Recently, however, Literary Licensing has offered print-on-demand reprints of the work. Perhaps because there was only the one edition with no contemporary republication, *Weapons of World War II* has become rather difficult to find. A nice copy of the book, with its green cloth still bright and the dust jacket intact, runs north of one hundred dollars in the out-of-print market.

Its contents are precisely what the title suggests; or, to use the characterization provided by Ray Riling in his *Guns and Shooting: A Bibliography,* the book is "an authentic account of small arms, machine guns, aircraft arms, etc., with illustrations and brief descriptions of each arm." Those descriptions and accompanying illustrations are the key to the book's value, for a reader can browse its pages and quickly determine whether a given gun was used in World War II, along with learning basic information about the weapon.

Evidently the final decade of Barnes' life was spent in relaxed retirement, because my researches found no indication of literary activity of any kind after 1951. Of course, it is quite possible he was involved in consulting, as one would expect of a man of his intellectual stature and accomplishments. Barnes died on November 15, 1961, and is buried in Arlington National Cemetery (Section 30, Grave 793).

This book, one that is all too often overlooked by military and weaponry historians, is of enduring value primarily from a reference standpoint. It belongs in the library of anyone keenly interested in World War II or the evolution of American weapons of war. As such it forms a logical and welcome addition to the Firearms Classics Library.

Jim Casada

ROCK HILL, SOUTH CAROLINA

WEAPONS

OF

WORLD WAR II

ORDNANCE-INDUSTRY TEAM IN ACTION

Left to right: Dr. Edgar C. Bain, Vice President, Carnegie Illinois Steel Corporation; Dr. F. B. Jewett, President, National Academy of Science; Dr. William D. Coolidge, Vice President, General Electric Company; Major General G. M. Barnes, United States Army; Mr. Rudolph Furrer, Vice President, A. O. Smith Corp.; Dr. F. Sperry (now deceased), Vice President, E. I. du Pont de Nemours & Co.; Mr. C. L. Bausch, Vice President Bausch & Lomb Optical Co.; Mr. Fred M. Zeder

WEAPONS
OF
WORLD WAR II

A Photographic Guide to Tanks, Howitzers, Submachine Guns,
and More Historic Ordnance

BY

G. M. BARNES

Major General, United States Army (Ret.)

Skyhorse Publishing

DEDICATED TO

THE OFFICERS AND ENGINEERS

OF THE

ORDNANCE DEPARTMENT, U. S. ARMY

PREFACE

The task of providing ultra-modern and effective weapons for our armies and the Allied Nations in the last war was of such vast scope that it is difficult adequately to discuss it in a short treatise of this character. Nevertheless, the Ordnance weapons used by our armies in World War II are displayed in this volume by means of developmental and action photographs, their characteristics are set forth, and the highlights of their development are discussed.

I have been careful to omit names of persons and companies making contributions to the success obtained, because to include them would require a separate volume. This work was done by the Science-Industry-Ordnance team working together to provide the best possible weapons and equipment for our armed forces. The team consisted of thousands of officers, scientists, engineers, industrialists, and workmen, all essential, all indispensable to the successful accomplishment of this mission. This book is intended as a tribute to those who through patriotism, sacrifice, and unselfish devotion to duty made possible these great accomplishments.

G. M. B.

Philadelphia, Pennsylvania,
January, 1947.

ACKNOWLEDGMENT

Acknowledgment is made, with appreciation, to the following officers and engineers of the Research and Development Service, Office of Chief of Ordnance, who have contributed so heavily to the successful development of ordnance materiel throughout World War II:

Colonel S. B. Ritchie, Deputy Chief.
Colonel I. A. Luke, Chief, Ammunition Development Division.
Colonel René R. Studler, Chief, Small Arms Development Division.
Colonel C. H. Morgan ⎫
Colonel W. R. Gerhardt ⎭ Chiefs, Artillery Development Division.
Colonel H. A. Quinn, Chief, Aircraft Armament Development Division.
Colonel G. W. Trichel, Chief, Rocket Development Division.
Major H. G. Jones, Jr., Rocket Development Division.
Colonel J. H. Frye ⎫
Colonel P. N. Gillon ⎭ Chiefs, Research and Materials Division.
Mr. Samuel Feltman, Chief, Ballistic Branch, Research and Materials Division.
Colonel J. M. Colby, Chief, Tank and Motor Transport Division.
Mr. W. F. Beasley, Chief, Tank and Motor Transport Liaison Branch.

CONTENTS

INTRODUCTION: THE ORDNANCE DEPARTMENT . . . 3
Purpose and Function 3
Peacetime Activities 3
Preparations for War 4
Organization 6
Ordnance Technical Committee 6
Cooperation with Industry 8
Ordnance Engineering Advisory Committees 8
Tank Committee 9
Small-Arms Weapon Committee 10
Ordnance Research Advisory Committees 10
The Gage Problem 12
Standardization Procedure 12

CHAPTER I: SMALL ARMS AND SMALL ARMS AMMUNITION . 15
U.S. Rifle, Caliber .30, M1 16
U.S. Rifle, Caliber .30, M1, with Grenade Launcher, M7 . . 20
U.S. Carbine, Caliber .30, M1A1 and M1A2 . . . 22
U.S. Rifle, Caliber .30, M1903A4 (Sniper's) . . . 25
Pistol, Automatic, Caliber .45, M1911A1 . . . 26
Browning Machine Gun, Caliber .30, M1919A6 . . . 27
Tree Mount, for Machine Gun, Caliber .30 . . . 28
Thompson Submachine Gun, Caliber .45, M1928A1 . . 29
Submachine Gun, Caliber .45, M3 30
Browning Automatic Rifle, Caliber .30, M1918A2 ("BAR") . 32
Browning Machine Gun, Caliber .30, M1917A1 . . . 33
Browning Machine Gun, Caliber .50, M2, Water-Cooled, Flexible 34
Browning Machine Gun, Heavy Barrel, Caliber .50, M2 . 35
Browning Machine Gun, Caliber .50, Ground Type . . 36
Browning Machine Gun, Aircraft, Caliber .50, M2 . . 38
Mount, A.A., Machine Gun, Caliber .50, M63 . . . 41
Small-Arms Ammunition 42
Launchers, Rocket, A.T., 2.36-inch, M9 ("Bazooka") . . 47
Recoilless Rifles, 57-mm and 75-mm 50
Body Armor 56

CHAPTER II: AIRCRAFT ARMAMENT 59
20-mm Automatic Gun, M3 (Aircraft Cannon) . . . 62
20-mm Feed Mechanism 64
Ammunition for 20-mm Automatic Guns 65
37-mm Automatic Gun, M4 (Aircraft Cannon) . . . 66
75-mm Gun, M4 (Aircraft Cannon) 68

CHAPTER III: AMMUNITION 71
   Explosives 73
   Propellants and Primers 76
   Flashless-Smokeless Developments in 76-mm Ammunition . . 78
   Flashless-Smokeless Developments in 3-inch and 90-mm
      Ammunition 79
   Flash Reducers 79
   Shaped Charges 81
   Artillery Fuzes 83
   V.T. (Variable Time) Fuzes 85
   High-Velocity Tungsten Carbide Core Armor-Piercing Ammunition 88
   Illuminating Projectiles 90
   Grenades 90
      Hand Grenades 91
      Rifle Grenades 92
   Mines, Antitank and Antipersonnel 93
   Mine Exploder 96
   Signal and Flare Ammunition 98
      Signals 100
      Flares 100
      Photoflash Munitions 100
      Target Identification Munitions 101
   Bombs 102
      Cluster Adapters 105
      Parachute Bombs 106
      Antiricochet Attachments for General-Purpose Bombs . . 107
      Semi-Armor-Piercing Bombs 108
      Chemical Bombs 108
      Bomb Fuzes 108

CHAPTER IV: ARTILLERY 111
   Mobile Artillery 113
   Light Artillery 114
      75-mm Pack Howitzer and Carriages 114
      105-mm Howitzer, M2A1, and Carriage, M2 . . . 118
      105-mm Howitzer, M3, and Carriage, M3A1 . . . 120
      37-mm Antitank Gun, M3A1 122
      3-inch Antitank Gun, M5, and Carriage, M6 . . . 123
   Medium Artillery 124
      155-mm Howitzer, M1 124
      4.5-inch Gun, M1 125
   Heavy Artillery 128
      155-mm Gun, M1A1, and Carriage, M1 128
      8-inch Howitzer, M1, and Carriage, M1 132
      8-inch Gun, M1, and Carriage, M2 134
      240-mm Howitzer, M1 136
   Artillery Fire Control 139

Antiaircraft Weapons 140
   37-mm Gun, M1A2, and Carriage, M3A1 140
   Caliber .50 A.A. Machine Gun 142
   Multiple Caliber .50 Machine Gun Mount, M45 . . . 143
   Twin 40-mm Gun Motor Carriage, M19 144
   40-mm Automatic A.A. Gun, M1 (Bofors) 146
   3-inch Gun, M3 (A.A.), Mount, M2A2 148
   90-mm Guns, M1 and M1A1 (A.A.), Mount, M1A1 . . 150
   120-mm Gun, M1, and Mount, M1 154
   Antiaircraft Artillery Fire Control 155
   Results of Antiaircraft Fire 158
Mortars and Ammunition 159
   60-mm Mortar, M19 160
   81-mm Mortar, M1 164
   105-mm Mortar, T13, and Mount, T12 168
   155-mm Mortar, T25 170
   914-mm Mortar (Little David) 172

CHAPTER V: ROCKETS AND LAUNCHERS 175
   Rocket, H.E.A.T., 2.36-inch, M6A3 178
   Rocket, Target, 3.25-inch, M2 180
   Rocket, H.E., 4.5-inch 182
   Launcher, Rocket, Multiple 7.2-inch 192
   Rocket Propulsion Units 194

CHAPTER VI: TANKS, GUN MOTOR CARRIAGES, AND
           MOTOR TRANSPORT 197
Medium Tank, M3 (General Grant) 200
Medium Tank, M4 (General Sherman) 203
Heavy Tank, M6 210
Heavy Tank, M26 (General Pershing) 214
Light Tank, M3 219
Light Tank, M5 222
Light Tank, M24 225
Light Tanks 228
Tank Guns 231
Swimming Devices, Tank 232
Gun Motor Carriages, Self-Propelled 234
   105-mm Howitzer Motor Carriage, M7 . . . 234
   3-inch Gun Motor Carriage, M10 238
   90-mm Gun Motor Carriage, M36 240
   76-mm Gun Motor Carriage, M18 244
   155-mm Gun Motor Carriage, M12 248
   Cargo Carrier, M30 250
   Heavy Gun Motor Carriages 252
      155-mm Gun Motor Carriage, M40 253
      240-mm Howitzer Motor Carriage, T92 . . . 255
      8-inch Gun Motor Carriage, T93 256

Army Transport Vehicles 258
   Truck, 1/4-ton, 4 x 4 (Jeep) 258
   Truck, 1 1/2-ton, 6 x 6, Cargo-Personnel 261
   Truck, 2 1/2-ton, 6 x 6, LWB, Cargo 262
   Truck, 2 1/2-ton, 6 x 6 (4DT) 263
   Tractor Truck, M26 267
   Semitrailer, M15 269
   Tank Transporters 269
   18-ton High-Speed Tractor, M4 271
   13-ton High-Speed Tractor, M5 275
   38-ton High-Speed Tractor, M6 278
   Truck, 1/4-ton, 4 x 4, Amphibian 282
   Truck, Amphibian, 2 1/2-ton, 6 x 6 (DUKW) 284
   Armored Car, M8 286
   Cargo Carrier, M29C 288

CHAPTER VII: RESEARCH AND MATERIALS 291
Materials 293
Specifications and Standards 293
Development of New and Improved Materials and Processes . . 294
Fuels and Lubricants 295
Technical Intelligence 297
Ballistics 299
Bombing and Firing Tables 299
ENIAC (Electronic Computing Device) 300
Supersonic Wind Tunnel 301
Aerodynamic Spark Range 302
Ballistic Service Teams 303
Blast Measurement and Penetration Determinations . . . 304
Ballistic Camera 304
Flash X-Ray Apparatus 304

CHAPTER VIII: CONCLUSION 307
Accomplishments 310
Postwar Plans 310

INDEX 313

Introduction

THE ORDNANCE DEPARTMENT

Introduction

THE ORDNANCE DEPARTMENT

Purpose and Function

The purpose of the Ordnance Department in this war was to equip our armies with fighting weapons. As it turned out, the Department furnished not only the fighting equipment for the American army but also a considerable part of the effective weapons used by the British, Russian, French, Chinese, and other Allied armies. While the Army Air Forces provided the airplanes, the Ordnance Department developed and supplied the weapons, bombs, and other types of armament used by both the Army and Navy Air Forces. Ordnance procurement in this war accounted for approximately forty-one cents out of every dollar spent by the Army for supplies and equipment.

The broad scope of Ordnance responsibilities is defined by the National Defense Act of 3 June 1916, by other statutes, and by Army Regulations No. 45-5. The responsibilities of the Chief of Ordnance * so defined include the design, development, procurement, storage, issue, and maintenance of all ordnance equipment required by the Army. In addition, by mutual arrangement, it equips the Marine Corps with its fighting weapons and provides many items used by the Navy.

Ordnance equipment includes all the weapons of the soldier—his grenades, rifles, carbines, machine guns, mortars, and their ammunition; artillery, from the small, 37-mm antitank gun, through the division, corps, army, and G.H.Q. artillery, including the 240-mm howitzer and ap-

* The Ordnance Department was established 14 May 1812.

proximately 150 different types of ammunition for these weapons. It embraces antiaircraft artillery from the 37-mm to the 120-mm "stratosphere" gun, and ammunition; it also includes directors, height finders, electric transmission systems, and electronic power control for the guns. It covers aircraft armament, including machine guns, automatic cannon, and their ammunition. It includes all types of bombs, except armor-piercing bombs, from the 4-pound fragmentation to the 45,000-pound demolition bomb, and the various types of bomb fuzes.

Ordnance equipment also comprises armored fighting vehicles—tanks, tank destroyers, armored cars, scout cars, personnel carriers; and motor transport for the Army, including the many types and sizes of trucks. And so on— through a list of approximately 1,800 major items and more than 600,00 principal components.

Peacetime Activities

During the years of peace between the First and Second World Wars, the officers, scientists, and engineers of the Department worked continuously on the development and perfection of new types of weapons and ammunition. This effort included the sending of selected Ordnance officers abroad to study foreign developments, to insure that the weapons being developed in this country were not lagging behind those of Germany, France, Italy, England, and other foreign countries.

Between 1921 and 1937 the Department was greatly handicapped by the meagerness of its annual appropriations. While the total appropriations for the Army were around 350 million dollars a year, the average annual Ordnance appropriation during that period was only 11 million dollars. This money had to cover the operation of the whole Department, including its six major manufacturing arsenals and Aberdeen Proving Ground. It was, therefore, impossible to produce weapons in quantity for the Army. Fortunately, however, as large parts as possible of these limited funds were spent in building new models of improved weapons, so that the Department would be able to go into immediate production in the event of a war emergency. The average annual sum allotted to research and development of these improved weapons was less than one million dollars.

At the beginning of the emergency, Ordnance had fewer than 350 officers with the necessary knowledge regarding design, development, production, storage, and issue of ordnance materiel, a number obviously inadequate for the task ahead. It is self-evident that if this small group of Ordnance officers and engineers, trained during the years of peace, had not been available in 1940, the War Department would have been in a distinctly critical situation.

During the period between wars, the Ordnance Department had been carrying out its plans for the industrial mobilization of the country. For procurement purposes the United States was divided into thirteen Ordnance Districts. One Regular officer, with a small office force, had been sent to each District and had surveyed the industries within its geographical limits. Plants were visited, and the various types of weapons which each manufacturer would be asked to produce were discussed with the management. Tentative war orders were placed with the plants—to become effective if and when an emergency arose. It is interesting to note here that some 85 per cent of the manufacturers so met accepted Ordnance war contracts.

Preparations for War

As war clouds began to gather, Congress increased the appropriation of the Ordnance Department for the fiscal year 1938 to 24 million dollars, and for the fiscal year 1939 to 112 million. These appropriations gave the Department its chance to accelerate its work and to revise and complete the drawings of equipment and to put them in the best possible condition for issue to manufacturers. Work was intensified on the development of important weapons, such as the 105-mm howitzer. Every effort was exerted to complete designs and proving-ground tests, and to urge the combat services to finish their Service Board tests so that the items might be standardized* and made ready for manufacture in case of war.

In September 1940 the first large war appropriation became available for expenditure. Of this money, the Ordnance Department received what was then considered to be the startling amount of one and a quarter billion dollars, for the manufacture of equipment. The plans for industrial mobilization had been so effectively worked out that within six weeks nearly all of this money had been obligated to manufacturers.

Throughout the years of peace, the Ordnance Department had repeatedly asked Congress to provide money for educational orders: that is, orders for complicated types of ordnance to be placed with selected manufacturers so that they might learn how such equipment could be produced. Small appropriations were obtained, and a number of important educational orders were placed for such items as gun recuperators, recoil mechanisms, and shell forgings. The firms, which had undertaken these educational orders had a considerable head start—which proved to be an important factor in the early delivery of certain vital types of ordnance equipment.

The Department's policy, from the beginning of the emergency, was to undertake a broad and vigorous program of research and development in all fields of ordnance equipment, to insure that our materiel would always be ahead of that of our enemies. The Department did not rest with the equipment which it had put into manufacture in the fall of 1940, but realized that these were merely initial orders and that, throughout the coming war, there would be accelerated de-

* "Standardization"—a military term meaning officially accepted and approved as a standard-type weapon by the War Department. See Standardization Procedure.

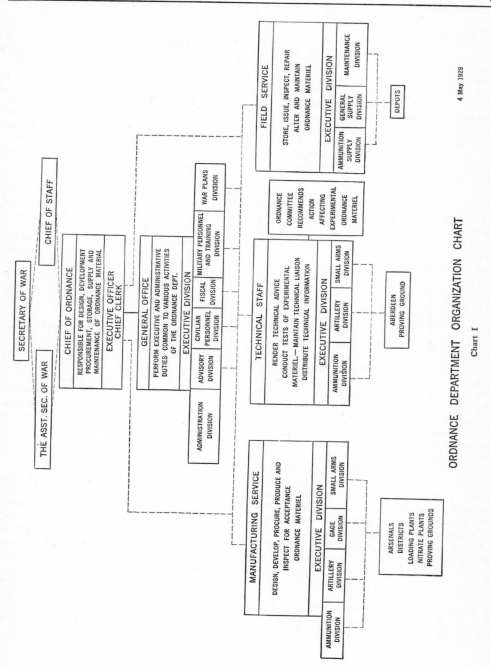

ORDNANCE DEPARTMENT ORGANIZATION CHART

Chart I

4 May 1929

velopments of all types of equipment. It fully realized that when millions of men used their weapons daily and when their lives depended upon the efficacy of those weapons, there would be constant and pressing demands for improved equipment.

It is a common belief that troops in the field develop new tactics which call for the use of new weapons. Actually, the reverse is true. Development of each new weapon requires new methods for the use of the weapon—the methods being TACTICS. The Ordnance Department, therefore, took the OFFENSIVE in this developmental work and did not wait for our troops on the battlefield to feel the need for new weapons. It turned vigorously to the task of conceiving new weapons; for even after a new item was satisfactorily tested and accepted by the using service, it would take at least a year to put it into the hands of troops in the field.

Organization

The organization of the Ordnance Department as of 1938 is shown in Chart I, dated 4 May 1929. In 1939, in anticipation of the huge task of research and development made necessary by the war program, the organization was changed to provide the Office of Research and Engineering. Under this reorganization the Office of Assistant Chief, Industrial Service for Research and Engineering, was created and was charged with research and engineering activities for the Department. The Technical Staff continued to exist, as an advisory group.

On 29 July 1941 the duties of the Chief of Research and Engineering were augmented so that they absorbed the Technical Staff. This change integrated the position of the Assistant Chief of Industrial Service for Research and Engineering, and made the office completely responsible for research, development, and engineering activities pertaining to the Office, Chief of Ordnance.

On 1 June 1942, upon the retirement of Major General C. M. Wesson as Chief of Ordnance, Major General (later Lieutenant General) Levin H. Campbell, Jr., was appointed Chief. On 26 June 1942 the Office of the Chief of Research

and Engineering was abolished and the Technical Division was established as an independent operating division, with authority to make contracts and to control all research and development funds. The Chief of the Technical Division was also made chairman of the Ordnance Technical Committee. The engineering responsibilities were taken over by the Industrial Division. This change constituted a great improvement in organization, since it placed research and development on a parallel with production, and permitted the necessary freedom of action.

Thus, in June 1942, for the first time in the history of the Department, research and development were recognized separately in the Ordnance organization, with authority to drive ahead at full speed on improving standard weapons and developing new ones. The results which have been achieved since the reorganization have demonstrated the soundness of this new plan of operation. A record number of projects was undertaken, and unusually large numbers of items were successfully developed and placed in production.

Since June 1942 there has been no further change except to replace the title of Technical Division with that of Research and Development Service, 1 July 1944 (see Chart II). The present organization of the Office, Chief of Ordnance, consists of four main services: Research and Development Service, Industrial Service, Field Service, and Military Plans and Training Service.

Ordnance Technical Committee

The Ordnance Technical Committee, organized in March 1919 by Major General C. C. Williams, then Chief of Ordnance, played an important part in this war. The purpose of the Committee was to provide a forum where research and development projects to be undertaken could be discussed, military characteristics be determined, and the action be approved jointly by Ordnance and by all of the technical services of the Army, Navy, and Marine Corps.

The Ordnance Technical Committee serves as an advisory body to the Chief of Ordnance, who appoints an Ordnance officer as chairman. It has

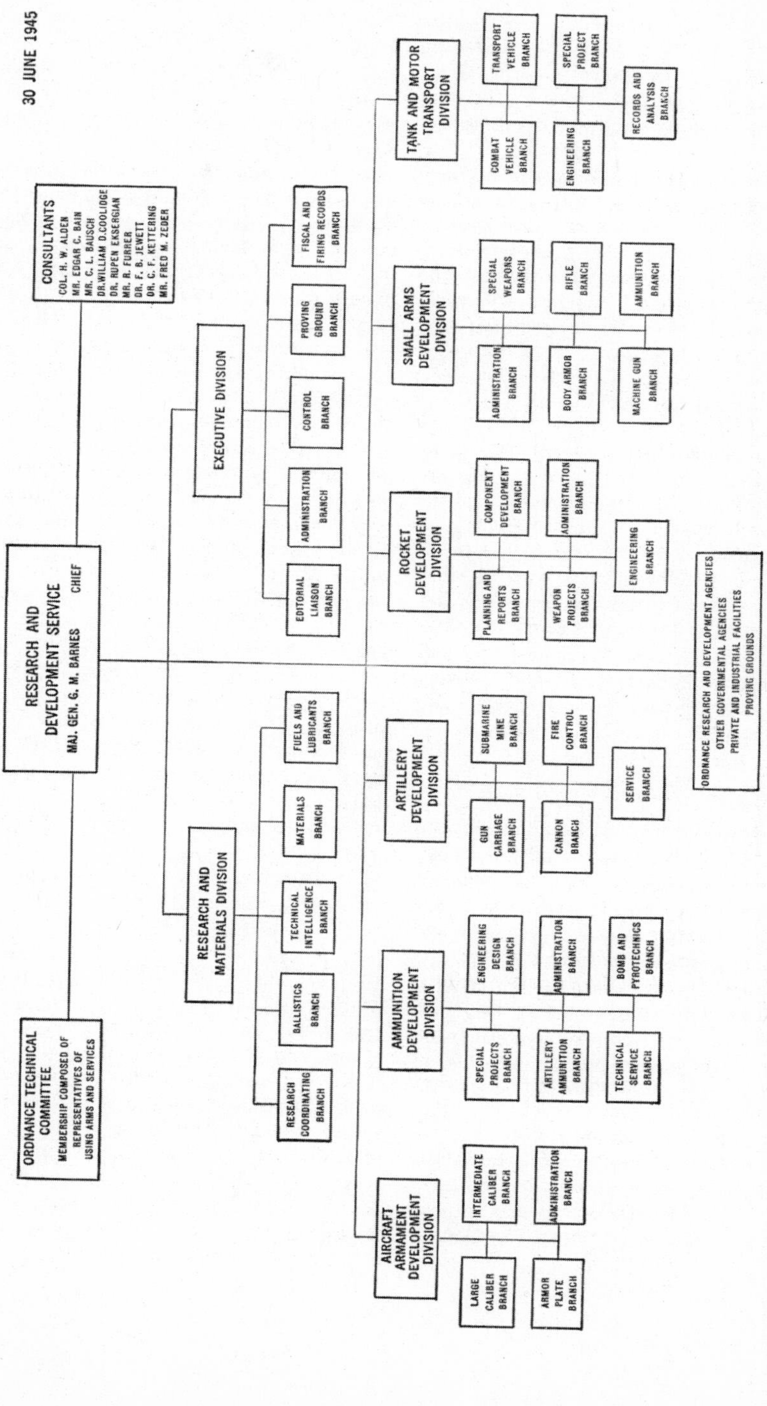
30 JUNE 1945
RESEARCH AND DEVELOPMENT SERVICE
MAJ. GEN. G. M. BARNES CHIEF
CONSULTANTS
COL. H. W. ALDEN
MR. EDGAR C. BAIN
MR. C. L. BAUSCH
DR. WILLIAM D. COOLIDGE
DR. RUPEN EKSERGIAN
MR. R. FURRER
DR. F. B. JEWETT
DR. C. F. KETTERING
MR. FRED M. ZEDER
ORDNANCE TECHNICAL COMMITTEE
MEMBERSHIP COMPOSED OF REPRESENTATIVES OF USING ARMS AND SERVICES
EXECUTIVE DIVISION
FISCAL AND FIRING RECORDS BRANCH
PROVING GROUND BRANCH
CONTROL BRANCH
ADMINISTRATION BRANCH
EDITORIAL LIAISON BRANCH
RESEARCH AND MATERIALS DIVISION
FUELS AND LUBRICANTS BRANCH
MATERIALS BRANCH
TECHNICAL INTELLIGENCE BRANCH
BALLISTICS BRANCH
RESEARCH COORDINATING BRANCH
TANK AND MOTOR TRANSPORT DIVISION
TRANSPORT VEHICLE BRANCH
SPECIAL PROJECT BRANCH
RECORDS AND ANALYSIS BRANCH
COMBAT VEHICLE BRANCH
ENGINEERING BRANCH
SMALL ARMS DEVELOPMENT DIVISION
SPECIAL WEAPONS BRANCH
RIFLE BRANCH
AMMUNITION BRANCH
ADMINISTRATION BRANCH
BODY ARMOR BRANCH
MACHINE GUN BRANCH
ROCKET DEVELOPMENT DIVISION
COMPONENT DEVELOPMENT BRANCH
ADMINISTRATION BRANCH
ENGINEERING BRANCH
PLANNING AND REPORTS BRANCH
WEAPON PROJECTS BRANCH
ORDNANCE RESEARCH AND DEVELOPMENT AGENCIES
OTHER GOVERNMENTAL AGENCIES
PRIVATE AND INDUSTRIAL FACILITIES
PROVING GROUNDS
ARTILLERY DEVELOPMENT DIVISION
SUBMARINE MINE BRANCH
FIRE CONTROL BRANCH
SERVICE BRANCH
GUN CARRIAGE BRANCH
CANNON BRANCH
AMMUNITION DEVELOPMENT DIVISION
ENGINEERING DESIGN BRANCH
ADMINISTRATION BRANCH
BOMB AND PYROTECHNICS BRANCH
SPECIAL PROJECTS BRANCH
ARTILLERY AMMUNITION BRANCH
TECHNICAL SERVICE BRANCH
AIRCRAFT ARMAMENT DEVELOPMENT DIVISION
INTERMEDIATE CALIBER BRANCH
ADMINISTRATION BRANCH
LARGE CALIBER BRANCH
ARMOR PLATE BRANCH

Chart II

been in continuous operation since its establishment and proved to be an important means of coordination between Ordnance and the using services throughout the war. Every important project undertaken in research and development was processed through this committee. The committee minutes (O.C.M.'s) were concurred in by those members who were concerned in a particular development; and these minutes, after approval by the committee chairman, were sent to higher authority and became directives approved by the War Department. In this way, all the services concerned in the development of a new ordnance item were given the opportunity to participate and to assure themselves that their special or peculiar needs would be met.

For example, if the Department initiates the design of a new tank which may weigh 60 or 70 tons, the Corps of Engineers knows of this development through the Ordnance Committee Minutes, which a representative of the Chief of Engineers must sign. In this way the Chief of Engineers is kept fully informed as to what bridge developments may be required to permit the proper use of this tank in the field. The Ordnance Committee Minutes form an important permanent record of the research and development projects carried out by the Ordnance Department since 1919.

Cooperation with Industry

No sooner had the Office of Research and Engineering been formed in 1939 than it was realized that it would no longer be practicable for the Department to continue its peacetime policy of conducting the major part of its research and development programs in its own establishments and with its own personnel. The Department immediately decided to form a partnership with American industry so as to utilize the vast reservoir of civilian engineers and laboratory facilities to work jointly with the Ordnance Department on its many projects.

Most manufacturers had had no previous experience in the production of munitions. It was obvious that they would encounter difficulties and would raise many questions concerning ordnance drawings and specifications. The Department therefore threw the manufacturing arsenals open to American manufacturers.

Each of the arsenals was skilled in the manufacture of certain classes of ordnance equipment. For example, information on small-arms ammunition manufacture, on shell production, and on the design and manufacture of fire-control equipment and mechanical time fuzes was centered at Frankford Arsenal. The Ordnance Department's non-ferrous metals laboratory was also at Frankford. Picatinny Arsenal had specialized in the manufacture and development of fuzes, pyrotechnics, and propellants. Rock Island Arsenal was concerned with the manufacture of tanks, mobile gun carriages, gun recuperators, and equilibrators. Watertown Arsenal had specialized in the manufacture of antiaircraft artillery, heavy artillery, and the centrifugal casting of gun tubes. Watertown also had the Ordnance Department's ferrous metals laboratory, which had pioneered development of armor and armor-piercing projectiles. Watervliet Arsenal was skilled in the finishing of guns and in the design and manufacture of breech rings and breech blocks. Springfield Armory was the center of small-arms information.

Manufacturers in great numbers visited the arsenals and were given all available data and information. In this way, Ordnance passed on its accumulated know-how to industry. Department policy was not to influence a producer to manufacture according to Ordnance methods, but rather to show him how the Department had produced these items in the past and to let him use his judgment, skill, and ingenuity in setting up his own manufacturing processes.

Ordnance Engineering Advisory Committees

It was to be expected that with the hundreds of items to be produced and hundreds of thousands of drawings issued to manufacturers, many questions would arise concerning metal specifications, tolerances, methods of manufacture, and reasons for making component parts according to certain designs or specifications. In order to provide an organization for the systematic transfer of technical information to manufacturers, and to provide a forum where engineering difficulties could be discussed, the Ordnance Engineering Advisory Committees were organized in the fall of 1940.

All manufacturers with Ordnance contracts were asked to designate one or more engineers from each company who would serve as their representatives and meet with qualified Ordnance officers and engineers to discuss difficulties encountered. It was found that the field of ordnance equipment could be broadly covered through the organization of the following 29 Engineering Advisory Committees:

Tank Committee
Half Track Vehicle Committee
Mobile Artillery Carriage Committee
Antiaircraft Carriage Committee
Automatic Cannon Committee
Fire Control Committee
Gun Machining Committee
Gun Forging Committee
Rifled-Bore Shell Committee
Smooth-Bore Shell Committee
Bar Stock Shell Committee
Small Caliber Armor-Piercing Shot Committee
Large Caliber Armor-Piercing Shot Committee
Demolition Bomb Body Committee
Pyrotechnics Committee
Bomb Fuze Committee
Cartridge Case Committee
20-mm Cartridge Case Committee
Artillery Fuze Committee
Adapter and Booster Committee
Primer and Detonator Committee
Loading and Assembly Committee
Mechanical Time Fuze Committee
Chemical and Practice Bomb Committee
Fragmentation Bomb Body Committee
Small-Arms Weapons Committee
Metallic Belt Link Committee
Small-Arms Equipment Committee
Small-Arms Ammunition Committee

Industry's response to the Ordnance invitation to send representatives to the meetings held in Washington, and at various arsenals and other places throughout the country, was spontaneous and complete. At the first meeting of each committee, the manufacturers' representatives voted unanimously in favor of having the committees formed on a permanent basis. The members then selected a chairman, and an Ordnance officer was designated as permanent secretary to conduct correspondence and to write and distribute the minutes of each meeting. The action taken at each meeting was recorded and the minutes were distributed to all members.

A résumé of the activities of one or two of the committees will indicate the value of the results achieved.

Tank Committee

The Tank Committee was especially active, because before putting the medium tank into quantity production the Department had to incorporate important changes found necessary by battle experiences in Europe. Armor thickness was increased, and a 75-mm gun was mounted. Tank manufacturers actively assisted in this redesigning, sending draftsmen and engineers to work cooperatively with Ordnance engineers. At each meeting of the committee, changes recommended by the members were discussed, and many of these suggestions were incorporated in the design. Ordnance drawings were sent out progressively as the work of redesign went forward. Ordinarily, manufacturers would have had to wait until all drawings were received before undertaking production. The use of the committee method thus saved several months' production time. At the same time, the manufacturers' suggestions and criticisms had been obtained almost daily and were put into effect before tooling and quantity production.

Another important feature of the committee's work was the coordination it achieved among manufacturers. Occasionally, when one manufacturer suggested a design change which would be beneficial to him, another manufacturer would be completely opposed to such a change. The committee thereupon debated such questions and made the best compromises to meet the general situation. Often a problem which presented itself to one manufacturer had already been solved by another, and all the manufacturers were able to benefit by this exchange of ideas.

Still another important result of the committee meetings was the exchange of information concerning sources of material. Subcommittees were established to aid in the procurement of special parts, especially those used in rather small quantities. The requirements of each manufacturer were not always sufficient to justify special tooling, but, by combining their limited needs for such items, they were able to order quantities large enough to prove of interest to reputable sources of supply.

Later, gage subcommittees were organized to coordinate the various manufacturers in regard to inspection difficulties.

Small-Arms Weapon Committee

The Small-Arms Weapon Committee, by solving such important problems as those concerning steel specifications, finishing of parts, and broaching of rifle barrels, greatly benefited both industry and the Ordnance Department. Perhaps Ordnance gained most, because it received the benefit of the advisory services of the principal engineers in each field of industry. In this manner, all designs and engineering principles of ordnance materiel were reviewed by many of the nation's best engineers. Industry was aided by increased understanding of service requirements for parts and equipment and of the reasons behind certain designs and manufacturing instructions. In committee meetings, Ordnance was able to point out military requirements which governed designs. Suggestions for design changes greatly facilitated production.

Later in the war, after production had started, the Ordnance Engineering Advisory Committees were reorganized as "Integration Committees" to handle production problems.

Ordnance Research Advisory Committees

In addition to the Engineering Advisory Committees, Research Advisory Committees, some of which had existed for a number of years, were enlarged and strengthened. These committees included the following:

Ferrous Metallurgical Advisory Board
  Subcommittee on Cast Armor
  Subcommittee on Rolled Armor
  Subcommittee on Welding of Armor
  Subcommittee on Helmet Steel
  Subcommittee on Body Armor
  Subcommittee on Aircraft Armor
  Subcommittee on Armor-Piercing Projectiles
    and Bullet Core Steel
  Subcommittee on Gun Forgings
Non-Ferrous Metallurgical Advisory Board
Scientific Advisory Committee of the Ballistic
    Research Laboratory
S.A.E. War Engineering Board
S.A.E. Ordnance Advisory Committee
  Subcommittee on Air Cleaners
  Subcommittee on Power Plants
  Subcommittee on Transmission Systems
  Subcommittee on Tracks and Suspensions
  Subcommittee on Rubber Products
Coordinating Research Council for Fuels and
    Lubricants
Committee on Corrosion
Committee on Paints, Varnishes, and Related
    Products
Committee on Petroleum Products and Lubricants
Ordnance Welding Committee

An illustration of the way in which these research groups functioned to assist the Ordnance Department is indicated by the subcommittees organized under the Ferrous Metallurgical Advisory Board. These subcommittees, covering critical categories in the Ordnance munitions programs, as indicated by their titles, included more than 200 individual companies and represented approximately 85 per cent of the total industrial steel capacity of the United States. The groups met frequently, especially during the early months of the emergency, to act promptly and effectively on research programs, on urgently needed production capacities, on specifications, on improvement of processes, and on the conservation of critical alloys.

By means of these committees and subcommittees, the best scientific and industrial talents and facilities were brought to bear in an integrated program on urgent Ordnance problems.

In 1940 the President established the National Defense Research Committee (N.D.R.C.), under the chairmanship of Dr. Vannevar Bush. This committee acted to mobilize further the scientific talent of the country, especially that more or less "latent" in educational institutions. It was later reorganized to become the Office of Scientific Research and Development (O.S. R.D.). The two main divisions of this organization were the National Defense Research Committee and the Committee on Medical Research.

A number of divisions and panels of N.D. R.C. assisted in carrying out Ordnance projects. Typical were the activities of the War Metallurgy Division, which worked closely with Ordnance in the solution of critical metallurgical problems. More than 200 Ordnance projects were sponsored with the N.D.R.C., of which approximately one-half had been completed by V-J-Day. Notable among these were the projects on VT fuzes and rockets.

In addition to these, there were many other groups organized by engineering and technical societies, as well as by the Ordnance Department, too numerous to mention here, which likewise rendered outstanding services in the war effort.

In all Ordnance development work the initiative remained in the Research and Development Service in Washington, where projects were conceived and general characteristics of weapons determined. These weapon projects were processed through the Ordnance Technical Committee to insure that they were the sort of things desired by the using services. Development contracts were then placed throughout the country with universities, laboratories, and manufacturing organizations for the development of materiel of these general designs. The results were far beyond expectations. Toward the end of the war, it was estimated that the Ordnance Department was at least a year ahead of the demands of the using services for most types of equipment.

It often occurred, when new equipment was devised, that no battlefield need could be seen at the time of its origin. In such instances, production orders were withheld until demands arose. This practice frequently brought about delays of a year or more in getting the equipment into the hands of the troops.

During the last two years of the war, however, a new system was introduced, whereby a limited number of a new ordnance item would be made: for example, the 75-mm recoilless rifle. This limited number would then be flown overseas, or shipped under special priorities, and given to selected troops for trial in battle. If they were found to be successful, large-scale production would then immediately be undertaken.

Some important types of new equipment, such as a new armor-piercing ammunition, were flown to theaters of operation with demonstration teams. Requisitions received from the theaters as a result of these demonstrations became the basis for mass-production orders.

The rate of production of new ordnance equipment toward the end of the war was so rapid that during the last three years of the war more than 1,000 new items were developed and brought into production. The rate was approximately 25 per month. Hundreds of thousands of draftsmen and engineers throughout the nation took part in this great plan of research and development conducted by the Department, and though the total number of draftsmen and engineers employed is unknown, Ordnance contracts involved more than 1,500 companies and thousands of subcontractors.

The development of the 240-mm howitzer is a good example of how the Ordnance-Industry team functioned. In 1940, development was begun on the now-famous 240-mm howitzer and carriage. General layouts were made in the Office, Chief of Ordnance. The design of the carriage for this huge howitzer was a difficult and complicated matter, involving the use of a large engineering staff. Consequently, an Ordnance development contract was placed with a capable company in the Middle West. A few Ordnance engineers with experience in gun-carriage design were sent with tentative layouts to work with the company engineers. After the design had been formulated, a wooden model was constructed and inspected by the Chief of Research and Development and his staff and by representatives of the Army Ground Forces. Upon approval of this design, the pilot carriage was placed under manufacture. The howitzer was shipped from Watervliet Arsenal and the fire control from Frankford Arsenal. The completed unit was then brought overland on its own wheels from the Middle West to the Proving Ground, where it was successfully fired. The ammunition was developed in a similar manner. The howitzer carriage was later tested by the Field Artillery Board and found to be satisfactory after minor modifications, and the item was then put into production. The 240-mm's great firepower was first used in battle in Italy and was of major importance in the successful drive into Germany. In a similar manner, hundreds of other ordnance items were developed and put into production during the war.

The Gage Problem

During the First World War, one of the greatest handicaps under which the Department labored in the production of equipment was the lack of proper gages. In the summer of 1938, therefore, a concerted effort was made to design gages for all items which would go into production when and if an emergency arose. Gages on hand at arsenals were brought up to date, and new gages were obtained for standard items. By renovating and modernizing gages on hand, it was possible to meet the early demands.

Between 1930 and 1939, the Ordnance Department had created 9 district gage laboratories at certain universities to train personnel in the use and surveillance of gages. In addition to these, the Department established complete laboratories at six manufacturing arsenals. Today there are 32 gage laboratories, together with several sublaboratories.

The emergency munitions programs issued in July 1940 indicated that the need for inspection gages would far surpass that included in any previous planning, on account of the excess load imposed by the aircraft, antiaircraft, tank, and ammunition programs, as well as by the British requirements, later superimposed. To meet these demands, estimates of the first wave of

gage requirments were met by analyzing the early programs and ordering gages to meet these needs before the appropriation of funds for component production.

Early in August 1940, a survey showed that the normal peacetime capacity of the gage-manufacturing industry would be inadequate to meet the requirements of the projected munitions program. After careful consideration, it was decided to expand seven of the outstanding commercial producers of gages. The Government gave Ordnance full responsibility to provide for capacity for all gages which would be required by the Navy, Army, Air Forces, and Allied nations.

Between August 1940 and June 1941, the gage industry was so greatly expanded that the annual procurement of Ordnance inspection gages rose from 50 thousand dollars to 30 million dollars. This expansion had been based on the general Ordnance procurement policy of centralized control in Washington with decentralized operation in the arsenals and procurement districts.

As a result of this planning and expansion, no serious delay in the production program was caused by gage shortages. The Navy and the Air Forces were, in turn, saved from serious production delays by this early and rapid expansion of the gage industry.

Standardization Procedure

Standardization, in the military sense, authorizes procurement from industry, determines quantities by providing for a basis of issue, and starts training and tactical agencies to work in planning for the use of the new equipment. The procedure for standardizing a new item of ordnance is outlined below.

The first step in standardization of an item after development by the Ordnance Department is its acceptance by the Service Boards of the appropriate branch of the Ground or Air Forces. This acceptance is then carefully reviewed by the top command of the using service in Washington—that is, headquarters of the Army Ground Forces or Army Air Forces. Headquarters, in addition to passing upon the acceptance of the new type of equipment by the Service Boards, determines the basis of issue which, when multiplied by the troop basis (or, in the case of theater stock-pile items, on the basis of anticipated theater requirements), determines the number to be procured.

These decisions are then transmitted to the Ordnance Technical Committee. The Committee then determines the many ramifications involved in standardization—that is, availability of material, and maintenance and spare-parts problems, Ordnance training, and general adaptability to American industry. (These factors were, of course, considered during the development stage by the Research and Development Service.) After these determinations are made and a number of other routine matters are considered, the final standardization papers are prepared in the form of an Ordnance Committee Minute (O.C.M.) which, when approved by formal action of the Committee and of higher authority, becomes the basis for production, storage, issue, maintenance, and field use.

By means of the Ordnance Technical Committee, complete agreement is reached between the designer and the user of a new piece of equipment before it is standardized. The "O.C.M." procedure through which an item must pass before it is standardized greatly minimizes the possibility of faulty design or of the item's failing to meet military requirements.

Once a weapon is standardized by the Ordnance Technical Committee and approved by higher authority, it is placed on the Army Supply Program and quantity production begins. The weapon is listed in tables of equipment; operation and maintenance manuals are published; and it becomes an accepted part of troop equipment. Occasionally standardization is a lengthy process, but its thoroughness assures that the Army will receive the very best weapon which can be designed.

Chapter I

SMALL ARMS AND SMALL ARMS AMMUNITION

Chapter I

SMALL ARMS

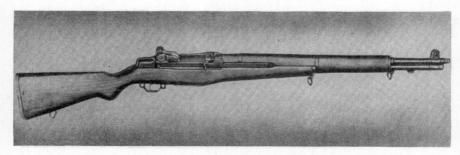

U. S. Rifle, Caliber .30, M1—Right Side.

U. S. RIFLE, CALIBER .30, M1

CHARACTERISTICS

Weight	9.5 lb. (with Bayonet, M1905: 10.5 lb.)
Length	43.6 in.
Length of barrel	24 in.
Length of rifling	21.30 in., 70.8 cals.
Rifling	
Number of grooves	4
R.H. twist, 1 turn in	33.3 cals., 10 in.
Depth of grooves	0.0040 in.
Type of mechanism	Gas-operated, semiautomatic
Feeding device	Clip
Capacity of feeding device	8 rds.
Rate of fire	Semiautomatic
Cooling	Air
Sight radius	27.9 in. at 100 yd. range
Trigger pull	7.5 lb. max., 4.5 lb. min.
Normal pressure	48,000 lb./sq. in. (copper)
Ammunition types	Ball, A.P., tracer

SMALL ARMS

The United States for many years has led all other countries in the development and manufacture of small arms, especially automatic weapons.

At the beginning of World War I, our troops were armed with the caliber .30 rifle, M1903, and its modifications. Popularly known as the Springfield rifle, it had the world-wide reputation of being one of the best rifles in existence, if indeed not the very best.

Soon after the 1918 Armistice, the Ordnance Department started working on a semiautomatic shoulder rifle to replace the Springfield. During the next twenty years, semiautomatic rifles developed in all countries were tested. Mr. John C. Garand, later employed at the Springfield Armory of the Ordnance Department, was working independently on his ideas for such a rifle. His ideas were combined with those which had been worked out at Springfield during this period. The result was the now famous semiautomatic shoulder rifle, M1, known as the Garand rifle.

In 1939, when the Ordnance Department received additional, funds for completing the development of new weapons then pending, the Department accelerated work on this rifle and made plans for its mass production. The rifle had been thoroughly tested by the Infantry Board and received its approval. At this time there were several competing semiautomatic shoulder rifles, some of which showed considerable promise. The proponents of these competing commercial rifles used every means in their power to bring about the adoption of their models instead of the Garand rifle. As a result of the publicity given to these efforts, a Congressional committee was appointed to make an investigation. The competing rifles were tested in the presence of the investigating committee; the result was that the Ordnance Department was allowed to proceed with its plans for the manufacture of the Garand rifle. This proved to be a wise decision, as the rifle has met all of the service demands and has been found to be thoroughly satisfactory in all the widely varying theaters of war.

The Garand rifle had its initiation early in this war, as General MacArthur's troops had been armed with the M1 shortly before the Japanese

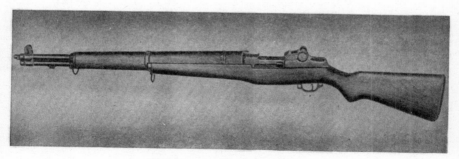

U. S. Rifle, Caliber .30, M1—Left Side.

attack. During the trying days of our retreat in the Philippines, General MacArthur took the time to send the following cablegram to General Marshall (20 February 1942): "Garand rifles giving superior service to Springfield, no mechanical defects reported or stoppages due to dust and dirt from foxhole use. Good gun oil required as lubricant to prevent gumming, but have been used in foxhole fighting day and night for a week without cleaning and lubricating. All these weapons are excellent ones even without any modifications such as suggested."

An Infantryman, crouched in his foxhole on the Vire front in France, fires his M1 rifle at the enemy through a gap in the protecting hedgerow. The M1 rifle had no equal in the war.

Sgt. Walter H. Kyle, Yreka, Calif., Infantry Squad Leader, demonstrates firing position for the mortar grenade, a combination of a mortar projectile and a rifle grenade.

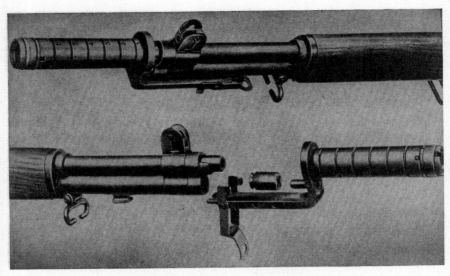

U. S. Rifle, caliber .30, M1, with Grenade Launcher, M7.

U. S. RIFLE, CALIBER .30, M1, WITH GRENADE LAUNCHER, M7

CHARACTERISTICS OF GRENADE LAUNCHER, M7

Weight	0.75 lb.
Length	7.5 in.
Outside diameter	0.86 in.
Diameter of bore	0.50 in.

U. S. RIFLE, CALIBER .30, M1, WITH GRENADE LAUNCHER, M7

General acceptance of the M1 rifle is indicated by a letter from the late General George S. Patton, Jr., Headquarters, 3rd U.S. Army, 26 January 1945, in which he asserted: "In my opinion, the M1 rifle is the greatest battle implement ever devised." General Eisenhower's headquarters reported from Algiers in 1943 that the M1 rifle was suitable for landing operations and that all units of the Center Task Forces who had used the M1 rifle in combat were enthusiastic about it, from the standpoints of both firepower and general serviceability. The commanding officer of an assault company, quoted in this report, said: "After one fight, the enemy asked if all American soldiers were armed with machine guns."

A true evaluation of the importance of this rifle may be obtained from the remarks of the users, as quoted above, plus the fact that for some time before the cessation of hostilities, every rifleman in the Army and Marine Corps was equipped with the M1 rifle, and so were members of the armed forces undergoing basic training in the United States.

To date, the American army is the only army in the world fully equipped with semiautomatic rifles.

Early in 1943, the M7 grenade launcher was adopted for use with the M1 rifle. A soldier equipped with a grenade launcher could fire antipersonnel and antitank grenades at ranges up to 235 and 330 yards, respectively, with a fair degree of accuracy. This device further permitted the firing of various types of signals and flares and so eliminated Ground Forces need for special-purpose pyrotechnic projectors.

U. S. Carbine, Caliber .30, M1 (Phantom View).

U. S. CARBINE, CALIBER .30, M1A1 AND M1A2

CHARACTERISTICS

Type of mechanism	Gas-operated
Feeding device	Magazine
Cooling	Air
Effective range	300 yd.
Sight radius	22 in.
Magazine Capacity	15 rounds
Rate of fire	Semiautomatic
Muzzle velocity	1,900 ft./sec.
Trigger pull	{ 6 lb. max.
	{ 4 lb. min.
Operating pressure (copper)	40,000 lb./sq. in.
Weight, without sling	5.2 lb.
Length, over-all	35.6 in.
Length of barrel	18 in.
Weight of ball cartridge, approx.	195 gr.
Weight of bullet, approx.	110 gr.
Weight of magazine, loaded	0.57 lb.
empty	0.17 lb.

U. S. CARBINE, CALIBER .30, M1A1 AND M1A2

In September 1941, the War Department announced the adoption of a new Infantry weapon —the carbine, caliber .30, M1. At that time, the need for a new weapon for the individual soldier was for one that would weigh little and hit hard. This need became apparent when it was noted that, thanks to the greater mobility of modern warfare, rear elements were often suddenly confronted by the enemy at close range.

The M1 carbine, weighing less than five and one-half pounds and with a 15-round magazine, was immediately put into mass production, and a total of five and one-half million were manufactured and supplied to the troops. A modification of the same carbine, equipped with a folding stock for use by airborne troops and called M1A1, was adopted in May 1942, and a large number of these were produced.

A holed-up Nazi, overlooked in initial mopping-up, emerges from his hideout and surrenders to Lt. Roy L. Rogers, Island Park, Minn., who is armed with a carbine, caliber .30, M1.

As the pace of the war speeded up, it was anticipated that more firepower would be needed. Consequently, the M1 carbine was converted to fire selective semi- and full-automatic with a minimum number of design changes. This modified carbine, designated as M2 and equipped with a 30-round magazine, was adopted in October 1944. More than 550,000 were produced and shipped with a priority of issue to front-line troops.

During assaults in 1942, 1943, and 1944, and during the invasion of France, the M1 carbine was used extensively in street fighting and close-in work, in both of which types of fighting it proved notably helpful. Early use of the M2 carbine by the 5th Army in the Mediterranean Theater produced expressions of enthusiasm. It was considered an excellent weapon for patrol work, and even more useful as a protective weapon for heavy gun emplacements. A report from E.T.O., Headquarters, 7th Army, stated: "The weapon [M2 carbine] was found to be particularly adapted to town and close combat fighting. Using personnel were very enthusiastic over the new weapon and were impressed by its rapid rate of automatic fire, thus providing a light hand weapon capable of greater firepower."

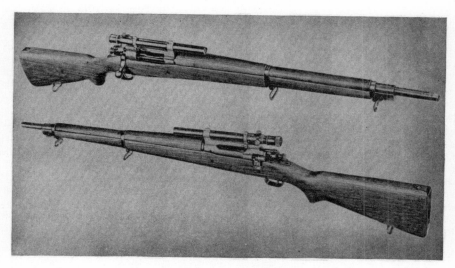

U. S. Rifle, cal. .30, M1903A4.

U. S. RIFLE, CALIBER .30, M1903A4 (SNIPER'S)

CHARACTERISTICS

Weight (without sight)	8 lb. 10 oz.
Weight (with Model 330 Weaver sight)	9 lb. 2 oz.
Weight (with Lyman Alaskan sight)	9 lb. 6 oz.
Sight magnification	2½ power
Eye relief	3 in. to 5 in.
Length of sight:	
Weaver sight	11.0 in.
Lyman Alaskan sight	10.9 in.

(Other measurements same as U. S. Rifle, caliber .30, M1903A1)

U. S. rifle, caliber .30, Springfield, was issued at the beginning of the war to our troops and used until the Garand rifle became available in such quantity as to permit it to replace the Springfield rifle. The latter was, however, used throughout the war as a sniper rifle and was equipped with a telescopic sight, of the Weaver and Alaskan types. Thus the inherent accuracy of the Springfield rifle was utilized throughout the war.

PISTOL, AUTOMATIC, CALIBER .45, M1911A1

The Colt automatic pistol, caliber .45, was adopted in 1911 and was used by the U. S. Army throughout World War I. After the war a board of Ordnance officers, reviewing the equipment which had been used during the war, recommended—on the basis of war experience—that no changes be made in this weapon. This is believed to be the only weapon which came through World War I with such a recommendation.

This pistol continued to be the standard hand weapon throughout World War II. During this war, however, the importance of the pistol as a military weapon declined, and its functions were largely taken over by the carbine.

The caliber .45 pistol remains in the U.S. Army primarily as a weapon for personal defense. Its excellence for this purpose is evidenced by the fact that many German officers, when captured, were wearing it.

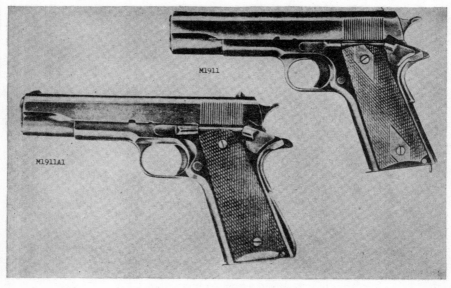

Pistol, Automatic, Caliber .45, M1911
Pistol, Automatic, Caliber .45, M1911A1.

Browning Machine Gun, caliber .30, M1919A6.

BROWNING MACHINE GUN, CAL. .30, BROWNING, M1919A6

CHARACTERISTICS

General Data

Weight	32.5 lb. w/metal stock
Length (over-all)	53 in.
Length of barrel	24 in.
Type of mechanism	Recoil
Feeding device	Metallic Link or Fabric Belt
Capacity of feeding device	250 rd.
Cooling system	Air
Rate of fire	400-500 rds./min.
Trigger pull	9 lb.
Type of sight	Leaf
Ammunition types	Ball, A.P., A.P.I., and tracer

The light machine gun used by American armies and marine corps in this war was the caliber .30 machine gun, M1919A6. This gun, an evolution of the original Browning machine gun, was used throughout the war in all theaters with complete success. It was sturdy and remarkably reliable even under the most trying field conditions.

Tree mount for caliber .30 machine gun, attached to a 9-inch diameter tree.

TREE MOUNT, T100E3, FOR GUN, MACHINE, CALIBER .30, M1919A4

CHARACTERISTICS

General Data

Weight	14 lb.
Maximum elevation	+20°
With repositioning lock	+60°
Maximum depression	−45°
With repositioning lock	−60°
Total traverse	110°

During the jungle fighting in the Pacific, a requirement arose for a method of permitting the caliber .30 machine gun to be fired using a tree as a firing platform or tripod. This need led to the development of the tree mount, T100E3. This mount could be readily attached to the trunk of any tree at any desired height and when so attached provided a rigid and stable firing mount for the gun. The mount was so arranged that a wide field of fire (of 110°) was possible.

Thompson Submachine Gun, caliber .45, M1928A1.

THOMPSON SUBMACHINE GUN, CALIBER .45, M1928A1

CHARACTERISTICS

Weight without magazine	10.8 lb.
Weight, 50-rd. magazine	2.6 lb.
Length (over-all) (with compensator)	33.7 in.
Length of barrel	10.52 in.
Length of rifling	22.8 cals.; 10.12 in.
Rifling	
Number of grooves	6
Right-hand twist: 1 turn in	36 cals.; 16 in.
Depth of grooves	0.0035 in.
Type of mechanism	Blowback
Feeding device	Magazine
Capacity of feeding devices	
box magazines	20 or 30 rd.
drum magazine	50 rd.
Rate of fire	600-725 rds./min.

The Thompson submachine gun, caliber .45, M1928A1, was issued to the troops in the early part of the war. These weapons were part of the equipment of all armored fighting vehicles and were included for the personnel protection of the crew under emergency situations. The gun was modified during the war and a new model Thompson machine gun, M1A1, was issued later. These weapons were later superseded by the submachine gun, caliber .45, M3.

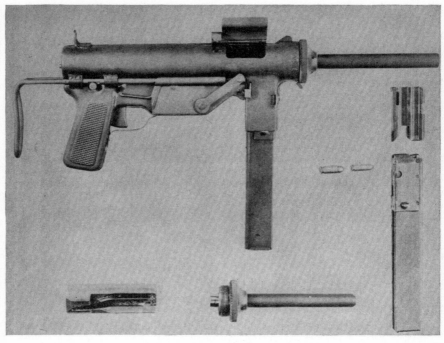

Submachine Gun, caliber .45, M3.

SUBMACHINE GUN, CALIBER .45, M3

CHARACTERISTICS

General Data

Weight	8.9 lb. w/magazine, oiler and sling
Length (overall)	
Stock extended	29.8 in.
Stock closed	22.8 in.
Length of barrel	8 in.
Type of mechanism	Straight blowback, fully automatic
Feeding device	Magazine
Capacity of feeding device	30 rd.
Cooling system	Air
Rate of fire	400 rds./min.
Trigger pull	5 to 7 lb.
Type of sight	Fixed Peep, 100 yd.
Ammunition types	Ball

SUBMACHINE GUN, CALIBER .45, M3

At the beginning of the war our troops were armed with the Thompson submachine gun, caliber .45. Thousands of these were manufactured and issued to all theaters. As the Thompson gun was expensive and difficult to manufacture, the development of a simpler and more reliable weapon was undertaken. This work resulted in the perfection and standardization of the caliber .45 submachine gun, M3. This weapon had the advantages of increased accuracy and improved reliability under the most difficult field conditions. Although at the beginning of the war, submachine guns cost the Government $55.00 each, the submachine gun, M3, was finally produced in great quantities for about $18.00 each, including extra barrel for German ammunition.

Rifle, Automatic, Caliber .30, Browning M1918A2—Right Side View.

BROWNING AUTOMATIC RIFLE, CALIBER .30, M1918A2 ("BAR")

CHARACTERISTICS

Weight, complete	19.4 lb.
Weight, less bipod	17 lb.
Weight of barrel	3.65 lb.
Length over-all	47.8 in.
Length of barrel	24.07 in.
Rifling length	21.41 in.; 71.1 cals.
No. of grooves	4
Twist	Right-hand, 1 turn in 10 in., 33.3 cals.
Depth of grooves	0.004 in.
Cross-sectional area of bore	0.074 sq. in.
Operation	Gas
Feed	20-rd. box magazine
Cooling	Air
Rate of fire	High-speed, 500-600 rds./min.
	Retarded, 300-350 rds./min.
Trigger pull	10 lb. max., 6 lb. min.

The automatic rifles and machine guns used in World War II were based largely upon the investigations and developments of John M. Browning, the world's most famous inventor of automatic weapons. It is a great tribute to the late Mr. Browning that his automatic weapons have been used throughout the last two wars by the U. S. Army and have formed the basis of many foreign automatic weapons.

The automatic shoulder rifle, caliber .30, known affectionately by the troops as the "BAR," was one of the weapons which was designed by Mr. Browning and accepted by the U. S. Army in 1917. Although this rifle has been under constant development before and during World War II, the basic principles of John Browning's invention have been retained. The BAR became and remained famous in all theaters because of its sturdiness and great reliability under all field conditions.

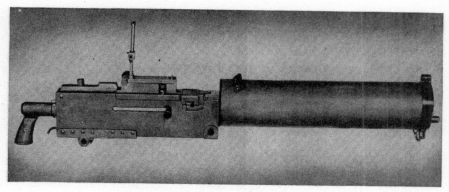

Browning Machine Gun, caliber .30, water-cooled.

BROWNING MACHINE GUN, CALIBER .30, M1917A1

CHARACTERISTICS

Weight, total .	32.6 lb. (less water)
Weight of recoiling parts	7.35 lb.
Weight of barrel .	. 3 lb.
Length, over-all .	. 38.64 in.
Length of barrel .	. 23.9 in.
Rifling, length	21.28 in., 71 cals.
No. of grooves	4
Twist .	Right-hand, 1 turn in 10 in., 33.3 cals.
Depth of grooves	. 0.004 in.
Cross-sectional area bore	0.074 sq. in.
Operation	Short recoil
Feed	Metallic Link or Fabric Belt, 250 rd.
Cooling .	Water, 8 pints
Rate of fire .	. 450-600 rds./min.
Trigger pull .	7 lb. min., 12 lb. max.
Breech pressure	48,000 lb./sq. in. (copper)

This is a water-type machine gun which was standardized for the use of the ground troops. Water-cooling the barrel makes it possible for the gun to fire much longer bursts than would be possible with the air-cooled type of barrel. These guns were extensively used by our troops in all theaters, and proved their worth on the field of battle. This weapon has the same reliable automatic feed mechanism as all the other types of Browning machine guns employed throughout the war. This reliability saved many American lives in Japanese attacks.

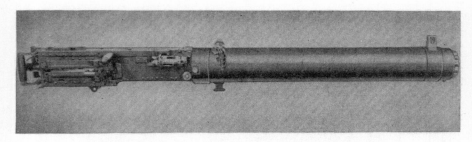

Browning Machine Gun, Caliber .50, M2. Water-cooled, Flexible.

BROWNING MACHINE GUN, CALIBER .50, M2, WATER-COOLED, FLEXIBLE

CHARACTERISTICS

Weight	121 lb. (less water, 100 lb.)
Length (over-all)	66 in.
Weight of recoiling parts	24.5 lb.
Weight of barrel	15.2 lb.
Length of barrel	45 in.
Length of rifling	40.91 in.; 81.8 cals.
Rifling	
Number of grooves	8
R.H. twist, 1 turn in	30 cals.; 15 in.
Depth of grooves	0.0050 in.
Cross-sectional area of bore	0.2021 sq. in.
Type of mechanism	Short recoil
Feeding device	Metallic link belt
Capacity of feeding device	As desired
Rate of fire	500-650 rds./min.
Cooling system	Water (capacity 10 qt., 6 oz.)
Firing-pin release	
Pressure applied to sear	10-20 lb.
Pressure applied to sear slide	30-35 lb.
Normal pressure	48,000 lb./sq. in. (copper)
Ammunition types	Ball, A.P., tracer, incendiary

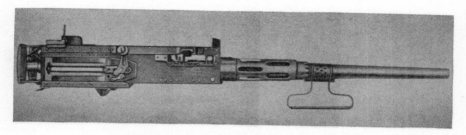

Browning Machine Gun, Heavy Barrel, Caliber .50, M2, H. B, Flexible.

BROWNING MACHINE GUN, HEAVY BARREL, CALIBER .50, M2, HB (Fixed, Flexible, and Turret Types)

CHARACTERISTICS

Weight, fixed	82 lb.
Weight, flexible	84 lb.
Length (over-all)	65 in.
Weight of recoiling parts	38.8 lb.
Weight of barrel	27 lb.
Length of barrel	45 in.
Length of rifling	40.91 in., 81.8 cals.
Rifling	
Number of grooves	8
R.H. twist, 1 turn in	30 cals., 15 in.
Depth of grooves	0.0050 in.
Type of mechanism	Short recoil
Feeding device	Metallic Links
Capacity of feeding device	As desired, in increments of 110 rds.
Rate of fire	450-575 rds./min.
Cooling system	Air
Sight radius	20 in.
Normal pressure	48,000 lb./sq. in. (copper)
Ammunition types	Ball, A.P., tracer, incendiary

BROWNING MACHINE GUN, CALIBER .50—GROUND TYPE

The ground-type caliber .50 machine guns developed during the years of peace preceding World War II were destined to play an important part against the Axis nations. Ships of the Navy, subjected to dive bombing and "suicide" attacks of Japanese fliers, depended heavily on the massed fire of batteries of caliber .50 water-cooled machine guns for close-in defense against those vicious attacks. Their reliability, plus that of their ammunition, was such that one naval officer expressed a desire for improperly loaded ammunition so that gunners might receive more practice in clearing stoppages, which did not occur.

These guns were used by thousands in the African, Italian, European, and Pacific Theaters of Operation as antiaircraft defense for airfields, command posts, artillery positions, supply depots, and other installations continually subjected to attacks by enemy aircraft.

During the precarious "Battle of the Bulge" and the relief of our forces encircled at Bastogne, Belgium, the caliber .50 air-cooled machine guns of the 4th Armored Division were credited with stopping a determined dive-bomber attack by the Luftwaffe. Basically the same weapon as the water-cooled machine gun, the air-cooled model was designed for use where a water supply for the gun might be critical or difficult to maintain. Fitted with a heavy-weight barrel to provide adequate cooling for firing long-bursts, it was an ideal weapon for the protection of truck

Sgt. George Brackemyre, left, Seymour, Ind., 3rd Army tanker, fires his caliber .50 Browning machine gun at a German sniper position in Saarburg, Germany. Note German sign on side of his tank.

convoys moving toward the battle fronts. It became the principal antiaircraft weapon of the armored divisions, and nearly all of the Army's larger vehicles were equipped with these guns. One winner of the Congressional Medal of Honor received his award for his efficient use of a caliber .50 heavy-barrel machine gun mounted on a tank destroyer. In this action, a serious enemy infantry counterattack was repulsed by the fire of this machine gun.

An official report from North Africa summarizes the general feeling toward this weapon: "The caliber .50 heavy-barrel gun was recommended by everyone."

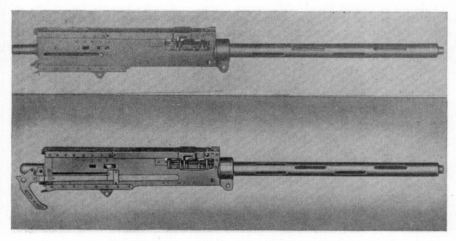

Browning Machine Gun, Aircraft, Caliber .50, M2 (Fixed).

BROWNING MACHINE GUN, AIRCRAFT, CALIBER .50, M2
(Fixed and Flexible)

CHARACTERISTICS

Weight of gun, fixed . . . . 64.5 lb.
Weight of gun, flexible . . . . 68.5 lb.
Weight of metallic-link belt, filled, 100 rds. . . . . 30.25 lb.
Weight of belt, empty, 100 links . . . . 4.00 lb.
Over-all length of gun, fixed . . . . 57.09 in.
Over-all length of gun, flexible . . . . 56.40 in.
Over-all length of barrel . . . . 36.00 in.
Maximum range, cartridge, M2, Ball and A.P. . . . . 7,125 yd.
Muzzle velocity, cartridge, M2, Ball and A.P. . . . . 2,810 ft./sec.
Rate of automatic fire . . . . 750-850 rds./min.

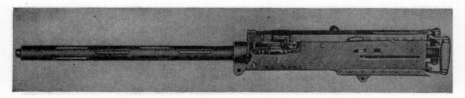

Browning Machine Gun, Caliber .50, Aircraft, M2 (Flexible).

BROWNING MACHINE GUN, CALIBER .50—AIRCRAFT TYPE

The caliber .50 aircraft-type machine gun in its present form is the most reliable and most famous machine gun in the world. Its perfection today is a tribute to the Ordnance-Industry team. Accepted by the Army and first produced in numbers in 1923, it was standardized in 1933. In 1940, improvements incorporated into the gun increased its rate of fire to 800 shots per minute, a speed which made it a superior aircraft weapon.

Typical of its combat efficiency is an action which took place during the Tunisian campaign. Approximately 35 P-40 type fighter aircraft fired a total of 25,000 rounds of caliber .50 ammunition in attacks on German transport aircraft, as a result of which 72 enemy aircraft were destroyed, WITHOUT A SINGLE MACHINE-GUN STOPPAGE.

A measure of the reliability of the aircraft machine gun may be taken from a report of the

Waist gunner of the B-17 Invader II (Flying Fortress)—L. to R., S/Sgt. Eldon R. Lapp, Fort Wayne, and S/Sgt. William D. King, Imperial, Texas, at their Caliber .50 machine guns, England, 17 March 1943.

IX Tactical Air Command: In a two-week period, during which 689,027 rounds were fired, a total of 89 stoppages occurred; the average was 7,742 rounds per stoppage; and the stoppages included 44 not attributable to the gun mechanism. That the confidence and belief of the Army Air Forces in the superiority of this weapon contributed in no small part toward the final victory is indicated by part of a letter from Major General Barney Giles, Chief of the Air Staff, to the Chief of Ordnance:

"1. The Commanding General of the Army Air Forces, with the full realization of the many outstanding achievements of the Ordnance Department in developing and producing large quantities of outstanding equipment for the United States Forces, wishes to commend specifically the Ordnance Department of the Army Service Forces for the magnificent achievement in furnishing the Army Air Forces with the most outstanding aircraft gun of World War II; namely, the Caliber .50 Aircrcaft Machine Gun.

"2. This weapon, together with its ammunition, is the backbone of offensive and defensive guns for American aircraft and was brought to such a state of perfection during the years of peace prior to the present conflict that it has enabled the Army Air Forces, the United States Navy, and the Marine Corps to show a definite superiority in aircraft gun power throughout this global war."

Despite the enviable record of the M2 aircraft gun, it became apparent that as the speed of aerial combat increased, corresponding increases in the rate of fire of aircraft weapons would be necessary to maintain our superiority. To meet this requirement, the Ordnance Department, in cooperation with several commercial facilities, developed the M3 caliber .50 aircraft machine gun. This gun, which has a rate of fire of 1,200 rounds per minute, provides an immediate increase of 50 per cent in the firepower of combat aircraft. Thus a fighter airplane carrying six of the new M3 guns had firepower equal to that of nine of the M2 guns. This increase in performance was remarkable in view of the fact that the M2 and M3 guns are essentially the same size and weight. The performance of the M3 gun is far superior to that of any weapon of comparable caliber or weight now in existence, and its use increases still further the superiority of our aircraft armament.

Antiaircraft machine-gun mount, M63, with extension handles in antiaircraft position.

MOUNT, AA, MACHINE GUN, CALIBER .50, M63

CHARACTERISTICS

General Data

Type of mount .	Light-weight, portable, antiaircraft
Armament .	Cal. .50 H.B. machine gun, M2
Weight .	144 lb.

Field of Fire

Elevation .	—29° to +85°
Traverse .	360° continuous
Fire power .	450 rds./min.
Fire control .	Machine-gun sight plus tracer control
Suspension .	Quadruped base and elevator

Principal Dimensions

	Emplaced
Base radius .	28 in.
Trunnion .	28 in.

Throughout the war there was constant demand for a light, portable weapon which could be used by the various services against low-flying aircraft. The caliber .50 antiaircraft machine gun and its ammunition were very effective against such low-flying aircraft, but the total weight of the gun and its mount made the weapon too heavy for general use. The antiaircraft machine-gun mount, M63, was developed for this purpose and provided an extremely light mounting for this effective machine gun. This mount permitted the caliber .50 machine gun to be readily used in front-line positions against low-flying enemy aircraft.

Complete rounds of Small Arms Ammunition
From left to right: Caliber .22 Cartridge; Caliber .45 Cartridge; Caliber .30 Carbine Cartridge; Caliber .30 Cartridge; Caliber .50 Cartridge.

SMALL-ARMS AMMUNITION

Some conception of the part which small-arms ammunition played in the late war may be gained from the fact that, since 1940, more than 47 billion rounds have been manufactured at a cost of approximately two and one-half billion dollars. With the single exception of the caliber .45 ball cartridge, the entire production consisted of types of ammunition developed during the past

Cartridge	Identification	Bullet Weight	Pressure-lbs per sq. in.	Velocity - ft. per second	Accuracy	Maximum Range	Striking Energy ft/lbs	Length of Trace	Penetration
Ball, Cal. .22 Long Rifle, M24	Plain Tip	40 grs.	22,000 Mean	1300' ± 25 at 25 feet, 24" Barrel	1" Mean Radius at 100 yd.	1400 yd.	150 at 25 ft.		
Ball, Cal. .30, M2	Plain Tip	152 grs.	52,000 Mean	2740 ± 30 at 78 ft., 24" Barrel	7.5" Mean Radius at 600 yd.	3500 yd.	2530 at 78 ft.		
Ball, Frangible, Cal. .30, M22	Green Tip White Annulus	108 grs.	5000 Approx.	1300 ± 30 at 53 ft., 24" Barrel	12" Mean Radius at 300 yd.	----	418 at 53 ft.		Must not penetrate 3/16" 24ST Dural at 25 yd.
Armor Piercing, Cal. .30, M2	Black Tip	168 grs.	54,000 Mean	2715 ± 30 at 78 ft, 24" Barrel	10" Mean Radius at 600 yd.	3160 yd.	2790 at 78 ft.		0.42" penetration in 7/8" Homogeneous Plate at 100 yd.
Incendiary, Cal. .30, M1	Light Blue Tip	140 grs.	52,000 Mean	2950 ± 30 at 78 ft, 24" Barrel	15" Mean Radius at 600 yd.	2875 yd.	2700 at 78 ft.		
Tracer, Cal. .30, M1	Red Tip	152 grs.	52,000 Mean	2700 ± 30 at 78 ft, 24" Barrel	15" Mean Radius at 600 yd.	3350 yd.	2470 at 78 ft.	900 yd. Min.	
Tracer, Cal. .30, M2	White Tip	152 grs.	50,000 Mean	2700 ± 30 at 78 ft, 24" Barrel	15" Mean Radius at 600 yd.	----	2470 at 78 ft.	500-50	
Tracer, Cal. .30, M25	Orange Tip	141 grs.	52,000 Mean	2665 ± 30 at 78 ft, 24" Barrel	15" Mean Radius at 600 yd.	----	2220 at 78 ft.	900 yds Min. Dim Trace 150-75 yd.	
Rifle Grenade, Cal. .30, M3	Rose Crimp	None	---	180 ± 10 at 5.5 ft, M11A2 Grenade	---	260 yd. With M7 Auxiliary Cartridge, 330 yds.			
Ball, Carbine, Cal. .30, M1	Plain Tip	110 grs.	40,000 Mean	1900 ± 30 at 53 ft, 18" Barrel	1.5" Mean Radius at 100 yd.	2200 yd.	880 at 53 ft.		
Tracer, Carbine, Cal. .30, M16	Red Tip	107 grs.	40,000 Mean	1850 ± 30 at 53 ft, 18" Barrel	4" Mean Radius at 100 yd.	1680 yd.	813 at 53 ft.	400 yd. Min.	
Grenade, Carbine, Cal. .30, M6	Rose Crimp	None	---	140 ± 5 at 5.5 ft, M11A2 Grenade	---	185 yd. With M7 Auxiliary Cartridge, 260 yds.			
Ball, Cal. .45, M1911	Plain Tip	230 grs.	17,000 Mean	820 ± 25 at 25 ft, 5" Barrel / 910 ± 25 at 25 ft, 10" Barrel	3" Mean Radius at 50 yd.	1640 yd. 5" Barrel / 1760 yd. 10" Barrel	343-422 at 25 ft.		
Shot, Cal. .45, M12	Red, waxed paper bullet containing 125-131 #7½ chilled shot		17,000 Mean	820 ± 25 at 25 ft, 5" Barrel	Shot Pattern, 50% in 30" circle at 25 ft.				
Shot, Cal. .45, M15	No bullet, Case contains 113-123 #7½ chilled shot retained by paper wad		17,000 Mean	750 ± 25 at 25 ft, 5" Barrel	Shot Pattern, 67% in 30" circle at 25 ft.				
Ball, Cal. .50, M2	Plain Tip	700 grs.	52,000 Mean	2810 ± 30 at 78 ft, 36" Barrel	9" Mean Radius at 600 yd.	7400 yd.	12,400 at 78 ft.		
Armor Piercing, Cal. .50, M2	Black Tip	700 grs.	53,000 Mean	2810 ± 30 at 78 ft, 36" Barrel	10" Mean Radius at 600 yd.	7400 yd.	12,400 at 78 ft.		90% Complete perforations in 7/8" Homogeneous Plate at 100 yd.
Tracer, Cal. .50, M10	Orange Tip	640 grs.	54,000 Mean	2860 ± 30 at 78 ft, 36" Barrel	20" Mean Radius at 600 yd.	5350 yd.	11,600 at 78 ft.	1600 yd. Min. Dim Trace 200-75 yd.	
Tracer, Cal. .50, M17	Maroon Tip	648 grs.	54,000 Mean	2860 ± 30 at 78 ft, 36" Barrel	20" Mean Radius at 600 yd.	5900 yd.	11,800 at 78 ft.	2400 yd. Min.	
Tracer, Headlight, Cal. .50, M21	Red Tip	700 grs.	54,000 Mean	2700 ± 30 at 78 ft, 36" Barrel	20" Mean Radius at 600 yd.	---	11,400 at 78 ft.	500 yd. Min.	
Incendiary, Cal. .50, M1	Light Blue Tip	630 grs.	54,000 Mean	2950 ± 30 at 78 ft, 36" Barrel	12" Mean Radius at 600 yd.	9960 yd.	12,200 at 78 ft.		
Incendiary, Cal. .50, M23	Dark Blue Tip, Light Blue Annulus	512 grs.	55,000 Mean	3400 ± 30 at 78 ft, 36" Barrel	12" Mean Radius at 600 yd.	---	13,000 at 78 ft.		
Armor Piercing-Incendiary, Cal. .50, M8	Silver Tip	660 grs.	55,000 Mean	2910 ± 30 at 78 ft, 36" Barrel	12" Mean Radius at 600 yd.	6375 yd.	12,400 at 78 ft.		80% Complete perforations in 7/8" Homogeneous Plate at 100 yd.
Armor Piercing-Incendiary-Tracer, Cal. .50, M20	Red Tip, Silver Annulus	620 grs.	55,000 Mean	2910 ± 30 at 78 ft, 36" Barrel	12" Mean Radius at 600 yd.	6375 yd.	11,700 at 78 ft.	1600 yds Min.	80% Complete perforations in 7/8" Homogeneous Plate at 100 yd.
Shell, Shotgun, All Brass, 12 Gage, No. 00 Buck, M19	All Brass Case	9 No.00 Buckshot	11,000 Mean	1070 ± 30 at 120 ft, 30" Barrel	Shot Pattern, 33-1/3% in 30" circle at 120 ft. 20" cylinder bore bbl.	590 yd.			

Performance Chart for Small Arms Ammunition

five years to meet the complex modern tactical requirements. This development covered more than thirty combat types of small-arms ammunition in seven different calibers, and included five new combat cartridges for the caliber .50 aircraft machine gun, which played such an important part in the attainment of Allied air superiority.

In keeping pace with the increased tempo of modern aerial warfare, the velocity of caliber .50 ammunition has been increased by as much as 500 feet per second, and its effectiveness has been greatly enhanced by the use of incendiary and armor-piercing incendiary projectiles. Before the United States' entry into the war, the standard ammunition for caliber .50 aircraft machine guns consisted of ball, tracer, and armor-piercing cartridges, but the performance of these had been rendered virtually obsolete by the rapid advances made in military aircraft. Realizing the urgent need for modern combat ammunition which would arise if the United States were drawn into the conflict, the Ordnance Department, in October 1940, initiated the

development of a radically new type of caliber .50 incendiary cartridge.

The round was designed specifically for use against the self-sealing fuel cells with which most military airplanes were equipped, and was given a velocity approximately 150 feet per second higher than that of existing types. Production was started early in 1942, and this cartridge achieved immediate success in aerial conflict against the Luftwaffe. The combat efficiency of this ammunition is indicated by an official report: "These pilots, who are in daily conflict with the enemy, swear by the effectiveness of the incendiary ammunition and would as soon go up without their machine guns as without this type of ammunition."

With the launching of full-scale bomber raids against the Continent in 1943, the ever-changing tactics of the German air force presented a new problem which threatened to jeopardize the success of the entire aerial offensive. Frontal attacks of German fighter planes against B-17 bomber formations rendered the caliber .50 in-

Night firing of Cal. .50 antiaircraft machine guns using tracer ammunition. For this type of operation, only one round in five is tracer and therefore visual in the photograph.

cendiary ammunition relatively ineffective because of the added protection afforded by the engine of the attacking craft. As a result, the Department was presented with an urgent requirement for a caliber .50 round with the combined properties of the M2 armor-piercing cartridge and the M1 incendiary cartridge.

Development of an armor-piercing incendiary cartridge was started in June 1943, and by October it had been made a standard item of issue. The combat performance of this cartridge won universal acclaim from the men whose lives depended upon the efficiency of their weapons. One pilot said: "As all hits are visible and it appears that the incendiary effect is more violent and destructive in that it penetrates to the more vulnerable sections of the enemy aircraft in the interior—A.P.I. ammunition is much superior to present ammunition in that it has both destructive and incendiary characteristics. Request that this ammunition be given the highest priority rating in a serious attempt to obtain it for all fighter aircraft." In the initial combat trials, one squadron of the Eighth Air Force destroyed 17 enemy aircraft while using this ammunition.

In the last phase of the war with Germany, the threat of enemy jet-propelled airplanes produced a request from the Air Forces for a new incendiary cartridge which would be effective against the low-grade fuels used for jet propulsion. The caliber .50 M23 incendiary cartridge was developed and put into production within three months. This contained double the quantity of incendiary mixture and had a velocity of 3,450 feet per second. On the first mission with this ammunition, the 63rd Fighter Squadron destroyed 20 enemy aircraft, and on the second, eliminated 44; a single pilot destroyed 10 aircraft on one four-hour combat flight.

The global aspects of World War II made necessary the development of radically different packagings for small-arms ammunition, to meet requirements of tactical operations in adverse climates and over difficult terrain. To supply the using services with small-arms ammunition in functional assemblies ready for use, the Department instituted factory and depot assembly of cartridges in combat ratios, packaged in unit

A Focke-Wulf 190 goes down in flames after the gas tanks are hit by caliber .50 incendiaries.

containers. Metal boxes and hermetically sealed cans of relatively small size and weight, packed in sturdy wooden shipping boxes, were developed. These were employed for all calibers of small-arms ammunition, and met with the universal approval of the services.

The packaging of small-arms ammunition to resist corrosion in the damp jungles of the Pacific constituted a difficult engineering problem, which was completely solved.

Pvt. Robert C. Starkey of Indianapolis, Ind., stands in front of a German tank he knocked out with a bazooka shell during a German counterattack. Near Hemich, Germany, 23 November 1944.

LAUNCHERS, ROCKET, A.T., 2.36-INCH, M9

CHARACTERISTICS

Assembled and ready for firing, the rocket launcher measures 55 inches over-all and weighs approximately 14½ pounds.

LAUNCHERS, ROCKET, 2.36-INCH, M9 ("BAZOOKA")

The 2.36-inch rocket launcher—which early in its development period was dubbed the "bazooka"—was originated by the Ordnance Department in 1942. Immediately upon completion of the development, production was rushed and the weapon was promptly put into action.

The bazooka was first used in the North African Theater of Operations. This new weapon provided the foot soldier for the first time in history with the equivalent of hand-carried, short-range artillery with enough power to stop tanks. Its use came as a complete surprise to the enemy; one enemy tank commander who surrendered when his tank was narrowly missed by a rocket stated that he thought he was under 155-mm gunfire.

This weapon was enthusiastically received by the troops. It later proved to be of inestimable value in every theater of operations, not only for use against tanks, but as a short-range anti-pillbox and antipersonnel weapon. Called by the Germans the "shoulder 75," it was used to destroy machine-gun and mortar nests. Where heavy bunker walls could not be penetrated, fire directed close to slits would stun occupants with concussion, and the fragmentation effect of the high-explosive rocket head proved effective against personnel.

Later in the war, the bazooka saw valuable service in the Pacific against Japanese tanks, caves, and bunkers. An officer on Okinawa reported: "The bazooka proved its worth when four Jap tanks came down the road, got through the front line and could have gotten through the Division C.P. and the beach, but decided to turn around. Bazooka teams got to the road and knocked them all out in three minutes. The regimental commander whose line was pierced said that the 37-mm guns were ineffective. Bazookas were also used on pillboxes and a great deal of success was secured in directing fire on the pillbox embrasures."

The greatest compliment to the bazooka, however, was that paid by the Germans, who copied the design.

Despite the development of newer weapons, the bazooka is still considered a highly effective short-range weapon, and was so popular that approximately 460,000 were produced during the war. Although improvements were incorporated continuously, the improved models of the bazooka are essentially similar to the origi-

Rocket Launcher, A.T., M9A1—Left Side.

nal design. The long tube has been broken into two piecees for ease in carrying; new sight and a new stock have replaced those originally used; and the batteries originally used to ignite the rocket propellant charge have been supplanted by an electrical magneto firing mechanism contained in the trigger grip. The use of aluminum has materially decreased the weight of the launcher, and the rocket itself has been improved in stability of flight and in penetrating power.

The possibilities of this type of weapon have not yet been fully explored, and its development will continue.

Rocket Launcher, M9A1 Broken Down.

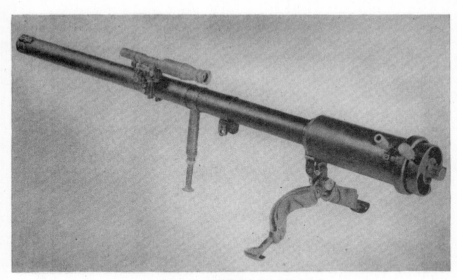

57-mm Recoilless Rifle, M18, Bipod Extended.

RECOILLESS RIFLES, 57-MM, M18, AND 75-MM, M20

CHARACTERISTICS

Gun Tube		57-mm	75-mm
Caliber		57-mm	75-mm
Weight (gun complete, for tripod mounting)		40.25 lb.	103 lb.
Rifling, Number of grooves and lands		24	28
Twist		Right-hand; one turn in 30 cals.	Right-hand; one turn in 22 cals.
Length		46.44 in.	64.8 in.

57-mm Recoilless Rifle, M18, with Bipod Folded.

RECOILLESS RIFLES, 57-MM, M18, AND 75-MM, M20—Continued

	57-mm	75-mm
Gun Tube		
Breechblock, type	Interrupted lug	Interrupted thread
Recoil mechanism	None	None
Range, maximum	4,400 yd. with Cartridge, H.E., 57-mm, M306	7,000 yd. Cartridge, H.E.A.T. 75-mm, M310
Muzzle velocity	1,200 ft./sec.	1,000 ft./sec.
Gun Mount		
Model	Tripod, cal. .30 M1917A1, Bipod T3 (with extendable handles T3 and T3E1	Tripod, cal. .30 M1917A1
Elevation, Maximum (on tripod)	+65°	+65°
Minimum (on tripod)	−27°	−27°
Traverse (on tripod)	360°	360°

75-mm Recoilless Rifle, M20, on M1917A1 Tripod Mount.

RECOILLESS RIFLES

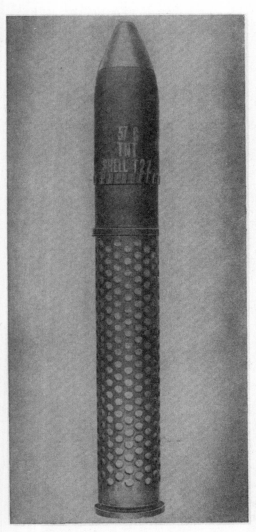

Complete Round, H.E., for 57-mm Recoilless Rifle.

The 57-mm and 75-mm recoilless rifles are among the most interesting weapons developed by the Ordnance Department in the last year of the War. These weapons, with ammunition and accessories, were standardized and quickly put into production. Each fires conventional artillery-type shells at velocities comparable with those of standard artillery, and each is made entirely recoilless by a design which permits escape of a portion of the propellant gases through exhaust ports in the breech. The resulting back-blast creates a characteristic triangular danger space to the rear of the firing position.

The 57-mm rifle, M18, may be fired from the shoulder or from an integrated bipod-monopod combination. It weighs about 45 pounds and has a range of more than two miles. The 75-mm rifle, M20, weighs 105 pounds, has a range of four miles, may be fired from any caliber .30 machine-gun mount, and is equipped with handles for hand carrying.

Both the 57-mm and 75-mm recoilless rifles were used in combat in the European and Pacific Theaters and proved highly effective for use against point targets, such as tanks, machine-gun nests, and pillboxes. Especially enthusiastic were reports of airborne operations in which the light weight, combined with the extreme accuracy and great firepower of the weapons, made them notably effective. The following reports from combat theaters are typical. An officer on temporary duty with the First Allied Airborne Army in Europe said of the 75-mm rifle: "Its effective range for direct fire is the limit of visibility. The gun is as accurate as an M1 rifle and a tank can be hit in any desired spot." A platoon leader of the 172nd Infantry, commenting on operations in the Pacific, stated: "For ranges under 1500 yards, the 75-mm rifle can't be beaten. My crew fired at caves of all sizes and into wooded ravines and scored direct hits in every case."

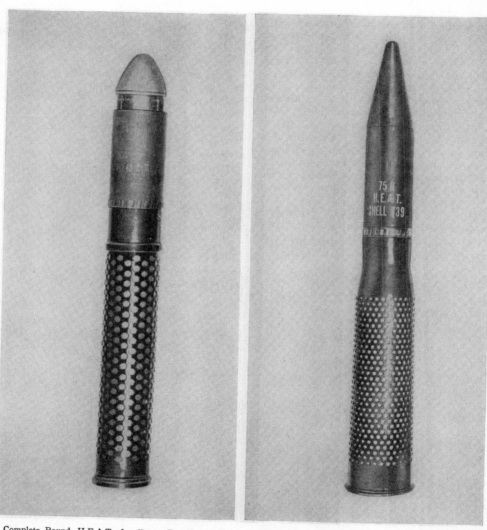

Complete Round, H.E.A.T., for 57-mm Recoilless Rifle.   Complete Round, H.E.A.T., for 75-mm Recoilless Rifle.

Describing one phase of the 17th Airborne Division's operation near Essen, Germany, the 75-mm rifle crew lieutenant said: "Whenever any fire was noticed interfering with the Infantry, we dropped 75's into them and the Infantry platoon leader always reported the firing stopped. We were with or ahead of the Infantry all day, during an advance of over three miles, with rifle, mount, and ammunition hand-carried."

Major General Miley, commanding the 17th Airborne Division, reported: "The 507th Parachute Infantry Regiment reports three Mark IV tanks immobilized and knocked out at 400, 450, and 600 yards range. One tank burned, two were hit above the tracks in hull. Total rounds fired at these tanks was 8.

"The 513th Parachute Infantry Regiment reports one Mark IV knocked out at 300 yards, three rounds fired and hit in turret and tracks.

One M24 T.D.* (being used by Germans) immobilized with one round at 300 yards by hitting bogie wheels. One Mark V [Panther] hit at 950 yards with a round below turret knocked out crew.

"The recoilless rifle is definitely a step in the right direction for the Infantry. The Airborne Division in particular has been particularly vulnerable to armor. With the addition of the 57-mm and the 75-mm recoilless weapons, airborne troops have the means to assist them against tanks and self-propelled guns. In my opinion, the recent operation has proven the practicability of the recoilless rifle and it should be issued to units, with high priority to airborne divisions. Modification designed for improving this weapon should be made as soon as possible. However,

* Tank destroyer.

A gun crew of the 383rd Infantry Regiment loads a shell into the new 57-mm recoilless rifle to fire against Jap pillboxes and caves on Okinawa, 10 June 1945. A new weapon of great importance.

the gun should be placed in the hands of troops without delay as improvements can be made on later models."

These weapons are now standard equipment for Infantry, Airborne, and other Ground Force units. Ordnance Department's opinion is that their development constitutes a great advance in firepower for the foot soldier.

A gun crew of the U. S. Army's new 75-mm recoilless rifle is seen in position to load the weapon. The gun was used for the first time in the Pacific during the Okinawa fighting. Okinawa, 9 June 1945.

BODY ARMOR

All helmets and body armor used by the Army during this war were developed by the Ordnance Department from 1941 to 1945. All models of helmets and body armor initially used manganese steel as a protective material. The M1 helmet was standardized in 1941 and more than 22 million were produced.

Early in the war, body armor and special helmets for the Army Air Forces were developed and several hundred thousand units were manufactured. These, of manganese steel, were widely used by crewmen of combat airplanes. Statistics from the Office of the Surgeon General showed that, in the cases studied, the wearing of armor produced a reduction of 50 per cent in deaths and of 80 per cent in wounds.

Standard Helmet, M1

In July 1943, the Ordnance Department received a suit of body armor which had been worn by Lieutenant Jack C. Fisher during a mission over enemy territory in Europe. This suit of armor had been stained and torn by numerous impacts of fragments from a 20-mm shell which had struck the plexiglass nose of the airplane. Although the shell fragments had penetrated the armor in many places, Lieutenant Fisher had been saved from serious injury. After inspecting this armor thoroughly, the Department decided that a test set-up should be established which would simulate as nearly as possible the conditions of attack in the actual use of armor. Before this time, armor materials had been evaluated by determining their ballistic limits with a caliber .45 bullet. This decision resulted in the establishment of a fragmentation test for armor materials. The test technique was developed and improved, and became known as the 20-mm triangular fragmentation test.

The development of this 20-mm triangular fragmentation test for light armor greatly aided the research for new and improved ballistic materials. Evaluation of a wide variety of test results showed that a combination of aluminum and nylon would produce superior body armor. These materials permitted a simultaneous reduction in weight and an increase in the degree of protection afforded.

As a result of the use of the aluminum-nylon principle of armor protection, body armor for the use of ground troops was developed and standardized near the close of the war. By the end of the war, aluminum-nylon had displaced Hadfield manganese steel as the ballistic material of every standard item of body armor, both for air and ground personnel.

Waist gunner of a B-17 firing a caliber .50 aircraft machine gun at enemy planes during a raid over Germany. Flyer's body armor protects him from shell fragments.

Chapter II

AIRCRAFT ARMAMENT

Chapter II

AIRCRAFT ARMAMENT

This chapter deals with aircraft cannon, 20-mm and larger. The caliber .50 aircraft machine gun and ammunition have been discussed in Chapter I (Small Arms).

It is a common tendency to judge the effectiveness of weapons by their size or caliber—the larger the weapon, the more destructive it is thought to be. The fallacy of this assumption is well illustrated by the caliber .50 machine gun and its ammunition. This projectile was large enough to be effective against all types of German and Japanese aircraft. At the same time, the relatively small caliber made it possible to obtain a very high cyclic rate with a machine gun. Each airplane could also carry a larger number of these machine guns and a greater quantity of ammunition.

Larger calibers of aircraft cannon were, however, constantly under development, so that if any enemy aircraft appeared too heavily armored for the caliber .50 aircraft machine guns, suitable weapons would be immediately available. Aircraft cannon of the larger calibers were extensively used in Army and Navy aircraft for special targets, such as enemy shipping.

Throughout the war there was considerable competition between the caliber .50 machine gun and the 20-mm aircraft cannon, and each had its ardent supporters. The postwar trend will be toward larger calibers as airplane structures become heavier and stronger to withstand the increased speeds at which future aircraft will be flown.

In 1936, the Ordnance Department undertook an extensive program, in cooperation with the Army Air Forces, to determine the calibers of guns required to destroy modern aircraft. The program required several months to complete. Shots were fired at critical sections of airplanes, and the results were analyzed by Ordnance and aircraft-structure experts. As a result of this experimental program, requirements for three new calibers of weapons (other than the caliber .50 machine gun) were established in the aircraft cannon field: the 20-mm (already mentioned), the 37-mm, and the 75-mm.

The introduction of cannon into aircraft brought several new problems. Weight and space are important factors in aircraft, and temperature extremes are great. In addition, special consideration had to be given to the distribution of the gun's recoil load in the aircraft structure. In firing at other aircraft, time on the target is but a small fraction of a second and it is important to obtain as many shots as possible while the target is in the sights; the requirement, therefore, is for automatic cannon with high cyclic rates of fire.

The considerations listed above make clear that the basic characteristics of aircraft cannon must be:

(1) Minimum silhouette, weight, and recoil load;

(2) Fully automatic operation under wide extremes of temperature; and

(3) High rates of fire and high muzzle velocities.

Several of these characteristics oppose each other, and therefore, to make a practical aircraft cannon, compromises are necessary.

20-mm Automatic Gun, M3.

20-MM AUTOMATIC GUN, M3

CHARACTERISTICS

Gun
Caliber 20-mm
Length (over-all) . . . . 77.75 in.
Length, gun tube . . . . 52.5 in.
Weight, gun tube . . . . 26.1875 lb.
Rifling, number of grooves 9
Twist . . . . Uniform, right-hand, 7° slope
Length . . . . 48.06 in.
Rate of fire . . . . 750-850 rds./min.
Ammunition
Types . . . . As listed
Powder pressure, Maximum . . . . 42,000 lb./sq. in.
Muzzle velocity . . . . 2,750 ft./sec

The following rounds were designed to satisfy the joint Army and Navy requirements for match within 0.1 second time of flight at 1,000 yd.:

Cartridge, A.P.-T, T9E5 (M95)
Cartridge, I, T18 (M96)
Cartridge, H.E. I, T23 (M97)
Cartridge, H.E., T16 (M98)
Cartridge, Practice, T24 (M99)

20-MM AUTOMATIC GUNS (AIRCRAFT CANNON)

Perhaps the best way to show the progress in aircraft-cannon development during the war period is by a comparison of characteristics. For example, this country entered the war with the 20-mm automatic cannon, M2. This gun, with a 60-round magazine, weighed 140 pounds and had a fire rate of 650 shots per minute. By the end of the war, a new 20-mm cannon (M3) had been developed which weighed, with its feeder, only 112 pounds and had a rate of fire of 800 rounds per minute. Ammunition for this new gun was automatically belt-fed so that its supply to the gun was limited only by the capacity of the airplane to carry the load.

An interesting characteristic of this new 20-mm automatic gun is its extreme flexibility. With one basic weapon, by changing bolts and solenoids, it is possible to fire either from the bolt-back position or the bolt-forward position, or to fire ammunition using electric primers. This flexibility is important when guns are used in wings synchronized to fire through propellers or are used in turrets.

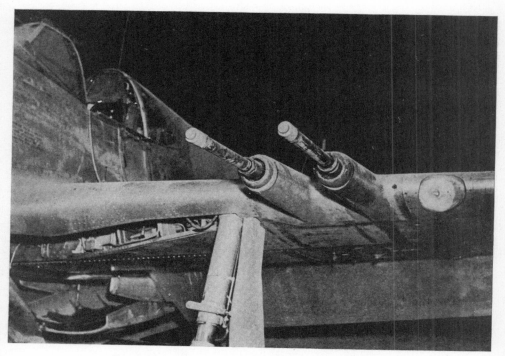

General view of 20-mm cannon, M2, installation in a P-51 airplane.

20-MM FEED MECHANISM

In order to increase the belt pull of 20-mm ammunition "belts," two new feeders were developed. One, taking energy from the recoil of the gun, was developed to the point where it would pull 70 pounds; another, using an electric motor, could pull 80 pounds. These developments more than doubled the available belt pull in the standard feeder. When the number of "G's" * under which a gun may be required to operate in aircraft is considered—with inertia affecting its moving parts—the importance of this "belt pull" can be realized.

* G = acceleration due to gravity. 1G = 32 ft./sec./sec.

20-mm Feed Mechanism, M3.

AMMUNITION FOR 20-MM AUTOMATIC GUNS

The discussion of any gun is incomplete if the ammunition is not considered. The gun itself is, after all, merely a device for starting a slug or a charge of explosive toward a target.

In the field of aircraft armament, three different projectiles are required: explosive, armor-piercing, and incendiary. The development of such ammunition is further complicated by the fact that all rounds must be the same length in order to pass through the feeder, and that all must have the same weight and shape in order that ballistics can be matched so that accurate fire can be delivered with any. The seriousness of the problem may be realized from the fact that the armor-piercing shot is solid steel and that the high-explosive round uses a comparatively heavy fuze (not present in the incendiary round).

However, the requirements were met by adding a cap to the armor-piercing round and by adjusting the weights of the shell in the other two rounds. The using service thus acquired three suitably effective rounds, meeting all ballistic requirements for the 20-mm automatic gun.

These 20-mm guns and ammunition of the Ordnance Department were used throughout the war by the U. S. Navy and the Marine Corps, as well as by the Army Air Forces. Operations included air combat, strafing attacks against Japanese aircraft, buildings, and fortifications, and close-support missions in cooperation with ground troops. One pilot's typical comment after attacking a Japanese fighter plane was that "Large pieces blew off the tail, the right wing broke off, and the plane disintegrated."

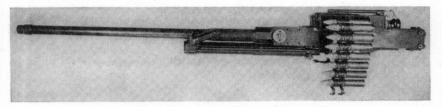

37-mm Gun, M4E3, with M55A1 Ammunition. Left side view.

37-MM AIRCRAFT GUN, M4

CHARACTERISTICS

Rate of fire . . . . 150 rds./min.
Muzzle velocity
   M54 . . . . 2,000 ft./sec.
   M55A1 . . . . 2,000 ft./sec.
   M80 . . . . 1,650 ft./sec.
Approximate range . . . . 4,000 yd.—12,000 ft.—2.2 miles
Weight of gun without magazine . . . . 213 lb.
Weight of 30-rd. magazine, empty . . . . 35.5 lb.
Weight of 30-rd. magazine, loaded . . . . 93.4 lb.
Length of gun, over-all . . . . 89.5 in.
Average length of recoil . . . . 9⅝ in.
Principle of operation . . . . Long recoil

AMMUNITION is in the form of fixed rounds, consisting of H.E. shell, M54, with P.D. fuze, M56; practice shell, M55A1, with dummy fuze, M50, A.P., and M80.

37-MM AUTOMATIC GUNS (AIRCRAFT CANNON)

Army Ordnance pioneered in the 37-mm automatic aircraft gun. At the start of the war, the 37-mm gun weighed, with magazine, 248 pounds and had a cyclic rate of 150 rounds per minute, at a muzzle velocity of 2,000 feet per second. The magazine had a 30-round capacity. Rapid development during the war led to its redesign and conversion into a self-fed type, using a disintegrating link belt. The gun then had these characteristics: Weight, 231 pounds; cyclic rate, 165 rounds per minute, with ammunition limited only by the capacity of the airplane. A still further development of this gun produced a weapon of greater muzzle velocity and firepower.

37-mm automatic gun, M9, mounted in aircraft.

37-MM AUTOMATIC GUN, M9

CHARACTERISTICS

Rate of fire	125 rds./min.
Muzzle velocity (approx.)	2,900 ft./sec.
Approx. maximum range	8,875 yd.
Weight of gun, without magazine	365 lb.
Length of gun, over-all	104 in.
Length of recoil	10¾ in.
Principle of operation	Long recoil

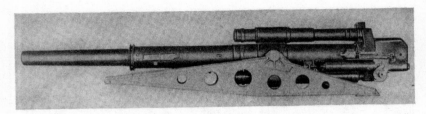

75-mm gun, M4—Mount, M6.

75-MM GUN, M4, MOUNT, M6

CHARACTERISTICS

Total weight (gun and mount)	1,297 lb.
Weight of gun (with loading tray and wrench)	900 lb.
Length of mount	140.94 in.
Length of gun	118.38 in.
Muzzle velocity (A.P.C. shot, M61)	2,050 ft./sec.
Maximum range	15,000 yd.
Maximum effective range	3,000 yd.
Maximum pressure	38,000 p.s.i.
Maximum elevation	6°
Traverse	0°

AMMUNITION is in the form of complete fixed rounds. It consists of H.E. shell, M48, with M.T. fuze, M43A4, or P.D. fuze, M57; A.P. shot, M72, and A.P.C. shot, M61, with B.D. fuze, M66A1.

75-MM GUN, M4 (AIRCRAFT CANNON)

In the desire to equip the Air Forces with aircraft cannon of still greater firepower, the Ordnance Department undertook the development of a 75-mm aircraft cannon—the largest gun used in any airplane during the war. Installation of this gun in aircraft produced entirely new problems. For example, the trunnion reaction of the gun had to be absorbed by the airplane. In the ground mounting of this type of weapon a recoil of 44 inches is permitted. In the airplane, however, space limitations prohibits such a long recoil; but shortening the recoil increases the trunnion load. Furthermore, the conventional recoil and counter-recoil systems, with the cylinders mounted above or below the gun tube, produce a gun silhouette which is entirely too large for aircraft installation. These problems were solved by carefully planned step-by-step development programs.

The first experiments were conducted in 1939 by installing a standard field gun in an existing airplane to prove that an airplane could stand the shock of firing a gun of such caliber, and that effective results could be expected from such an installation. After prolonged ground and air trials at Aberdeen Proving Ground, the test unit was moved to Eglin Field, Florida, where firings against aerial targets were conducted. The tests showed that, even with the crude fire-control equipment then available, accurate firing was possible at ranges of 2,000 yards and more, far beyond any ranges considered possible with existing aircraft weapons.

A project was thereupon initiated to design the gun, airplane, and fire-control system to take advantage of this new firepower. Out of this project came a fully automatic 75-mm gun which included a fuze setter rammer and a 20-round magazine. At about the same time, a requirement was presented for a 75-mm hand-loaded gun to be used against ground targets. A light weapon was designed, built, and installed in the B-25 airplane. This weapon proved to be very effective against light surface vessels, including destroyer classes, antiaircraft batteries, tanks, and similar water and land targets.

In developing this weapon, the problems referred to above were all solved. The preliminary tests proved that an airplane could stand the trunnion loads resulting from firing the standard 75-mm field gun. The accelerations resulting from this firing amounted to 1/4 G. Discussion among Ordnance and Air Forces engineers, and crew members, indicated that an airplane could easily withstand an acceleration resulting from firing equal to 1 G,* and that the airplane crew would not be adversely affected either physically or mentally by this shock. The recoil stroke was therefore limited to 22 inches, with a resulting load of 3/4 G being applied to the airplane. A new recoil mechanism was designed, in which the cylinder was concentric about the gun tube and thus reduced the silhouette and weight. Finally, for the first time in gun design a steel having an elastic limit of 160,000 pounds per square inch was employed in the gun tube. The result was the lightest and most compact 75-mm gun and recoil mechanism ever built. In these developments the weight of gun and recoil mechanism were reduced from 1,500 to 800 pounds. In fact, in the final design the weight of gun, recoil mechanism, feed mechanism, and 20 rounds of ammunition were less than the weight of the original gun and recoil mechanism installed in an airplane.

When completed, this gun looked promising for use as a tank gun, and so the M24 light tank was built around it. This, one of our outstanding tanks, appeared on the battlefields in 1945.

An example of the operational use of the 75-mm gun in the B-25 airplane, is given in the following citation in the award of an Air Medal to Colonel John T. Murtha, Jr. (since killed in action): "For meritorious achievement while participating in an aerial flight over Wake Island on 18 May 1944. Colonel Murtha was air coordi-

---

* See note, p. 64 above.

nator of an amphibious operation against this enemy-held island. Piloting a B-25, he was in a position to observe the difficulties encountered by our ground forces, who were being fired upon by an enemy pillbox, which was so well camouflaged that it could not be seen by the men on the beach. Since no air support patrols were in the area at this time, Colonel Murtha volunteered to attack the pillbox. Descending to minimum altitude, he made three runs, raking the emplacement with machine-gun and cannon fire. On the third run, all return fire from the enemy ceased and the troops resumed the advance. The courage and devotion to duty displayed by Colonel Murtha on this occasion are worthy of commendation."

Another example of the potentialities of the 75-mm aircraft cannon is contained in the account of an attack on a large destroyer by two airplanes on 23 July 1943. The attack occurred off the coast of Cape Gloucester and the aircraft involved were B-25 bombers. On the first run, seven shots were fired; the first two were misses, which the gunners credited to lack of experience. Hits in order of sequence were observed near the 6-inch gun turret, the front deck, the aft deck, the forward turret, and the control bridge. On the second run, the first two shots were again misses; the following five, however, were direct hits approximately 75 feet apart through the entire length of the ship, which was, by that time, in a sinking condition.

Throughout the war, the Ordnance Department supplied both the Army and the Navy with all their aircraft armament and ammunition. The caliber .50 machine gun and its ammunition constituted by a wide margin the best weapon in the air and gave our aviators a tremendous advantage over the German and Japanese fliers. Our aircraft cannon likewise provided superior firepower for ample coverage over a wide variety of land and sea targets.

A 75-mm aircraft gun destroys a Japanese freighter.

Chapter III

AMMUNITION

Chapter III

AMMUNITION

The design and development of military ammunition utilizes all sciences. It covers all forms and shapes of missiles and their components such as shells, bombs, grenades, mines, pyrotechnics, flares, fuzes, propellants, explosives, and rockets. It requires specialists in metallurgy, physics, thermodynamics, aerodynamics, and chemistry and engineering in many fields for the successful development of any given item. The multiplicity of types, running to thousands of items, caused the expenditure of the greatest amount of energy, funds, and manufacturing facilities, as compared with the production of other weapons of war.

Although a number of items had been standardized before the war, most of them were available only in limited quantities. Just before World War II, steps were taken toward quantity production. The global character of the war, as the conflict progressed, called for new and improved types of ammunition.

Explosives

At the beginning of the war, military explosives had been brought to a point where lead azide had almost completely replaced the less stable mercury fulminate as an initiator of detonation. Highly satisfactory substitutes had been developed to meet a possible shortage of T.N.T.; new processes for the production of high-grade Tetryl had been established; and improved fuze powders had been provided for standard applications. The increased tempo of warfare, the advent of new weapons and devices, and the demand for increased power and precision of ammunition characterized World War II throughout, and necessitated corresponding improvements in explosives, which were met as new situations and demands arose.

Very early there arose a demand for explosives of higher shattering effect (brisance) than T.N.T. The increased availability of Tetryl—the highly brisant standard booster explosive for artillery ammunition and bombs—permitted its use in the development of special-purpose, castable explosives. The Tetrytols (mixtures of Tetryl and T.N.T.), which are much more brisant than T.N.T., resulted from this development. These were employed as burster charges for chemical shells and as new demolition charges which were developed by the Corps of Engineers.

The enormous extension of bombing led to a requirement for an explosive with greater blast effect than T.N.T. but suitable for melt-loading in the same manner as T.N.T. To meet this need, two large-scale processes were developed for the manufacture of R.D.X.—the continuous and batch processes. R.X.D. has too high a melting point (204° C.) for melt-loading and is much more sensitive to shock than T.N.T. The requirement was met and the disadvantages of R.D.X. overcome by the use of Composition B, a desensitized mixture based on R.D.X. Composition B, about 35 per cent more brisant than T.N.T., was suitable for melt-loading from steam-heated kettles and was not unduly sensitive to shock. This was used chiefly for loading bombs.

A similar development was the use of pento-

73

lite, a mixture of P.E.T.N. (pentaerythritol-tetranitrate) and T.N.T. Even more sensitive to shock than R.D.X., P.E.T.N. offered the advantages of being nearly as highly brisant and more readily detonated by fuze-booster systems. The composition finally adopted has a brisance 30 per cent higher than that of T.N.T., and had special advantages with respect to loading, since it could be produced, during the purification of the P.E.T.N., by coprecipitation with or precipitation on T.N.T. The explosive so prepared can be handled in a dry state and subjected to both melt and press loading. It has been used extensively in detonators, in bazooka grenades, in special boostering devices, and in shaped charges of H.E.A.T. (high explosive antitank shell).

Further advantage was taken of the high brisance and ease of initiation of R.D.X. in Composition A3 and Composition C3. These explosives consist of R.D.X. desensitized with suitable ma-terials. Composition A3 was used to some extent as a charge for boosters and small-caliber projectiles, and Composition C3 was used extensively as a demolition explosive.

The use of bombing with the objectives of achieving a high incendiary effect and widespread disruption instead of localized shattering action led to the development of Tritonal, a mixture of T.N.T. and powdered aluminum, which can be prepared from dry materials in steam-heated melting kettles and then can be melt-loaded. Tritonal, in bombs, was used extensively in the latter phases of the war.

In the other direction there was a requirement for an explosive less sensitive to shock than T.N.T. and more brisant than ammonium picrate, the standard explosive for armor-piercing shells. The new explosive had to be suitable for melt-loading into semi-armor-piercing bombs. The requirements were met by Picratol, a mix-

Effects of high-explosive munitions (bombs and artillery shells) on Aachen, Germany.

ture of ammonium picrate and T.N.T. which possesses essentially the best characteristics of each of its ingredients.

In addition to these, a number of other explosives were developed which, at the end of the war, were just about to be produced in quantity. Among these were Haleite and its mixture with T.N.T. (Ednatol), mixtures of Cyclonite and T.N.T. (Cyclotols) and ternary mixtures of explosives, such as P.T.X.-2 which has unusually high brisance.

Although no pressing need arose during this war for a new initiating agent, diazodinitrophenol was used to some extent as a substitute for lead azide. As it had both satisfactory stability and marked ease of ignition, diazodinitrophenol was suitable for use in detonator and priming elements.

Special phases of tactical bombing required delayed functioning of the dropped bomb, to permit the airplane to escape beyond the bomb's radius of destruction. Ordinary fuze powders burned too rapidly in delay elements to be suit-

able. This combustion speed was due, in part at least, to the pressure of confined gaseous products of combustion causing acceleration of burning rate. This difficulty was overcome and the problem solved by the application of two newly developed powder compositions which form only solid combustion-products and which burn at constant, predetermined rates. This type of composition offered definite advantages, and a similar composition was developed and used in hand-grenade delay elements instead of black powder.

The development of improved explosives does not constitute the entire story of explosives development during World War II. Process development was also an important contribution.

As pointed out above, the development of large-scale processes for the production of R.D.X. was necessary before this explosive could be standardized for use in Compositions A3, B, and C3. The methylaminedinitrochlorbenzene process led to greatly increased production of Tetryl with existing facilities. In connection

Static Detonation of 10,000 lb. Bomb. Explosive: RDX Composition B, 30 June 1943.

with the development of other new explosives, a new process for the production of raw material used in the manufacture of Haleite was developed. A manufacturing process for the new gasless delay powders was placed in operation, and manufacturing procedures were developed which permitted large-scale production of the ternary explosive P.T.X.-2.

The story of the T.N.T. processes is even more outstanding. Before World War II a shortage of T.N.T. was anticipated because of the limited amount of toluene available from the coal-tar industry. In the early stages of the war, however, a process was conceived for the production of toluene from petroleum. Thus toluene was made available in ample supplies to meet the requirements. Shortly afterward, there was introduced a "direct-nitration" process which increased the daily output of a T.N.T. line from 25,000 to 140,-000 or more pounds. This resulted in such a flood of T.N.T. from the plants that the use of

all substitutes was discontinued and it became the universal solvent of military explosives, and was produceable at a cost of only six cents a pound.

Propellants and Primers

Experience in World War I with the weaknesses of the simple pyro-cellulose type of propellant indicated that changes had to be made in the propellent powder for improved combat uses. The pyro powders were hygroscopic and gave a very large muzzle flash. These were serious disadvantages—the first because moisture had a deleterious effect on accuracy, and the second because flashes too readily betrayed the position of the weapon or battery.

During the period between wars, active research was undertaken in the development of a non-hygroscopic propellant, which was flashless in the small and medium caliber weapons. How-

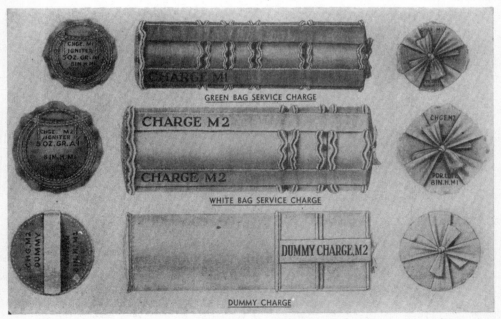

Our medium and heavy guns and howitzers used separate loading ammunition, that is, the propellent and projectiles were loaded separately into the gun. The calibers of artillery using this system were the 4.5-inch gun, 155-mm howitzer, 155-mm gun, 8-inch howitzer, 8-inch gun, and 240-mm howitzer.

ever, this too often increased the amount of smoke to an undesirable or even a prohibitive degree. The advent of intensive mechanized warfare with weapons of high power and under conditions of practically point-blank aim intensified the problem of smoke and flash as expressed in the word "obscuration." Similarly, obscuration became a serious problem in the case of small-caliber direct-fire antiaircraft weapons and, indeed, in the case of any ground weapons where tactics called for direct-fire operation.

As a general introduction to the propellant and primer development carried out in World War II, the more important requirements which arose from modern warfare conditions are as follows:

1. Reduction of obscuration of tracer, point of impact of projectile, and target, particularly for direct-aim weapons. For indirect-fire weapons, and for aircraft weapons, smoke was of secondary importance, although always undesirable.

2. Increase of muzzle velocity, to provide greater striking power against armor and to provide flatter trajectories for better aim and shorter times of flight. The flat trajectory and short time of flight were especially vital for airplane weapons, in direct proportion to the speed and maneuverability of the aircraft itself.

3. Reduction of the temperature coefficient of the propelling charge as a whole, and most especially control of the dispersion in muzzle velocity and pressure at extreme temperatures. This was a requirement brought about by warfare in all conceivable climates and at stratospheric altitudes.

4. Development of suitable propelling charges for various special types of ammunition and weapons, such as the following:

(A) High-velocity armor-piercing (H.V. A.P.) projectiles, the principle of which was to utilize a light-weight projectile containing a hard core and fired at hyper-velocities.

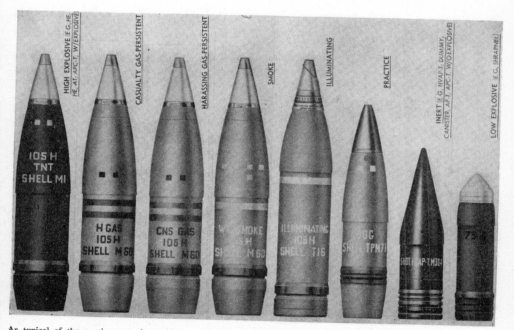

As typical of the requirements for artillery ammunition, 13 different types of ammunition were required for the 105-mm howitzer alone. Eight of these are here shown.

(B) Increasingly large caliber mortars. Many of these weapons were designed for jungle warfare, to propel a large volume of explosive power over relatively short ranges but with great accuracy.

(C) Reduced-velocity, short-range, high-angle rounds of high-explosive ammunition for barrage fire and for medium-caliber weapons whose primary purpose was tank or anti-tank usage. The obvious advantages of this special type of H.E. ammunition were: Improved accuracy, certainty of functioning, ability to reach targets over obstacles, ease of flash and smoke control (important because of vulnerable position).

(D) Suitable propelling charges for recoilless weapons.

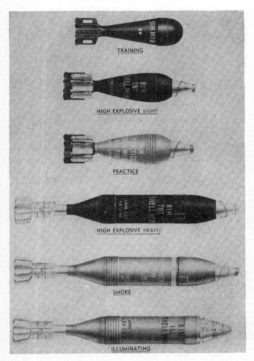

81 M Mortar ammunition. As in artillery ammunition, many different types of mortar ammunition were required to meet the demands of the tactical situations encountered on the battle field.

(E) Propelling charges for new weapons with increased chamber capacity, length of tube, and greatly increased muzzle energy.

5. Improved accuracy of ammunition in general, and particularly reduction in dispersion and velocity between different lots of ammunition of precisely the same type.

It must be noted that the phenomena occurring in a firearm at or near the muzzle are not alone functions of the propellant but, rather, are tied up intimately with the gun and ignition system. This fact became more and more evident as the attempt was made to meet simultaneously all the complex requirements imposed by modern warfare and tactical situations. Hence it became regular practice in developing complete propelling charges to design the ignition system to fit the designs of chamber and propellant as effectively as possible. This was a means of improving the efficiency and smoothness of the heat engine (the weapon), just as a spark plug is designed to obtain the most power from an internal-combustion engine.

Also, other factors influence the performance of the weapon in varying degrees. The basic characteristics of the weapon itself, such as chamber size and shape, length of projectile travel and use of muzzle attachments, all have their effect on the perfomance of the propellant. Even the use of a particular design of tracer in the base of the projectile have some influence on muzzle flash and smoke.

It was apparent, therefore, that performance must be calculated as an integrated effect of all influencing factors rather than merely of the propellant alone. This was at once an advantage and a disadvantage. It meant that there were more factors to bring into play to solve a given problem, and also that the problem of analyzing a particular difficulty was correspondingly more complex.

Flashless-Smokeless Developments in 76-mm Ammunition

To meet the necessity for increased striking power for tank guns, the 76-mm gun (2,600 f.s.) was developed. This gun was designed to be fitted into the same tank space as that formerly occupied by the 75-mm gun (2,000 f.s.). It was equipped with the standard type of non-hygroscopic M1 propellant, but the ballistic requirements made large muzzle flash inevitable. To solve this flash problem, various methods of attack were tried:

1. A small percentage of inhibiting salt, such as potassium sulfate, was added. This salt completely eliminated the flash, but gave a cloud of smoke which obscured the projectile tracer and the point of impact for as much as ten seconds. This was considered unsatisfactory, and so steps were taken to develop a more suitable flash reducer.

2. It was noted that, in addition to the large amount of smoke, the same round gave erratic ballistic performance at low exterior temperatures. This was extremely serious, in view of the global scope of the war, which meant that all ammunition had to be fired under extreme variations of temperature. Immediately suspicion was directed at the ignition system, which, at the time, consisted of a standard M28 primer, 10 inches long, loading a 300-grain A1 black powder, venting on the sides. An extended series of tests conducted at a temperature of —40° F., with many variations in loading and ignition, indicated the type of primer which would give satisfactory ignition. This new primer was appreciably longer—19 inches—than the M28. The most important feature, however, of the new primer was that the venting was entirely in the forward portion of the primer body, and the end was left open except for a thin cardboard disk. This primer furnished front ignition and gave smooth and uniform ballistic results even at extreme temperatures.

3. During the course of the experimental firings to improve the ignition and low-temperature performance, various types of propellants were investigated. These tests indicated that the new forward-venting type primer, when used with M1 propellant even without potassium salts, eliminated flash and gave very small quantities and densities of smoke. The new primer was standardized, and complete rounds of the 76-mm ammunition loaded with this primer were officially identified as flashless and smokeless, and removed the objections of the using services.

Flashless-Smokeless Development in 3-inch and 90-mm Ammunition

The 3-inch and 90-mm guns were used, in the early phases of the war, as antiaircraft guns, for which purpose they had been primarily designed. It was realized, however, that they would also be used as antitank guns, and in 1939 armor-piercing ammunition was developed and manufactured for these weapons. The 90-mm gun was well suited to tank purposes with no change in basic interior ballistics. This gun was the American answer to the German 88-mm gun as a tank and antitank weapon.

To obtain still more striking power and armor penetration, however, it was desirable to increase the muzzle velocity for the armor-piercing round. Further, it was necessary to obtain flashlessness with reduced smoke (obscuration) to provide protection against enemy observation and to afford our gunners more opportunity to observe hits. To obtain the increase in velocity to 2,800 feet per second with M1 propellant, it was necessary to increase the pressure limit. In view of the high density of loading, however, the ignition of this propelling charge with the standard primer was inadequate. Increasing the length of the primer to 19 inches, as for the 76-mm gun, gave better results. But this was not entirely satisfactory because of flarebacks inside the tank when the breech was opened. Another disadvantage was that only a small percentage of the rounds were flashless.

These disadvantages were eliminated by the addition of a supplementary igniter pad. This assembly proved to be virtually flashless except for a small residual flame in or near the muzzle brake. Thus the flash and smoke problems were solved, for these weapons.

Flash Reducers

It had been recognized, in the past, that an optional method of reducing the flash in the 155-mm gun would be highly desirable. It was also known that reduction of flash was accompanied by an increased volume of smoke. Therefore, if an optional means could be developed wherein the flash would be reduced or eliminated for night firing and the flash accepted during day firing without smoke, it would be a very desirable combination. Between 1917 and 1942 several attempts were made to attain this result. Trials frequently gave flashless performance but were not consistent. Because of the critical need for an effective flash reducer, experimentation was intensified in April 1943.

During these experiments many substances were tried, such as black powder, potassium sulfate, potassium nitrate, and potassium bitartrate. These were all tested, either alone or in combination with black powder. They were tried as pads in front of charge, pads between base and increment section, and as annular rings placed in different positions around the charge. Finally, a pair of longitudinal strips, consisting of three channels in each strip, were used. The finally adopted flash-reducer strip gave consistently flashless results; the flash was reduced so much that at night only a small muzzle glow was visible.

Immediately after achieving success with the flash reducer in the 155-mm ammunition, work was undertaken to develop a similar optional means of reducing flash in the 105-mm, the 155-mm, and 8-inch howitzers. These weapons were considered essentially flashless, but there were circumstances in which—with certain powder lots, worn weapons, or extremely humid atmosphere, either singly or in combination—they occa-

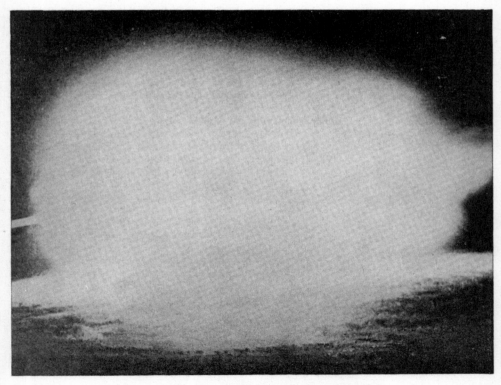

155-mm gun, M1, firing super-charge round without flash reducer.

sionally flashed. It was felt, therefore, that an optional flash reducer, for use at the discretion of the battery commander, should be made available. For all these howitzers, a wafer-type flash reducer was developed.

Shaped Charges

The term "shaped charge" is applied to special high-explosive ammunition, the distinguishing feature of which is the cavity (usually conical) covered by a thin metal liner (usually steel) conforming to the shape of the cavity. Despite the reduction in weight of explosive, on account of the cavity, such ammunition displays certain remarkable characteristics, notably its ability to penetrate armor and other resistant targets. In this respect, it equals or exceeds the effects of the best armor-piercing projectiles and, what is even more remarkable, its penetrating power is not a function of the velocity or angle of impact.

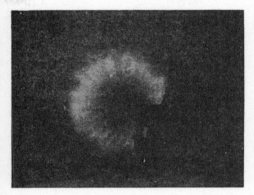

155-mm gun, M1, firing super-charge round with flash reducer.

Night photograph of detonation and jet from 15-lb. demolition shaped charge, fired into space. Vertical range of jet about 300 feet.

In fact, the penetrating power of shaped charges is greatest when static.

The principle of the shaped charge has been known for considerably more than one hundred years, but it could not be utilized efficiently for military purposes until the development of new and more powerful high explosives made possible the design of suitable ammunition. Although much basic work on shaped charges was done by Munroe, in this country, more than sixty years ago, the theory of the shaped charge was not well established until World War II. It has now been improved sufficiently to make great progress.

Briefly, the shaped charge functions by virtue of an extremely high-velocity jet of metallic particles, derived from the cavity liner and projected at velocities in excess of the detonation velocity of the explosive. Initial jet velocities of the order of 30,000 feet per second have been measured, from charges whose rate of detonation is of the order of 25,000 feet per second. When this stream of particles impinges on the target, the metal at the point of impact flows forward and laterally, to form a hole.

Two essential requirements for effective development of the shaped-charge effect are: (1) Initiation of detonation of the charge must be at the end opposite to the end containing the cavity, and (2) the charge must detonate at a suitable distance, or stand-off, from the target.

The military shaped charge was first introduced in late 1940. Its potentialities were immediately recognized, and active secret work, at once initiated, produced two designs of rifle grenade, one machine-gun grenade, and two calibers of artillery projectiles by the time we entered the war in December 1941. The machine-gun grenade, in the early spring of 1942, was modified by development of a rocket tail and provision of a suitable projector, and in July 1942 was introduced into combat as the now famous "bazooka," which the Germans later copied and used against us.

Shaped-charge artillery projectiles, in 75-mm and 105-mm calibers, were effectively used by tanks and tank destroyers in all theaters. They are credited with having helped to destroy Rommel's Afrika Korps in the German retreat from Tobruk to Bizerte, and were employed effectively in reducing fortifications in Italy, France, Germany, and the Pacific.

An especially interesting and novel shaped charge was developed on urgent request from the Air Forces, for use in cutting glider tow cables. This device, attached to the towing plane, would instantly sever the cable, whether stationary or being paid out. The full quantity

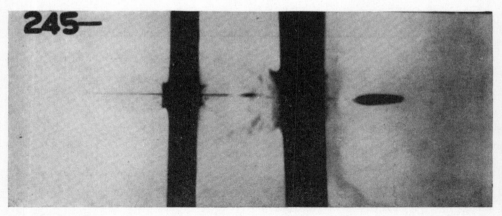

X-ray photograph of jet shaped charge, showing penetration of multiple targets. Note small diameter of needle-like jet compared with diameters of holes in targets, and also comparative sizes of holes in steel (left) and aluminum (right). Photo approximately full size. Oval object at right is residue of collapsed liner, known as the "slug."

required for operational use by the 14th Air Force was manufactured in less than 30 days. Theater reports indicated that this device was effectively used during the operations of Merrill's Marauders.

Of the shaped-charge demolition devices produced for the Corps of Engineers, the 15-pound and 40-pound sizes were widely used in both Europe and the Pacific. Designed to perforate reinforced concrete walls from three to six feet thick and provide a hole large enough for the insertion of a bangalore torpedo or a flame thrower, these charges proved to be especially effective against Japanese fortifications and shelters. Because of the poor quality of Japanese concrete, these shaped charges would frequently demolish the entire sides of small pillboxes. Against log and earth bunkers, they were used to perforate the walls or roofs and spray the occupants with super-high-velocity particles.

Artillery Fuzes

The fuze is the most important element of a complete round, as the functioning of the fuze initiates the detonating train and explosive of any type of ammunition. The performance of American fuzes during the war was outstanding, with a minimum percentage of malfunctions. The Ordnance Department can be justly proud of its fuzes and their efficiency record during World War II.

During World War I, our fuze system for point-fuzed high-explosive artillery shells did not have a common contour and weight. Thus a large number of firing tables were necessary, because the ballistics were different for each type of fuze; also, fire adjustment was necessary when changing from one type of fuze to another.

From 1918 on, the Ordnance Department had developed for manufacture, or had in process of development, many of the artillery and mortar

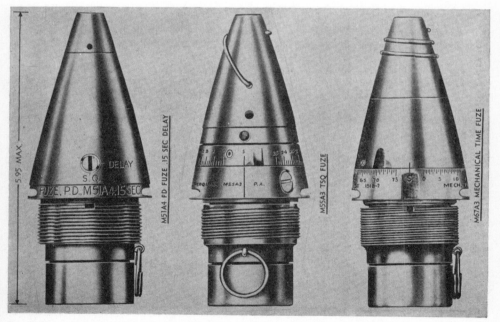

The Ordnance Department designed and industry manufactured more than 150 types of artillery fuzes to meet every requirement of the ground forces.

fuzes now standard (157 types). The most notable achievement in this field was the establishment of a common contour and weight for fuzes and boosters for point-fuzed, high-explosive artillery shells, which would be suitable for interchangeable employment in calibers from 75-mm to 240-mm inclusive. Millions of these standard fuzes were manufactured during the war. Reports from the battlefields indicated that the functioning of these fuzes was far superior to that of any enemy fuzes; our number of "duds" was fewer than those of either the Germans or the Japanese. In addition, the standard contour of fuzes made possible a considerable reduction in the number of firing tables which would otherwise have been required. Our Army thus enjoyed certain distinct advantages over the enemy.

These fuze systems covered selective superquick and delay types, selective time and superquick types, and the single-purpose mechanical time type, all with the same contour. The fuze for smooth-bore mortars (the 60-mm and the 81-mm) also had a similar contour and weight with integral booster.

Beginning shortly after the start of World War II, new field requirements constantly arose, necessitating certain changes in ammunition already in existence in order to maintain superiority over enemy ordnance in all tactical situations. New weapons also necessitated new series of ammunition, which, in turn, required additional fuze development.

One of the outstanding fuzes of the war was the concrete-piercing type. This was a direct product of an urgent requirement for a means of neutralizing concrete or similarly constructed fortifications. It was designed for use with the standard high-explosive shell, and could readily be substituted for the standard fuze in the field. This fuze placed in the hands of the using arms an effective resistant-target or concrete-penetrating ammunition in a very short time. A considerably longer time would have been required to provide a special high-explosive and high-capacity concrete-piercing projectile and fuze. Furthermore, a new type of ammunition for all calibers would have complicated the supply and production programs.

As the war progressed, it was determined that suitable base detonating fuzes were necessary for armor-piercing projectiles of the explosive type. During the early part of the war, only solid armor-piercing shot were manufactured

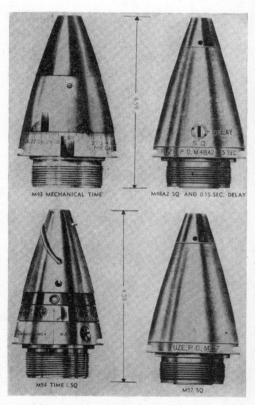

Every artillery shell fired at the enemy had to have a suitable fuze. Ordnance artillery fuzes meet all requirements as to reliability and accuracy.

and issued. Base detonating fuzes for armor-piercing, high-explosive projectiles were designed and standardized for the 57-mm, 75-mm, 3-inch, and 90-mm guns.

With the development of shaped-charge ammunition, fuzes for the effective detonation of this type of ammunition for 75-mm and 105-mm guns were rapidly developed and manufactured.

The early completion of this design materially increased the effectiveness of these weapons in the destruction of armored vehicles and tanks.

For use in the Pacific war, especially in jungle operations where air burst was desired, development of a time and super-quick fuze was undertaken, and rapidly and successfully completed. This type of fuze was of immeasurable aid to the using services in jungle warfare.

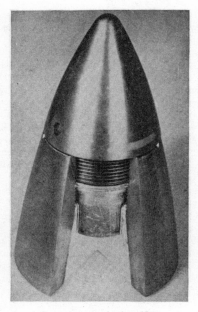

Fuze, concrete piercing, M78.

V.T. Fuzes

The radio proximity fuze was one of the outstanding scientific products of this war. This fuze is as simple in principle as it is complex in design and functioning. It consists of a minute radio transmitting and receiving oscillator, an amplifier, an electrical firing circuit, and a series of electrical and mechanical safety devices which assure its proper operation. It is one of the safest types of fuze: its record of "prematures" is approximately one per million.

The radio transmitter broadcasts a continuous signal which, on approach to an airplane, the ground, or other suitable target, is reflected back to the fuze and is received by the same oscillator. This sets up an interference, known as the Doppler frequency, and when its frequency and intensity reach the proper values, for which the amplifier is tuned, the signal passes through the amplifier and actuates the firing circuit, thereby detonating the projectile. The mechanism of the fuze is so designed that detonation occurs when the shell, bomb, or rocket to which it is assembled comes within lethal range of the target.

Aside from its importance as a unique scientific development, the V.T. fuze was significant because it permitted naval vessels to operate in enemy waters and to combat both land- and carrier-based enemy aircraft on terms approaching equality. In 1921, the Ordnance Department's development of 2,000- and 4,000-pound bombs, then the largest in the world, and their successful use by General Mitchell in sinking capital ships, had proved that surface fleets were vulnerable to air power. In World War II, the proximity fuze for antiaircraft artillery proved to be the best answer of the surface ship to air power. It was effective not only in shooting down enemy bombers and fighters, but also in countering the deadly Japanese KAMIKAZE (suicide) bombers.

But this was only a part of the value of the V.T. fuze. It was also effective in multiplying the destructive power of field artillery, bombs, rockets, and mortar shells. Through its effective air burst, which is adjusted to occur at the optimum location to obtain the maximum effects from high-velocity fragments, the V.T. fuze increases the deadliness of projectiles against targets suitable for such attack by a factor that varies from three to twenty, depending upon the projectile employed and the target attacked. It was deadly against personnel in the open or in the trenches, in that it permitted delivery of accurately registered time fire, without observation, up to the maximum range of artillery, and at any time of day or night. In bombs, it permitted the attainment of optimum height of burst of fragmentation types, for attacks on personnel or light materiel; of demolition types, for maximum effects of blast; and of chemical types, for the most effective distribution of fire, smoke, or chemicals. In rockets or aircraft cannon, it greatly increases the effectiveness of plane-to-plane and plane-to-ground attacks, as it yields results far superior to those obtainable with conventional time fuzes.

The "V.T. fuze" is not a single item of ordnance, but is a generic term applied to a large family of similarly functioning devices, each different from the others and each designed for a specific weapon or purpose. For United States and British field artillery, rotated rockets, and antiaircraft use, nine types of fuzes were developed and manufactured in large quantities, while a number of additional types were in development or in limited procurement. Of the

Typical Examples of V.T. Fuzes
At left — MK 53 for Navy 5"/38 gun
        T75E6 for 120-mm A.A. gun
        T74, T76, T80 type for 90 mm A.A. gun and Army
        Howitzers.
At right—M166 (T51) for Bombs (Bar type)
        M168 type for Bombs (Ring type)
        T2005 for non-rotated rockets
        T132 for mortar shells (81-mm and larger).

non-rotated types—which were developed by the Ordnance Department and Division 4 N.D.R.C., and manufactured under Signal Corps, Ordnance, and N.D.R.C. contracts for the Army, Navy, Marine Corps, and the British—five types of bomb fuzes and four types of rocket fuzes were manufactured in large quantities, while a number of additional types were in development or in limited procurement. In addition, other types of V.T. mortar fuzes were in the final stages of development.

V.T. fuzes were first used in combat by the cruiser HELENA on 5 January 1943 to destroy a Japanese airplane. From that date on, they were used continuously and effectively by both the United States and British navies. On account of the danger of compromise, reproduction by the enemy, and use against our growing air power, V.T. fuzes were placed under direct control of the Combined Chiefs of Staff, and their use over land was prohibited until the military situation was such that it was virtually certain that their capture or recovery by the enemy could not influence the progress or outcome of the war. Only then, in the fall of 1944, were Allied nations permitted to fire V.T. fuzes into or over enemy territory.

In the spring of 1944, when it became known that Germany was about to start the V-1 attack on England, the use of V.T. fuzes in antiaircraft guns defending the Channel coast was permitted. Fuzes were shipped to England and stored there under guard. Ordnance personnel were sent to make the necessary preparations and to instruct both British and American antiaircraft personnel. The rest is history: the British have officially credited the V.T. fuze, assisted by United States antiaircraft artillery radar and fire control, with saving London from the buzz-bombs. During the last four weeks of the V-1 attacks, V.T.-fuzed projectiles destroyed 24, 46, 67, and 79 per cent, respectively, of the targets attacked.

It had been planned to introduce the Germans to V.T. field artillery fire on Christmas Day, 1944, but Von Rundstedt's drive in the Ardennes Forest made necessary its earlier employment. The results were effective, not only against personnel in the open but also against those under substantial cover, and against transport, bivouacs, and barracks. V.T. fuzes contributed decisively toward the collapse of the German offensive. German prisoners of war were unanimous in stating that never had they been subjected to such devastating artillery fire, and many complained that it must be contrary to the laws of warfare. V.T. fuzes contributed materially to the defense of Bastogne and to its eventual relief. The late General Patton in a letter to General L. H. Campbell, Jr., said: "The new

Air burst of 155-mm H.E. shell with V.T. fuze, over German barracks at Camp Bitsche. Dust rising from roofs is caused by impacts of fragments. The troops called this "Rain on the Roof." Shell fragments would penetrate such roofs and destroy occupants.

Battalion "Tot" of 105-mm howitzer shells with V.T. fuzes, over valley in Holland. Low-angle fire, showing how height of burst rises with the ground on far side of valley. Note dust rising from fragment impacts on the ground. Such concentrations are deadly against troops in the open, in trenches, or in foxholes.

shell with the 'funny fuze' is devastating. . . . I think that when all armies get this fuze, we will have to devise some new method of warfare." To illustrate the amazing effectiveness of V. T. fuzes, it is necessary to cite only one other occasion, when a battalion of German infantry attempted to cross the Sauer River in rubber boats. A battalion concentration of 105-mm V.T. fuzed shells was delivered, after which 702 dead Germans were counted.

V.T.-fuzed bombs were first used in the Pacific theaters, where they were employed from 12 to 17 February 1945 in highly effective pre-invasion saturation bombing of airfields, antiaircraft defenses, and beach positions on Iwo Jima. They were subsequently used in quantity, in both bombs and rockets, in all of the Pacific operations. Toward the end of the war, carrier aircraft were fuzing from 30 to 50 per cent of their bombs and aircraft rockets with V. T. fuzes. In the Italian and European theaters, V.T.-fuzed bombs were used with deadly effect against German antiaircraft batteries and in "carpet bombing" for close support of ground forces. The aviators liked V.T.-fuzed bombs especially for attacking antiaircraft positions, as these afforded them a highly effective weapon for combating the accurate German antiaircraft fire.

High-Velocity Tungsten Carbide Core Armor-Piercing Ammunition

In anticipation of requirements for ammunition with greater armor-penetrative ability than was possible with conventional types of armor-piercing shot, experimental work was undertaken on high-velocity, tungsten carbide core, armor-piercing shot early in the emergency period. Tests of a variety of designs showed that the "composite rigid" type was found to have the best combination of exterior ballistics and effect on the target. This type of ammunition was found to have approximately 50 per cent greater penetration than standard armor-piercing ammunition of the same caliber. This increased penetrative power resulted from two factors: (1) The use of a tungsten carbide core, which has both high density and extreme hardness; (2) the high velocity, which is made possible by

reducing the weight of the assembled shot to about 60 per cent of the normal weight, by the use of an aluminum-steel carrier for the core.

In spite of the known improvements in armor penetration which would be gained by the use of this type of shot, none was made for service use at that time. The reason was that existing 75-mm and 3-inch armor-piercing ammunition was capable of defeating any enemy armored vehicles which had so far been met on the battlefield. In addition, the supply of tungsten was extremely critical, and the available amounts were needed to meet demands for cutting tools and similar purposes.

Shot, HVAP, 90-mm, for 90-mm Gun, M3.

With the appearance of the more heavily armored German "Panther" and "Tiger" tanks, it became apparent that ammunition of much greater penetrating power than even the 3-inch M62 and 90-mm M82 was necessary if either of these tanks were to be defeated by frontal attack. Consequently, designs based upon the earlier development work were prepared for both 3-inch and 76-mm H.V.A.P. shot. This ammunition was manufactured and rushed to the battlefields under special priorities.

Complete round, H.V.A.P., M93, for 76-mm guns, a highly lethal round for destroying German tanks.

Battle reports for this ammunition indicated the improved destructive effect against tanks:

REPORT ON FIRING OF H.V.A.P. AMMUNITION (Platoon Leader, 1st Plt., Co. "B," 893rd T.D. Bn.): "Enemy tanks were reported at long range in the vicinity of Vossenack. I gave the glasses to Sergeant Griffith for further identification and he spotted four (4) more enemy tanks moving from Kommerscheidt to Vossenack; they were coming straight down the forward slope of the hill to Vossenack. Four (4) destroyers [3-inch guns] of the First Platoon, Company "B," moved into firing position and opened fire. The first tank, a Mark IV, was hit by the first round fired by No. 1 gun. The crew of the tank jumped out of the vehicle and were destroyed by H.E. fired by No. 1 gun. The other three guns were firing upon three (3) Mark V's and one (1) Mark VI during this time. Direct hits were obtained on all tanks. No. 3 gun hit one Mark V [Panther] at a range of 2,600 yards.

. . . The Mark VI [Tiger] tank was overwatching for the others and at one time, it was taken under fire, when it was 3,500 yards away. A.P.C. was used by No. 1 gun at this range; the range was correct but the round struck a few yards left of the tank. No. 1 gun then fired one round of H.V.A.P. using 3,000 yards range and scored a direct hit on the right front sprocket and stopped it cold. They then fired one more round of H.V.A.P. scoring another direct hit on the tank. They then fired H.E. destroying the crew. Total ammunition expended was 31 rounds A.P.C., 2 rounds H.V.A.P., and 16 rounds H.E. . . . IN MY OPINION H.V.A.P. IS WONDERFUL AMMUNITION."

REPORT ON USE OF H.V.A.P. (C.O., 893rd T.D. Bn.): "On the 5th of November, the 3rd Platoon of Company B was in the town of Kommerscheidt, Germany, where heavy fighting was going on. At about 1500 hrs., on this day, the destroyer commanded by Sergeant Sicena-

Effect of H.V.A.P. projectile on German Panther tank (Mark V).

vage sighted a Mark VI tank parked by the side of a house, at a range of 1,400 yards. The destroyer was in defilade when the tank was sighted, so it was pulled out into a firing position. The visibility was very good at the time and the destroyer fired 3 A.P.C. shots directly at the front of the stationary tank. Hits on the tank were observed but there was no apparent damage. One round of H.V.A.P. was then fired directly at the glacis plate and the tank burst into flames."

Illuminating Projectiles

In the fall of 1942, the trend in warfare, especially in the Pacific Theater, indicated the need for a means of illuminating inshore areas, as the methods available at that time were considered inadequate. Searchlights, both naval and land, were considered too vulnerable to enemy fire; aircraft flares illuminated not only the shore line but also the attackers; and the 60-mm mortar shell had insufficient range to handle most situations.

In addition, the using services indicated that the illumination of land targets was desirable in preventing night infiltration, in detecting enemy night movements, and in locating targets for night artillery fire. As a result of these needs, development was undertaken on illuminating shells for the 81-mm mortar, the 76-mm, 3-inch, and 90-mm guns, and the 105-mm and 155-mm howitzers.

The 81-mm design was modeled on the 60-mm type. The candle for this shell as developed had a minimum burning time of 60 seconds, produced 275,000 candlepower, and had a maximum range of 2,200 yards. The 76-mm, 3-inch and 90-mm, 105-mm, and 155-mm illuminating projectiles were all of a similar design; they differed materially from the non-rotating mortar shells by reason of higher velocities, higher chamber pressures, and high rotational velocity. The 3-inch and 76-mm shells developed 120,000 candlepower for 25 seconds; the 105-mm illuminating shell provided 250,000 candlepower for 60 seconds; and the 155-mm shell gave 400,000 candlepower for 60 seconds.

Grenades

Never before has the grenadier had available to him the quality and diversity in type of grenades that were issued in this war. The incidence of fatal malfunctions caused by poor quality was remarkably low considering the magnitude of the output. The frequency of accidents due to mishandling was no less remarkable, considering the constant need that the soldier had for grenades. To cite one frequently used type, the antitank rifle grenade, malfunctions from all causes were only one per million. This record is a distinct tribute to the engineering skill in design, production, and inspection applied to this important item.

In 1940, no military requirement for a rifle grenade existed, and none was available, although in World War I slight use had been made of unsatisfactory types. The development in 1941 of the rifle launcher, which permitted

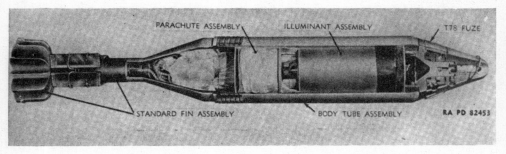

Shell, Illuminating, 81-mm, M301. An important shell for illuminating enemy positions at night.

grenades to be launched efficiently and easily from the rifle and carbine without damage to the weapon, resulted in a flood of requirements. So rapid were the tempo and changes of scene during this war that all of our successful rifle grenades were developed and put into service since early 1941.

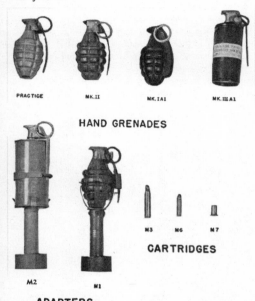

PRACTICE   MK.II   MK. IA1   MK.III A1

HAND GRENADES

M3   M6   M7

CARTRIDGES

M2   M1

ADAPTERS

Hand Grenades, Adapters, and Grenade Cartridges.

Hand Grenades

The hand grenade dates virtually from the discovery of explosives, and history records its use as early as the fifteenth century. It was not until this war, however, that research in fragmentation and in establishment of sound criteria for casualty-producing fragments provided means for designing hand grenades that, for effectiveness, have no equals anywhere in the world.

Throughout this war the standard hand grenade used by troops was, outwardly, the "pineapple" type of World War I. An important internal change, however, was the introduction of a high-explosive filler which increased the number of lethal fragments from 50 to 1,000.

In jungle areas and in terrain containing dense underbrush, fighting frequently took place under conditions in which the opponents were invisible to each other. The former hand-grenade fuze, although reliable, gave forth a flash, a report, and a trail of smoke and sparks as the grenade left the hand, and so revealed the position of the thrower. In 1944 a new fuze was developed which was noiseless, smokeless, and flashless. This offered superior advantages of concealment to the American soldier besides providing additional safety features. It had a $4\frac{1}{2}$-second delay element. Special delay powders of the gasless type had to be developed for this type of fuze. All future grenade fuzes of the U. S. Army will incorporate these characteristics. Many millions of these new fuzes were manufactured and issued with the Mark II T.N.T. grenade.

To make possible projection of the Mark II grenade over a greater range and to provide increased scope to the activity of the Infantry soldier, an adapter (M1) was devised. The M1 adapter could be readily attached to the hand grenade and the assembly launched from the rifle or carbine. Effective air burst could then be accomplished with the delay fuze. This simple device provided a dual-purpose ammunition. A private of the 28th Infantry Division in the battle for France said: "The Mark II fragmentation hand grenade was fired from the rifle, using a grenade projector adapter M1 and is very effective in firing into pillbox doors."

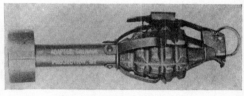

Adapter, Grenade, Projection, M1.

Other hand grenades included a series of chemical grenades with white phosphorus, or white, red, yellow, green, or violet smoke fillings. The white phosphorus was used for smoke screening as well as against personnel. Since it was a bursting type, it provided a screening cloud quickly. The other smoke grenades were of the burning type, the colored ones being used for signaling purposes. To project these chemical grenades over greater ranges, a readily attachable adapter was developed to permit projection from the rifle or carbine.

In thick woods or dense underbrush, it sometimes became necessary to suspend a smoke grenade in a treetop for signaling purposes. An ingenious tree-suspension device was developed, using a standard smoke grenade, the adapter, a length of cord connecting them, and a setback ring. When the grenade was fired from the rifle, the setback ring separated the adapter from the grenade, upon which the cord paid out and became entangled in the tree.

Rifle Grenades

The projection of fragmentation and chemical grenades by means of rifle adapters has already been described.

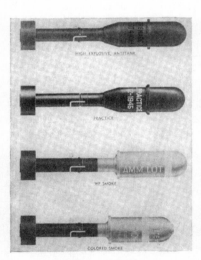

Identification of Rifle Grenades.

Early in the war it became apparent that it was desirable to provide the infantryman with a weapon that could defeat tanks. For this purpose, the shaped-charge antitank rifle grenade was developed. It was effective against three to four inches of armor plate. It was also a very effective weapon against bunkers and pillboxes, in that it could be projected into embrasures where its excellent fragmentation characteristics were particularly valuable against personnel. A first lieutenant of the 45th Division reported, concerning this rifle grenade: "In March, during street fighting in a German village, I saw a replacement knock out a Mark VI [Tiger] tank with a rifle grenade fired from an M1. The G.I. was partially concealed in a house about 15 feet from the tank as it came down the narrow street. He fired one round which hit the turret, blowing up the ammunition in the tank and killing the entire crew. Our battalion has knocked out about 10 German tanks with rifle grenades over a period of 18 months."

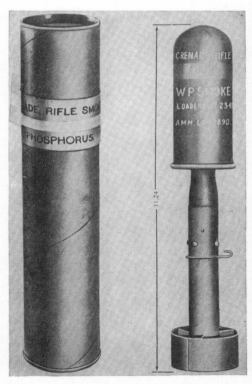

Grenade, Rifle Smoke (WP), M19, and Container.

The white phosphorus rifle grenade and rifle smoke grenade were devised for smoke-screen work, but the former provided good antipersonnel effect as well, by dispersal of burning phosphorus. The colored-smoke rifle grenades, M22, were provided in red, yellow, green, and violet, for signaling. The stabilizer and fin assembly were built into them, and no adapter was required for rifle launching.

A series of colored-smoke rifle grenades, M23, was provided to fill a special requirement for ground-to-air signaling in densely wooded areas, known as the streamer smoke type. On being launched from a rifle the grenade was ignited immediately, leaving a stream of smoke of the desired color over most of the trajectory, which reached heights of about 600 feet. These smoke streams could be seen by airplanes flying at heights of two miles. Among other uses, they were employed for marking the front lines of our troops as an aid to bombers attacking enemy troops.

Mines, Antitank and Antipersonnel

For a number of years before World War II, the tactical possibilities of the land-mine in both defensive and offensive warfare had been recognized by the U. S. Army. The fluid character of modern warfare clearly established the need for such a device, especially as a weapon to be used against tanks and armored vehicles. The land-mine in this country is a modern military development, and the first type was standardized before our entry into this war.

The first satisfactory antitank mine was developed in 1940. This mine is a squat cylindrical container of light steel, holding $5\frac{1}{2}$ pounds of explosives. It was capable of disabling light tanks and armored vehicle, and could be used in multiples for greater effect against heavily armored vehicles.

During the North African campaign the heavy German tanks, such as the 65-ton Tiger, made their appearance and created a requirement for a still heavier mine. To meet this need, a heavy,

American soldier fires rifle grenades into an underground hideout of German snipers during the battle for Cherbourg, France.

high-explosive mine containing 12 pounds of explosive was manufactured. In addition, a newly designed chemical-type fuze was conceived. This heavy mine is now the principal

The new heavy antitank mine, capable of stopping any German tank or vehicle.

antitank mine used by the U. S. Army. It can be emplaced on the surface of the ground, or beneath the surface, and in water, such as stream crossings, to a depth of five feet. It will effec-

tively damage tank tracks, suspension parts, and, in many cases, the hulls, thus immobilizing the tanks. Against light-weight vehicles, it will kill or disable the occupants and set fire to the vehicles.

Experience indicated a need for a hasty defense against light tanks and vehicles. A light, compact, portable mine, which could be quickly set and armed, was designed. This mine could be easily converted to antipersonnel and demolition use by inserting any of the standard Army firing devices in the activator well provided for that purpose. Both the light and heavy tank mines were produced in large quantities and were used effectively and efficiently in operations against both Germany and Japan.

The possibilities of antipersonnel mines were recognized in the months immediately preceding the Pearl Harbor attack. Antipersonnel mines depend for their initiation upon some action of the enemy. In addition, they are primarily intended for use against personnel on foot, so that it is necessary to take full advantage of oppor-

U. S. Army troops plant mines in a snow-covered field somewhere in France, 10 January 1945.

tunities for concealment. Two basic types of antipersonnel mines were produced. The first was the "bounding mine," which was actually a small mortar that projected a shell which exploded three to six feet above ground; the second was a fragmentation type of cast-iron case loaded with high explosive which could be emplaced either on or beneath the ground surface. Both types of antipersonnel mines were extensively used in all theaters.

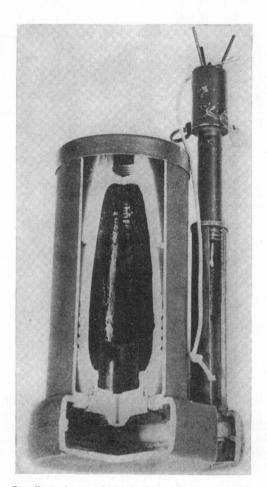

Bounding antipersonnel mine (sectionalized). Used to booby-trap a position. When wire is tripped, the mine throws the grenade waist-high, at which height the grenade explodes.

Mine Exploder, T1E3.

MINE EXPLODER, T1E3

CHARACTERISTICS

Type of Construction—Two units of large roller disks, mounted one unit in front of each track and driven from the sprocket by means of a chain. This equipment to be used with M4 series tanks

Type of Drive . . . . Chain drive, from driving sprocket of tank

General Data

Turning radius	82½ ft.
Maximum speed	15 MPH
Length (including tank)	360 in.
Length (including tank and rear bumper)	384 in.
Width, over-all	131½ in.
Width (each unit)	33¾ in.
Weight	58,500 lb.
Diameter of Disk	8 ft.
Thickness of Disk	2¾ in.

In all their operations, the Germans planted extensive mine fields. Throughout the operations in Africa, Italy, and France, many tanks and other types of vehicles were destroyed by German mines. Many devices were employed in attempts to neutralize these mine fields. The mine exploder, T1E3, was one of these devices. It consisted of a series of disks, eight feet in diameter, mounted loosely on a horizontal shaft. As the disks were made of armor plate, an exploding mine would not damage the rollers. As many as four German mines could be exploded simultaneously without damage. This unit was especially useful in exploding mines planted on German roads. A tank equipped with this exploder could move along the road at from 10 to 15 miles an hour exploding mines as it went along. It could be used cross-country provided the mine fields were not too soggy. The rollers had such great weight (30 tons) as to insure exploding all mines over which it passed. This device was used to a limited extent during the advance across France into Germany.

The British type of mine exploder attached to the American M4 medium tank. This type of mine exploder, known as the Scorpion, was successfully used by the British 8th army in Africa. A number were manufactured here for the American army. The cylinder to which the chains were attached was driven by a power take-off from the tank's engine. The chains whipped the ground, setting off any concealed tank mines.

SIGNAL AND FLARE AMMUNITION

Although the use of pyrotechnics dates from the discovery of black powder, items for military use were not adopted and standardized for Ordnance issue until World War I. The nature of warfare at that time, involving continuous movement of military units by land, water, and air, required the development of devices to provide illumination of ground areas at night and to provide visual signals for day and night use, both for recognition and the transmission of emergency messages.

Since World War I the Ordnance Department has maintained a continuous program for the investigation and development of the numerous types of flare and signal ammunition required by the different branches of the service. Comparisons indicate that, in both quality and quantity, the items of flare and signal ammunition furnished to our forces were in advance of those of other countries.

During this war, 119 separate pyrotechnic items were developed.

Military pyrotechnic items now in use by the services may be grouped under four general classes, as follows:

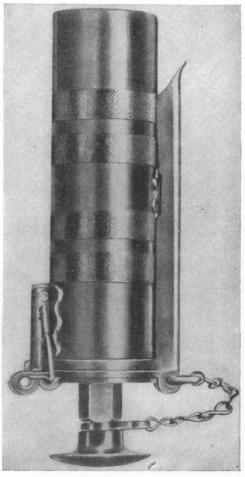

Pyrotechnic Pistol Mount, M1.

Projector, pyrotechnic, hand, M9, with safety set at safe.

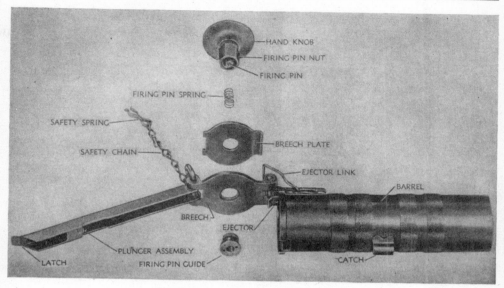

Projector, pyrotechnic, hand, M9, disassembled.

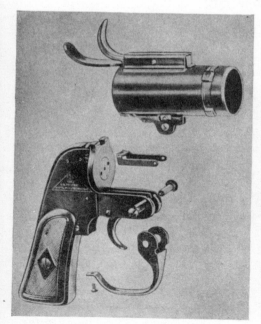

Pistol, pyrotechnic, AN-M8, disassembled.

PYROTECHNIC PISTOLS
AND PROJECTORS

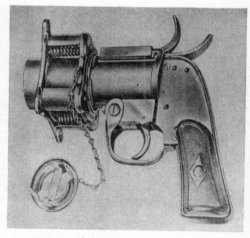

Pistol, pyrotechnic, AN-M8—Left side view, with mount, M1.

SIGNALS, AIRCRAFT, SINGLE STAR, AN–M43 TO AN–M45

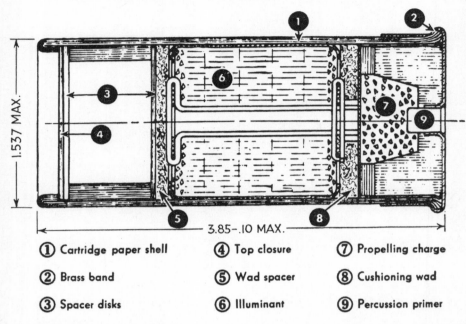

1.537 MAX.

3.85–.10 MAX.

① Cartridge paper shell   ④ Top closure   ⑦ Propelling charge

② Brass band   ⑤ Wad spacer   ⑧ Cushioning wad

③ Spacer disks   ⑥ Illuminant   ⑨ Percussion primer

Signals: Signals include colored light or smoke units generally intended for communication between military groups or from isolated parties in distress. They may be projected into the air by means of pistols, rifles, mortars, or artillery weapons.

Flares: Aircraft flares, trip flares, and flares, projected from pistols, rifles, mortars, or artillery weapons, are for the general purpose of pro-

viding illumination. The candlepowers range from 40,000 for the smaller units to 1,000,000 for the aircraft flares.

Photoflash Munitions: Photoflash bombs and cartridges are for the general purpose of providing light for night photographic reconnaissance. Automatic cameras are operated in conjunction with the photoflash units, which develop candlepowers ranging from 25,000,000 for the cart-

BOMB, PHOTOFLASH, M46

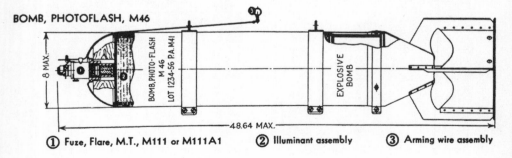

① Fuze, Flare, M.T., M111 or M111A1   ② Illuminant assembly   ③ Arming wire assembly

ridges to 1,000,000,000 for the bombs, with a flash duration of the order to 40 milliseconds, or 0.040 of a second.

Target Identification Munitions: Colored light and smoke and illuminating units are contained in bomb cases for general use as either ground or sky markers for the identification of specific targets for bombardment missions.

Signal and flare composition developments for the various pyrotechnic types listed above were covered by continuing research and development programs, which sought to improve the light efficiency of illuminating flares and the purity and effectiveness of colors of the light-emitting and smoke-producing signals, as well as the stability in storage for long periods under service conditions of the chemical mixtures used.

Target identification bombs from 100- to 1,000-pound sizes were designed for use by aircraft groups to indicate location or bomb-release line for bombing operations. The special targets or bomb-release points were identified by various types of colored light or smoke-producing devices. Varied effects were provided so that the enemy could not quickly duplicate the local effect at other locations and so mislead our bombardiers.

Targets were usually identified by "Pathfinder forces" using illuminating flares. The markers were released to function by selective fuze settings, so that a colored smoke cloud or streamer would indicate the bomb-release line to following aircraft in the formation. The pyrotechnic units included candles with and without explosive charges. Explosive charges, when used, were intended to discourage enemy attempts to interfere with the marker patterns.

In the course of the war, it proved necessary to devise flares to give warning of infiltrating hostile troops. For this purpose, trip flares were designed. One type was, in effect, a one-shot mortar fired by a trip wire which projected a parachute-supported candle of 100,000 candlepower. Another flare, resembling a hand grenade, had a bracket for attachment to a tree or post, and gave approximately 40,000 candlepower.

A considerable number of ground signals were

manufactured for the purpose of signaling from one ground unit to another or between ground troops and aircraft. Among these ground signals were some containing colored-smoke composition in the form of clustered smoke-producing units. For the numerous uses of ground signals,

Pointing the way. Among the varied targets for U. S. Army 8th Air Forces heavy bombers on the seventh consecutive day of large-scale attacks, were Nazi airfields. Here explosive bombs follow marker bombs down to hangers and other installations at the Schwabisch-Halle airdrome.

and also to provide different colors and series, thirteen different types, all of which looked alike externally, were produced.

The Air Forces asked Ordnance to provide an assembly marker to aid elements of a squadron or group forming for a mission under poor-visibility conditions. Flares developed for this purpose were visible for approximately ten miles when towed at 5,000 feet altitude. Three types of flares, with candlepowers varying from 80,000 to 200,000, were evolved and manufactured.

When bombing planes returned during the early morning after night raids, the general location and runway illumination of the airport were usually determined by the planes' own equipment, radio, or other navigational aids. For some time, there had been serious need for a flare to indicate the ends of runways of fog-bound airfields. Therefore, an airport flare was designed to burn for a minimum of five minutes at an intensity of 600,000 candlepower, with a deep yellow light that effectively penetrated fog. During the last few months preceding V-E Day, this flare was credited with aiding the safe landing of 1,000 planes on airfields in England.

Bombs: The nature of a war fought on many fronts, each presenting special tactical and strategical situations requiring the use of air power, called for the development of bombs capable of maximum effect against many different types of targets. As the war went on, the steadily increasing load capacities of aircraft and the need for greater concentrations of destructive power resulted in the design of heavier and more powerful bombs. Although a primary objective of bombing was demolition, the proved effectiveness of bombing employed against troops, convoys, parked airplanes, and other lightly protected targets led to the development of more lethal fragmentation bombs.

As the tempo of the war quickened, the bomb's role became increasingly important. The weight of bombs supplied by the Ordnance Department and dropped by the Air Forces and by naval fliers grew with each major bombing attack. Between Pearl Harbor and V-J Day, millions of tons of bombs fell from American airplanes to blast the enemy in Europe, Asia, and the Pacific. These consisted of many types, each designed to produce a definite effect on a specific type of target. They varied in size from the small, anti-

Standard Bombs. From left to right: Fragmentation, 20-lb., M41; Fragmentation, 23-lb., M40; Parachute-fragmentation, 100-lb., M30; Demolition, 300-lb., M31; 500-lb., M43; 1000-lb., M44; 200-lb., M34; S.A.P., 500-lb., M58; 1000-lb., AN-M59; Demolition, light-case, 4000-lb., M56. All standard fuzes except nose fuze, 4000-lb., M56.

personnel fragmentation bomb to great block-busters. Each type required one or more types of fuzes according to the results desired. Fuzes were designed to burst these bombs effectively in the air, instantaneously on impact, and with delays ranging from a few seconds to hours. The bombs, explosives, and fuzes of the Ordnance Department were standardized for both the Army and the Navy. The great numbers and variety of the bombs and fuzes required and provided proved to be one of the greatest achievements of the Ordnance Department in this war.

A major development—occasioned by the need for concentrating bombs of small size against personnel or unprotected ground targets in a given area—was the design of various cluster adapters to permit light fragmentation, general purpose, smoke, or incendiary bombs to be car-ried in multiple suspension on the bomb racks. Cluster adapters containing 20-pound fragmentation bombs were utilized with great success in "carpet bombing" of enemy airfields, while the vast burned-out areas in Tokyo, Yokohama, Nagoya, and Osaka resulted from incendiary clusters dropped by B-29 superfortresses.

Although low-level bombing was especially destructive to parked enemy aircraft, particularly on Japanese island bases, it involved the solution of problems connected with the safety of the bomber and the exact placing of the bomb. The blast of a bomb dropped in the normal manner from an airplane flying at a very low altitude might easily damage or destroy the bomber itself, and the unpredictable ricochet of the bomb after impact often caused it to detonate far from the intended target. These disadvantages were

Holiday greetings for Nazis—B-17 Flying Fortresses of the U. S. 8th Air Force drop their holiday greetings from open bomb-bay doors, high over Germany, on December 24. This was part of the record force which attacked Nazi targets.

Bombing Brest. Bombs from U. S. Army 8th Air Force planes are seen in various stages of exploding as they crash into a gun emplacement and small quay on the Brest peninsula during attacks.

overcome by the development of an antiricochet parachute which enabled the bomb to fall at a low enough speed for the bomber to escape blast and fragmentation effects, and which also permitted more accurate placement of the bomb in relation to the target by eliminating ricochet.

quently, fragmentation bombs with weights of 90 and 260 pounds respectively were devised and standardized. The larger fragments produced by these bombs made them effective against targets such as gun positions and heavy automotive equipment not protected by armor plate.

Cutting Nazi engine production. This pile of ruins was all that remained of the Matford Factory in Strasbourg after a two-minute bombing by 53 heavies of the U. S. Army 8th Air Force. The attack stopped a monthly production of 200 to 300 German airplane engines.

This device alone made it possible for our airmen to penetrate under enemy air defenses and lay 100-, 250-, and 500-pound general-purpose bombs exactly where they desired.

The 20-pound fragmentation bomb—our only bomb of this type during the early part of the war—had been designed for use mainly against aircraft, airdromes, personnel, and light transport vehicles. Although considerable weight of opinion indicated that this was the most effective fragmentation bomb, some targets made larger fragmentation bombs seem desirable. Conse-

Cluster Adapters

The need for increased bomb loads in the large bombers for "carpet bombing" and for maximum effects at the target brought about the development of cluster adapters to permit simultaneous release of a large number of bombs. These adapters made possible the assembly of 20-pound fragmentation bombs in groups of six in one type of cluster and twenty in another. The latter type filled the space provided for a 500-pound bomb. A six-bomb cluster of 90-pound fragmentation bombs likewise fitted the 500-pound station.

Cluster AN M1A1 modified for shipment of bombs without fuzes (top). Cluster AN M1A1 modified and fuzed (bottom).

The device functioned by a fuze setting that permitted immediate or predetermined-height opening. Hook-and-cable type cluster adapters were produced in an assortment of lengths which allowed the clustering of two or three 100-, two 250-, or two 500-pound bombs, to be carried on one bomb rack station. With this type of adapter, bombs could be loaded in combination. For example, one 500-, one 250-, and one 100-pound bomb could be carried on one station, depending on space and weight limitations. These devices made possible the delivery of increased volume of our bombs at the target, with consequent greater destructive effect.

Parachute Bombs

The successful operational use of the 20-pound fragmentation bomb equipped with a parachute to delay its impact and detonation after release from low-flying aircraft suggested the development of a similar parachute for the 90-pound fragmentation bomb. This parachute, like that for the 20-pounder, was housed in a metal container that replaced the fin assembly.

Multiple suspension of general-purpose bombs became desirable to increase the number of the smaller bombs that could be carried in the larger aircraft. Two cluster adapters were developed

5th Air Force Over Luzon—Photo shows parachute bombs, used in low-level bombing, falling on Jap railroad installation in southeastern Luzon.

for assembling the 100-pound G.P. bomb into clusters before loading into aircraft.

Antiricochet Attachments for General-Purpose Bombs

The successful use of fragmentation bombs in low-altitude attack suggested similar use of general-purpose bombs. Variations in the length of post-impact ricochet, however, made aiming difficult; some means was needed of limiting or preventing ricochet.

The first antiricochet device used was a heavy steel spike made to screw into the bomb nose in place of the nose fuze. It was intended to stick into the sides of railroad embankments or to the wooden crossties, depending on the direction of approach. It was only moderately successful, and was used in some theaters and not in others.

The need for low-altitude attack against targets other than railroads indicated the advantage of a retarding parachute to replace the usual fin

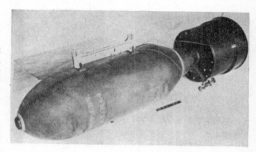

500-lb. G.P. bomb with antiricochet attachment.

assembly of the bomb. These antiricochet parachutes were highly successful. They not only prevented ricochet on both land and water surfaces, but also retarded the bomb's fall enough to permit the bomber to get away before the detonation. As a result, these were developed and issued for all the commonly used general-purpose bombs.

5th Air Force Over Luzon. Photo shows freight cars left in smoke after attack by low-level bombers somewhere in southeastern Luzon. More than 300 freight cars and 26 locomotives were destroyed by our air force which continued attacking railroad installations. Note chutes which carried bombs lying beside the tracks at right.

Semi-Armor-Piercing Bombs

The existence in numbers of highly resistant targets such as heavy reinforced-concrete gun emplacements increased the importance of this type of bomb. However, as the largest standard S.A.P. bomb, the 1,000-pound, had an explosive capacity of only 300 pound, a larger bomb appeared to be essential, and so one of 2,000 pounds was developed. This bomb had an explosive capacity equivalent to that of the 1,000-pound general-purpose bomb. It could perforate approximately 7 feet of reinforced concrete, 4 inches of armor plate, and other targets invulnerable to even the 2,000-pound G.P. bomb.

Chemical Bombs

So that chemical bombs of sizes comparable with the high-explosive bombs of the general-purpose series might be available for emergency requirements, Ordnance undertook the development of 250-, 500-, 1,000-, and 2,000-pound bodies for chemical loading.

The 500-pound chemical bomb body, equipped with a cylindrical igniting charge of white phosphorus surrounding the axial burster, was loaded with jellied gasoline to provide an incendiary bomb of the intensive type. This filled the need for a large-capacity incendiary bomb that could be accurately aimed against important targets, particularly from aircraft at relatively low altitudes.

Bomb Fuzes

During the war, new bombing techniques evolved requirements for many new types of bomb fuzes. Low-level bombing and the desire for bombs to function at times varying from a fraction of a second to hours or days after impact made imperative the development of delayed-action fuzes. Other fuzes were designed to provide air bursts of bombs at predetermined heights above the ground, and mechanical time fuzes were developed to open bomb clusters properly at the desired instant. It even proved expedient to adapt a modified version of an

American fuze to captured Japanese bombs, which we could then use against the enemy.

The effectiveness of fragmentation bombs and of such devices as the "butterfly bomb," against personnel, was largely attributable to the fuzes with which they were armed. This was particularly true of the "butterfly bomb," in which fuzes caused the small bombs to burst in air, on impact, on the ground after varying periods of delay, or upon being disturbed.

Development was undertaken on a total of 115 types of bomb fuzes, of which 48 were standardized during the war. To make new and improved fuzes available to combat air forces as soon as possible after a new requirement arose, pilot quantities of such fuzes were often rushed through manufacturing and loading plants even faster than detailed drawings for the fuze could be laid down and standardization effected. Here are a few of the more important bomb fuzes:

The M123 and M132 series of tail bomb fuzes were designed early in the war to give delayed detonation, ranging from five minutes to several days. The shorter delays were used mainly for low-altitude raids by large bomber formations, to permit all the airplanes to clear the target area before the explosions started. A rush shipment of these fuzes to the African Theater was instrumental in making possible the daring raid on the Ploesti oil fields that marked the beginning of the concentrated program for destruction of Germany's fuel-producing facilities.

The longer-delay fuzes permitted neutralization of enemy activity-points, such as railroad yards and dock areas, for an extended period with only one raid. They proved to have a highly demoralizing effect on enemy personnel. This was heightened by a booby-trap feature in the fuze designs, which blew up a bomb immediately if any attempt were made to remove the fuze. Their effectiveness is testified to in a report (January 1944) from the 14th Air Force: "Reports have been received that out of three 500-lb. bombs dropped recently, with two-hour delay fuzes, two were dug up by our oriental enemies and their population has been decreased by a total of 75. The first bomb killed 60, and the second wiped out another 15. They decided to leave the third bomb alone in the ground to detonate, after such costly experience. Word of such success with this type fuze makes it more popular with us over here than ever."

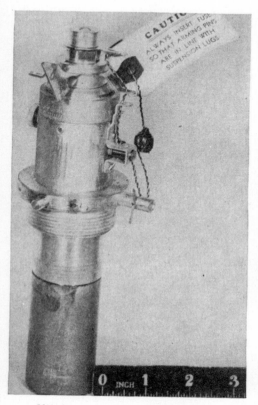

M135 fuze, preparatory to assembly to bomb.

Three fuzes were produced for obtaining above-ground burst of large bombs to increase their effect against personnel and equipment protected by slit trenches or revetments. Two of these were mechanical time fuzes, the M135 for use from high altitudes and the M136 for use from low and medium altitudes. These fuzes contained accurately adjusted clockwork mechanisms that started running upon release of the bomb from the plane and exploded the bomb at the expiration of the time set. Aerial burst was

obtained by setting the fuze for slightly less than the time of the bomb's fall.

The third fuze developed for aerial burst (the M149 nose fuze) contained a simple but effective pressure-actuated firing device. The bombing technique employed with these fuzes involves dropping a string of bombs at close intervals across the target. The first bomb detonates on impact, and the blast wave from this bomb operates the fuze of the next bomb before it reaches the ground, and each succeeding bomb is detonated in the air by similar action.

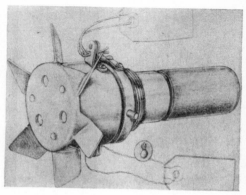

M149 fuze, preparatory to assembly to bomb.

Among the reasons for the almost total lack of employment of small, scatter-type incendiary bombs by our aircraft in the early phases of the war, was inability to bomb targets accurately with them from high altitudes, because of the unpredictable flight of light-weight bombs. Anticipating the great potential usefulness of incendiary bombs against the cities of Japan, the Chemical Warfare Service subsequently started an all-out program of development and manufacture of large clusters of incendiary bombs designed especially for use from high altitudes. These clusters, before opening, were heavy enough and sufficiently streamlined to have ballistics approaching those of large explosive bombs. By opening the clusters a few thousand feet above the target, the individual bombs could be scattered just enough to get good target coverage without sacrificing accuracy. The Chemical Warfare Service investigated various fuzing possibilities and then called upon the Ordnance Department to develop mechanical time fuzes that would accomplish reliable cluster opening and that, at the same time, could be produced soon enough and copiously enough to keep pace with the cluster program that was already under way. A nose bomb fuze and the M152 tail bomb fuze were successfully produced to meet these needs. The use of incendiary bomb clusters fitted with these fuzes paid the anticipated dividends when they were finally loosed upon Japan.

The steady trend toward bigger bombers led to a corresponding trend toward clustering of all types of bombs except the very largest, to increase the pay-load of the bombers. Among the clusters that required special fuzing to open at the right time was a cluster containing 20 of the 20-pound fragmentation bombs; a proper fuze for this purpose was quickly developed.

Chapter IV

ARTILLERY

Chapter IV

ARTILLERY

MOBILE ARTILLERY

During this war, for the first time in its history, the United States Army was equipped with a complete system of artillery of all required types, namely, light, medium, and heavy. Before World War I, the Army had only a few types, and even at the close of that war still lacked many essential weapons. In 1940 a few artillery weapons designed during World War I, such as the 155-mm howitzers, Model 1918, were still in service. These weapons had been modernized by increasing their speed through the use of rubber tires and of roller bearings in the axles. As new weapons were designed and manufactured, the old ones were rapidly replaced, so that during the last years of World War II only the new types were in use. The Army's present system of artillery was based upon a long, comprehensive study of calibers, and each caliber of gun and howitzer was selected to cover a selected area of fire. Thus, enemy positions could be brought under effective fire from the minimum ranges of the light artillery to the maximum ranges of the heaviest calibers.

The design of all this artillery was influenced by the consideration that it would be used in all parts of the world. Recoil and recuperator mechanisms, elevating and traverse mechanisms, had to be so designed and lubricated that each artillery piece would function equally well at the Arctic Circle or at the Equator. Several years of research before the war had brought about the redesign of carriage structures to permit the use of welded steel plates. This gave the United States a distinct advantage over all enemy countries in lightness of construction and speed of production. The devastating, concentrated fires of our artillery surpassed those of all other countries and insured success in our attack against both the German and Japanese armies.

75-mm pack howitzer, M1A1, on carriage, M1.

75-MM PACK HOWITZER, M1A1—CARRIAGES M1, M8

CHARACTERISTICS

Howitzer

Caliber	75-mm.
Weight	341 lb.
Over-all length	59 in.
Length of bore	15.93 cals.
Muzzle velocity	700, 810, 950, 1,250 f./s.
Volume of chamber	57.3 cu. in.
Travel of projectile in bore	39.2894 in.
Maximum powder pressure	26,000 lb./sq. in.
Type of block mechanism	Sliding block
Rate of fire	6 rds./min.
Range, M41	9,760 yd.

Recoil Mechanism

Type	Hydropneumatic
Weight	211 lb.
Normal recoil	28 in.
Maximum recoil	33 in.
Maximum piston rod pull	5,188 lb.

Carriage

Total weight without howitzer	927 lb.
Length of carriage (muzzle to spade)	144 in.
Width over hub caps	47 in.
Maximum height at 0°	34 in.
Type box trail	Axle traverse
Elevation (maximum)	45°
Depression (maximum)	−5°
Traverse (right)	3°

75-MM PACK HOWITZER, M1A1—CARRIAGES M1, M8—Continued

Carriage

    Traverse (left) . . . . 3°
    Total weight of howitzer, recoil mechanism, and car-
    riage in firing position . . . . 1,440 lb.

Ammunition

	M41A1	M48	H.E.A.T. M66
Weight of complete rounds	17.16 lb.	17.87 lb.	16.3 lb.
Weight of projectile	13.76 lb.	14.60 lb.	13.27 lb.
Weight of projectile explosive charge . . .	1.11 lb.	1.47 lb.	1.0 lb.
Weight of propelling charge		15.55 oz. (approximate)	
Type of ammunition		Semi-fixed	

ABERDEEN PROVING GROUND
75-mm Howitzer Carriage, M8. Firing Position (45° elevation).

A section of men from a field artillery battalion. The piece is a 75-mm pack howitzer in firing position Kiska,
20 October 1944.

75-mm howitzer M8, assembled after parachute drop. A few minutes ago, these men and the gun were in the air. They
bailed out of their C-47 plane, the gun coming down in sections. Nine paratroopers having assembled the gun, it is now
moved to a less vulnerable position.

75-MM PACK HOWITZER, M1A1

The Ordnance Department, before the war, had developed a highly effective 75-mm pack howitzer. This howitzer could be broken into mule-pack loads and so was suitable for mountain warfare. A light carriage with rubber-tired wheels was also designed which could be towed behind a jeep or other suitable prime mover. The remarkable characteristic of these weapons was a range of 9,760 yards with a 14-pound projectile, although the unit weighed but 1,440 pounds. The 75-mm howitzer was manufactured in large quantities and was used in all theaters.

It was an important weapon in Pacific island-hopping and in the mountainous country of Sicily and Italy, as well as in China, as it could be flown in and easily transported over roadless country. It could also be disassembled, packed in special containers called "paracrates," and be dropped by parachute from airplanes to paratroops or isolated units. Large quantities of these howitzers and ammunition were supplied to China under lend-lease.

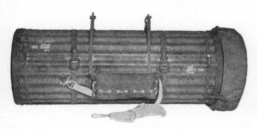

This photograph shows a typical standard steel paracrate for one of the nine 75-mm pack howitzer loads. Each paracrate is built for a specific load. The loads are held rigidly in place by felt-faced transoms which are formed to fit the loads. Paracrates may be built to land on the end, in which case a crash pad is used to cushion the shock. Others land on their sides, without the crash pad. A control pattern, consisting of canvas ties which are folded in sacks on the sides of the paracrates during flight, holds the loads together and thus limits the dispersion of landing.

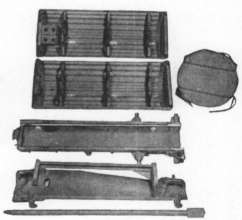

Paracrate for Carriage, howitzer, 75-mm, M8. Parachute, M4A2, and load—Cradle and Top Sleigh.

105-mm Howitzer, M2A1, on Carriage M2, at 60° elevation.

105-MM HOWITZER, M2A1—CARRIAGE, M2

CHARACTERISTICS

Howitzer
Caliber	105-mm
Weight	1,080 lb.
Over-all length	101.35 in.
Length of bore	22.5 cals.
Muzzle velocity	1,550 f./s.
Volume of chamber	153 cu. in.
Travel of projectile in bore	81.67 in.
Maximum powder pressure	28,000 lb./sq. in.
Type of breech mechanism	Sliding
Rate of fire	4 rds./min.
Range	12,500 yd.

105-MM HOWITZER, M2A1—CARRIAGE, M2—Continued

Recoil Mechanism
  Type . . . . M2 hydropneumatic
  Weight . . . . 457 lb.
  Normal recoil . . . . 42 in.
  Maximum recoil . . . . 44 in.
  Maximum piston rod pull . . . . 12,980 lb.
Carriage
  Total weight without howitzer or recoil mechanism . . . . 3,570 lb.
  Height of lunette (limbered position) . . . . 18 in.
  Length of carriage (muzzle to lunette) . . . . 236 in.
  Width over hub caps . . . . 80.875 in.
  Tread width . . . . 70 in.
  Height in traveling position . . . . 65.75 in.
  Trail spread (included angle) . . . . 28° left, 29° right
  Elevation (maximum) on wheels . . . . 64° 15′
  Depression (maximum) . . . . −4° 45′
  Traverse (maximum, right) . . . . 22° 30′
  Traverse (maximum, left) . . . . 22° 30′
  Total weight of gun, mechanism, and carriage . . . . 4,980 lb.
Ammunition
  Weight of complete round (with M1 H.E. shell) . . . . 41 lb. 12 oz.
  Weight of projectile . . . . 33 lb.
  Weight of projectile explosive charge M1 . . . . 4.8 lb.
  Weight of propelling charge (approximate) . . . . 44.8 oz.
  Type of ammunition . . . . Semi-fixed

The backbone of the American artillery was the 105-mm howitzer, M2. This weapon had been under development for many years before the war, but lack of funds had limited manufacture and so the design had not been frozen. In 1939, Ordnance, with its increased appropriations, accelerated this project, and, working with the Field Artillery Board, completed the present design of the 105-mm howitzer, M2. After thorough testing at Aberdeen Proving Ground and at the Field Artillery Board, it was standardized and put into production in 1940. It is worth noting that when Ordnance placed this howitzer under quantity production, only two carriages had previously been manufactured and tested. Fortunately, it was not necessary to make any major changes in this weapon throughout the war. Troops in the field reported that it could withstand the roughest service.

The importance of the 105-mm howitzer, M2, and its ammunition cannot be overstated. The weight of the projectile, 33 pounds, was ideal for a light artillery weapon and could be easily handled. Its effect was devastating. This was the weapon for which Ordnance provided the most complete series of ammunition. There are some 13 different types of 105-mm ammunition, including high-explosive shell, hollow-charge armor-piercing ammunition, illuminating shell, several colored smokes for signaling, propaganda shell for distributing leaflets, and white-phosphorus ammunition.

105-mm Howitzer, M3, on Carriage, M3A1, in firing position with weapon at center traverse and maximum elevation.

105-MM HOWITZER, M3—CARRIAGE, M3A1

CHARACTERISTICS

Caliber of howitzer 105-mm
Weight of howitzer . . . . 955 lb.
Weight of projectile
  H.E., M1 . . . . 33 lb.
  H. E. A. T., M67 . . . . 29 lb.
Muzzle velocity . . . . 1,020 f./s.
Twist of rifling . . . . Uniform, right-hand, 1 turn in 20 cals.
Length of bore (approximate) . . . . 16 cals.
Maximum range, 30° . . . . 7,250 yd.
105-mm Howitzer Carriage, M3A1
Weight of howitzer and carriage without accessories . . . . 2,495 lb.
Length, over-all (traveling position) . . . . 155 in.
Width, over hub caps . . . . 67 5/16 in.
Width, of tires, c. to c. . . . . 56 11/16 in.
Height, over-all . . . . 44 in.
Height to center of bore . . . . 34⅛ in.
Height of lunette (limbered position) . . . . 29 in.
Elevation . . . . 30°
Depression . . . . —9°
Traverse right or left from center line . . . . 22° 30'
Size of combat tires . . . . 7.50 x 16
Type of recoil mechanism . . . . Hydropneumatic
Normal recoil . . . . 27 in.
Equilibrators . . . . Spring
Weight of recoil mechanism and cradle . . . . 379 lb.

105-MM HOWITZER, M3

The 105-mm howitzer, M3, was designed to provide a weapon of greater firepower than the 75-mm field howitzer. Under this project, begun in 1941, the barrel of the 105-mm howitzer was shortened and mounted on the 75-mm field howitzer carriage. The result was a weapon weighing 2,500 pounds, which had a range of 7,000 yards with a 33-pound high-explosive shell.

More ammunition was fired from the 105-mm howitzer, M3, than from any other artillery weapon during the war, except for the standard 105-mm howitzer, M2. This weapon was available for the early North African operations and for the Italian campaigns. Although initially used in some artillery battalions, it was specifically assigned to infantry cannon companies. Reports from the South Pacific theater indicate that this howitzer fulfilled all requirements for close support; it was capable of extreme accuracy and such a rapid rate of fire that prisoners inquired about our automatic artillery.

In the first months of the Pacific war, troops thought that the difficult jungle terrain prohibited the use of medium or even of light artillery. A few initial engagements marked by heavy losses brought the realization that, regardless of the work involved, it was necessary to bring in artillery and ammunition. Thereafter, in all our engagements, our troops were backed up by these excellent artillery weapons, emplaced in the jungles after days and nights of hard work in building roads and paths. One combat report from Luzon tells of an occasion when 15 Japanese were seen digging in a hill about one and a half miles distant. With a delay fuze, the 105-mm howitzer scored a direct hit just below the crest of the hill. The top of the hill was blown off and Japanese bodies were seen flying through the air in all directions.

37-mm Antitank gun, M3A1.

37-MM ANTITANK GUN, M3A1

CHARACTERISTICS

Weight (Gun only)	191 lb.
Length (over-all) of gun	82½ in.
Muzzle velocity	2,900 f./s.
Volume of chamber	19.92 cu. in.
Maximum powder pressure	50,000 lb./sq. in.
Type of breech mechanism	Vertical drop block
Rate of fire	25 rds./min.
Maximum range	12,850 yd.
Recoil mechanism	Hydrospring
Weight of carriage (without gun)	721 lb.
Height of lunette (limbered)	29½ in.
Length of carriage, muzzle to lunette	130½ in.
Width over hub caps	63½ in.
Height (traveling position)	37⅞ in.
Trail spread (maximum) (included angle)	60°
Elevation	10° to 15°
Traverse	30° right to 30° left

The 37-mm antitank gun was one of the most versatile light antitank and anti-personnel weapons used during the war. This weapon weighed but 900 pounds yet was capable of penetrating armor of most German tanks. Thanks to its lightness and mobility, it could be put into position under the most difficult terrain conditions. The 37-mm antitank gun was invaluable in stopping the Japanese attacks at Guadalcanal. In addition to armor-piercing ammunition, high-explosive and canister ammunition were available for this weapon. The canister was very effective against massed Japanese attacks. On several such occasions, the 37-mm antitank gun saved our limited troops from annihilation by the Japanese. The 37-mm antitank gun was likewise used on the light tanks and on the armored cars, M8.

3 Inch Gun M5 on Carriage M1. The Carriage M6 differs
in minor details from the M1.

3-INCH ANTITANK GUN, M5, ON CARRIAGE, M6

The weapon fires high-explosive and armor piercing ammunition, the 15.43-pound A.P.C. projectile, M62, having a muzzle velocity of 2,800 feet per second. This projectile can pierce 4.5 inches of homogeneous armor at 20° from normal at 500 yards, and 3.31 inches at 2,000 yards. Sighting and fire control equipment for this gun consists of Panoramic telescope, M12A6; Telescope mount, M41A1; Telescope, T108; Telescope Mount, M5, and Elbow telescope, M29. The 3-inch antitank gun, M5, and carriage, M6, are standard items of ordnance.

By mounting the high-powered 3-inch gun on a mobile carriage, an effective antitank weapon was made available in large quantities for American troops. This 3-inch high-powered gun was capable of penetrating armor of all German tanks at battle ranges. Hundreds of these units were employed by our troops in all theaters during the war.

155-mm howitzer, M1, on carriage, M1.

155-MM HOWITZER, M1

CHARACTERISTICS

Howitzer
Caliber 155-mm
Weight . . . . 3,825 lb.
Over-all length . . . . 150 in.
Length of bore . . . . 20 cals.
Muzzle velocity . . . . 680, 770, 880, 1,020, 1,220, 1,520, 1,850 f./s.
Volume of chambers . . . . 725 cu. in.
Travel of projectile in bore . . . . 120.675 in.
Maximum powder pressure . . . . 32,000 lb./sq. in.
Type of block mechanism . . . . Interrupted screw
Rate of fire . . . . 2 rds./min.
Range (maximum) . . . . 16,000 yd.
Recoil Mechanism
Type . . . . T2 hydropneumatic
Weight . . . . 1,570 lb.
Normal recoil variable (super charge, Zone VII) . . . . . 58 in. at 0° to 41 in. at 65°
Maximum piston rod pull . . . . 64,000 lb. at 65° elevation
Carriage
Total weight without howitzer . . . . 8,975 lb.
Height of lunette (limbered position) . . . . 29 in.
Width of carriage (over-all) . . . . 95½ in.

155-MM HOWITZER, M1—Continued

Carriage

Tread width	81½ in.
Trail spread (included angle)	30° right, 30° left
Elevation (maximum) (on firing base)	65°
Depression	2°
Traverse (maximum, right) (on firing base)	26° 30′
Traverse (maximum, left) (on firing base)	26° 30′
Total weight with weapon (without cover or accessories)	12,800 lb.

Ammunition

Weight of complete round, H. E. M107	108.42 lb.
Weight of projectile	95 lb.
Weight of projectile explosive charge	15.87 lb.
Weight of propelling charge	13.42 lb.
Type of ammunition	Separate loading

4.5-inch gun, M1, on carriage, M1, in firing position at 0° elevation, the carriage resting on the firing jack.

4.5-INCH GUN, M1

CHARACTERISTICS

Gun

Caliber	4.5 in.
Weight	4,200 lb.
Over-all length	193.69 in.
Length of bore	42 cals.
Muzzle velocity	1,820 and 2,275 f./s.
Volume of chamber	531 cu. in.
Travel of projectile in bore	162.16 in.
Maximum powder pressure	40,000 lb./sq. in.
Type of block mechanism	Stepped-thread interrupted screw
Rate of fire	4 rds./min.
Range (maximum)	21,125 yd.

4.5-INCH GUN, M1—Continued

Recoil Mechanism, M5

Type	Hydropneumatic
Weight	1,671 lb.
Normal recoil, variable	43 in. at 0° to 29 in. at 65°
Maximum piston rod pull	48,000 lb.

Carriage

Total weight without gun	8,270 lb.
Length of carriage (muzzle to lunette)	312 in.
Over-all width	95½ in.
Width of tread (c/—c/of wheels)	81¼ in.
Height of lunette (limbered position)	29 in.
Over-all height (traveling)	83½ in.
Trail spread (included angle)	60°
Elevation (maximum) (firing base)	60°
Depression (maximum) (firing base)	0°
Traverse (maximum, right)	26° 30′
Traverse (maximum, left)	26° 30′
Total weight of gun, mechanism, and carriage (limbered)	12,455 lb.

Ammunition

Weight of complete round (M65 H.E.)	61.963 lb., 66.315 lb.
Weight of projectile	54.90 lb.
Weight of projectile explosive charge	4.49 lb.
Weight of propelling charge	7.063 lb., 11.415 lb.
Type of ammunition	Separate loading

155-MM HOWITZER, M1, AND 4.5-INCH GUN, M1

In 1939 the Ordnance Department pushed forward plans for designing new types of medium artillery. Two new weapons were conceived: the 4.7-inch gun with a range of 20,000 yards with a 50-pound projectile, and the 155-mm howitzer with a range of 16,000 yards with a 95-pound projectile. Both the gun and the howitzer could be mounted on the same carriage, weighing approximately six and one-half tons, designed for high-speed, cross-country transportation.

So that ammunition might be interchangeable with the British types, the caliber of the 4.7-inch gun was changed to 4.5 inches, using the 55-pound British shell. In service, however, artillery trooper found that the 4.5-inch British shell, though it had excellent range, did not have sufficient payoff in explosive to justify its use. The 155-mm howitzer, on the other hand, with its 95-pound projectile and explosive charge of nearly 16 pounds, was considered the ideal weapon. It had uncanny accuracy at all ranges and was universally popular in the service.

In Normandy, the 155-mm howitzer was used for firing at road intersections, for harrassing and neutralizing fires, and for keeping the Germans in foxholes. When V.T. fuzes were issued to the troops for the various types of ammunition, it was the burst from the 105-mm and 155-

mm howitzer shells which caused the greatest destruction among Germans caught in the open. As our troops advanced into Germany, the German resistance was pulverized by the accuracy of the American long-range artillery fire.

155-mm howitzer in position in Italy.

155-mm gun, M1A1, in firing position.

155-MM GUN, M1A1—CARRIAGE, M1

CHARACTERISTICS

Gun

Caliber	155-mm
Weight of gun complete	9,595 lb.
Length of bore	45 cals.
Length of gun	23.7 ft.
Muzzle velocity	2,800 f./s.
Weight of projectile	95 lb.
Weight of powder charge	30 lb.
Maximum rated pressure	40,000 lb./sq. in.
Number of grooves	48
Twist	Right-hand—uniform
Rate of fire	1 rd./min.
Range (maximum)	25,715 yd.

Recoil Mechanism

Type	Hydropneumatic, variable recoil, M3
Weight	3,890 lb.
Normal recoil	65 in. at 0°, 32 in. at 65°
Maximum recoil	70½ in.
Maximum piston-rod pull at 65°	96,500 lb.

Carriage

Type	Split trail
Weight of carriage with gun	30,600 lb.
Maximum elevation	65°
Traverse (maximum, right)	30°
Traverse (maximum, left)	30°
Maximum spread of trails	60°
Over-all height (traveling position)	102 in.

155-MM GUN, M1A1—CARRIAGE, M1—Continued

Carriage

Over-all length (traveling position)	34.3 ft.
Over-all width (traveling position)	99 in.
Recoil mechanism	Hydropneumatic, variable recoil
Bogie	4 dual wheels
Brakes	Air, on each bogie wheel

Ammunition

	M101 H.E.	M112 B1 A.P.
Weight of complete round	126.97 lb.	131.03 lb.
Weight of projectile	94.71 lb.	99 lb.
Weight of projectile explosive charge	15.13 lb.	1.44 lb.
Weight of propelling charge	32.26 lb.	26.17 lb.
Type of ammunition	Semi-fixed	Semi-fixed
Armor penetration homogenous plate, 20° from normal		3 in. at 6,000 yd.

155-mm guns (Long Toms) in action in the Pacific.

155-MM GUN, M1A1

Fortunately, the Ordnance Department had been working on heavy guns and howitzers before the war. The 155-mm gun, affectionately known by the service as "Long Tom," was adopted and standardized in 1938. At the beginning of the war this unit was placed under quantity production and became one of the vital weapons. The 155-mm "Long Tom" had a range of 25,000 yards, as compared with 18,000 yards for the 155-mm gun used in World War I. Further-

more, it was mounted on a carriage of such design that it could be pulled cross-country at the highest possible speeds. The 155-mm gun was extremely important in the attack on the Siegfried Line, thanks to the development of the concrete-piercing fuze. This fuze, when attached to the high-explosive shell of the 155-mm gun, made it possible to penetrate the thickest concrete pillboxes at ranges up to several miles.

Members of a division loading their American 155-mm gun, 5th Army, Gabbinano Area, Italy. All American artillery weapons functioned equally well in snow or at the equator.

An American field artillery unit is putting a shell in the chamber of the 155-mm gun in preparation for firing on the German lines in France. July 26, 1944.

8-inch howitzer, M1—carriage, M1.

8-INCH HOWITZER, M1—CARRIAGE, M1

CHARACTERISTICS

Howitzer

Caliber . . . . 8 in.
Weight . . . . 10,240 lb.
Over-all length . . . . 209.59 in.
Length of bore . . . . 25 cals.
Muzzle velocity . . . . 820, 900, 1,000, 1,150, 1,380, 1,640, 1,950 f./s.
Volume of chamber . . . . 1,485 cu. in.
Travel of projectile in bore . . . . 173.83 in.
Maximum powder pressure . . . . 33,000 lb./sq. in.
Type of block mechanism . . . . Interrupted-screw type
Rate of fire . . . . ½ rd./min.
Range . . . . 18,510 yd.

Recoil Mechanism

Type . . . . Hydropneumatic, M4
Weight . . . . 3,890 lb.
Normal recoil . . . . 63 in. at 0° to 32 in. at 64°
Maximum recoil . . . . 70 in.
Maximum piston rod pull at 65° . . . . 139,850 lb.

Carriage

Total weight of carriage and limber without howitzer . . . . 21,460 lb.
Height of lunette (limbered position) . . . . 27 in.
Length of carriage (muzzle to lunette) . . . . 40 ft.
Width over hub caps . . . . 95¾ in.
Width over-all of bogie . . . . 98⅞ in.
Tread width (c/—c/of wheels) (limber) . . . . 83½ in.
Height in traveling position . . . . 102¼ in.
Trail spread (included angle) . . . . 60°

8-INCH HOWITZER, M1—CARRIAGE, M1—Continued

Carriage
Elevation (maximum) (firing base)	64°
Depression (maximum) (firing base)	0°
Traverse (firing base) (right)	30°
Traverse (firing base) (left)	30°
Total weight of gun, mechanism, and carriage	31,700 lb.

Ammunition
Weight of complete round	213.96 lb.
	228.75 lb.
Weight of projectile shell, M106	200 lb.
Weight of projectile explosive charge	29.6 lb.
Weight of propelling charge	10.75 lb. (approx.)
Type of ammunition	Separate loading

The 8-inch howitzer, which became famous throughout the Army for its accuracy, could be mounted on the same carriage as the 155-mm gun. The 155-mm gun and the 8-inch howitzer were both valuable for destroying strong buildings and the houses of cities employed by the Germans as fortifications. Field reports tell the story. "Our artillery were attacking German strong points in a stone building which was holding up the advance of our Infantry which had surrounded it and were standing by at a distance of some 300 yards. The first round from the 8-inch howitzer, fired at a range of 11,000 yards, hit 30 yards to the right. The next three rounds eliminated the strong point." In the North African campaign the 8-inch howitzer was extensively used for destroying the many stone bridges which were encountered. On one occasion, the 8-inch howitzer, at a range of 15,000 yards, in 10 rounds knocked out a heavy stone bridge abutment and so caused an entire span to fall into the river. Every howitzer of this battalion had a bridge painted on the gun shield.

A battery of 8-inch howitzers, M1, ready for an attack in the Pacific. Judged the most accurate artillery weapon in the war.

8-inch gun, M1, carriage, M2, in firing position, at 10° elevation.

8-INCH GUN, M1—CARRIAGE, M2

CHARACTERISTICS

Gun
Weight	29,800 lb.
Over-all length	409.5 in.
Length of bore	50 cals.
Muzzle velocity	2,950 f./s.
Volume of chamber	5,156 cu. in.
Travel of projectile in bore	338.58 in.
Maximum powder pressure	38,000 lb./sq. in.
Type of block mechanism	Rotating drop type breech block
Rate of fire	1 rd./min.
Range—maximum (approx.)	35,000 yd.
Range—minimum (approx.)	22,000 yd.

Recoil Mechanism, M7
(Including cradle)
Type	Hydropneumatic
Weight	7,021 lb.
Recoil	50 in. at 50°
	47 in. at 10°

Carriage
Weight without gun	39,300 lb.
Trail spread (included angle)	45°
Elevation (maximum)	50°
Elevation (minimum)	10°
Traverse (maximum, right)	20°
Traverse (maximum, left)	20°
Total weight of gun, mechanism, and carriage	69,300 lb.

Gun Transport Wagon, M1
Weight (loaded)	49,200 lb.
Weight under front tires (loaded)	15,200 lb.
Weight under rear tires (loaded)	34,000 lb.
Over-all length (loaded)	501 in.
Over-all height (loaded)	84 in.
Over-all width	111½ in.
Wheel tread	92 in.
Wheelbase	192 in.

Carriage Transport Wagon, M3
Weight (loaded)	46,900 lb.
Weight under front tires (loaded)	14,360 lb.
Weight under rear tires (loaded)	32,540 lb.
Over-all length (loaded)	429½ in.
Over-all height (loaded)	128¼ in.
Over-all width	111½ in.
Wheel tread	92 in.
Wheelbase	264 in.

8-INCH GUN, M1—CARRIAGE, M2—Continued

Truck Mounted Crane, M2
    Gross weight . . . . 53,000 lb.
    Wheelbase . . . . 168½ in.
    Over-all length (without boom) . . . . 298½ in.
    Over-all height . . . . 130½ in.
    Over-all width . . . . 108 in.
Ammunition
    Type of shell . . . . H.E. M103
    Weight of complete round . . . . 347.24 lb.
    Weight of shell as fired . . . . 240.37 lb.
    Weight of charge, propelling, N.H. powder . . . . 106.77 lb.
    Weight of charge, bursting, T.N.T. . . . . 20.90 lb.
    Weight of primer, percussion, electric Navy Mk. XIM1 . . . . . 10 lb.

8-inch mobile gun, M1, in firing position—Range 20 miles.

8-INCH GUN, M1, AND 240-MM HOWITZER, M1

Ordnance realized that in the final assault upon the German homeland all of our guns and howitzers would have to be used to destroy the Germans' mighty fortifications. Starting in 1940, therefore, the Department undertook the design of the now famous 8-inch gun and 240-mm howitzer, which were completed and standardized in 1942. The carriage was so designed that the 8-inch gun and the 240-mm howitzer could be interchangeably mounted. The weight of the gun and howitzer made it necessary to divide the weapon into two parts and to transport the gun or howitzer and its recoil mechanism as one load and the carriage proper as a second load.

Because of this division, the maximum load for crossing bridges did not exceed 22 tons.

The 8-inch gun and the 240-mm howitzer became famous throughout the Army for their accuracy and great destructive power. During the period when it was doubtful that the Anzio beachhead in Italy could be held, the arrival of the 240-mm howitzer changed the complexion of the campaign. In Italy the 240-mm howitzer was found necessary for destroying the heavy masonry buildings and bridges which formed vital targets along our lines of advance. On one occasion, at a range of ten miles, it quickly succeeded in destroying a vital bridge which offered

Rough terrain is no obstacle to the prime mover shown here pulling the U. S. Army's 240-mm howitzer into position somewhere on the Italian front. This was the largest mobile gun used by the U. S. Army on the Italian front.

a target area of only 40 square feet. Allied bombers had tried for weeks to drop this bridge but had found it too small a target. Major General Lewis, 5th Army Artillery Officer, said: "The 8-inch gun is the answer to the German 170-mm which outranges our artillery by some 7,000 yards. When in North Africa the 170-mm was too many times in a position to fire upon our troops without being shelled in return." The 8-inch gun gave our troops a weapon with a range of 35,000 yards.

Front view of a 240-mm howitzer on the Italian front just before firing into German-held territory. 30 January 1944.

240-mm howitzer, M1, on carriage, M1, in firing position at maximum left traverse and 15° elevation.

240-MM HOWITZER, M1—CARRIAGE, M1

CHARACTERISTICS

Howitzer
Weight	25,100 lb.
Over-all length	336 in.
Length of bore	34 cals.
Muzzle velocity	2,300 f./s.
Volume of chamber	4,430 cu. in.
Travel of projectile in bore	268.16 in.
Maximum powder pressure	36,000 lb./sq. in.
Type of block mechanism	Interrupted step thread
Rate of fire	1 rd./min.
Range (maximum)	25,255 yd.
Range (minimum)	12,000 yd.

Recoil Mechanism
Type	Hydropneumatic, M8 (including cradle)
Weight	6,980 lb.
Recoil	60 in.

Carriage
Total weight without howitzer (including cradle and recoil mechanism)	39,425 lb.
Trail spread (included angle)	45°
Elevation (maximum)	65°
Elevation (minimum)	15°
Traverse (maximum)	22½°
Traverse (minimum)	22½°
Total weight—howitzer, mechanism, and carriage	64,525 lb.

240-MM HOWITZER, M1—CARRIAGE, M1—Continued

Howitzer Transport Wagon, M2
  Weight under front tires (loaded) . . . . 18,595 lb.
  Weight under rear tires (loaded) . . . . 21,100 lb.
  Over-all length (loaded) . . . . 398 in.
  Over-all height (loaded) . . . . 84 in.
  Over-all width . . . . 107⅝ in.
  Wheel tread . . . . 80 in.
  Wheelbase . . . . 192 in.

Carriage Transport Wagon, M3
  Weight under front tires (loaded) . . . . 16,740 lb.
  Weight under rear tires (loaded) . . . . 25,440 lb.
  Over-all length (loaded) . . . . 370 in.
  Over-all height (loaded) . . . . 120 in.
  Over-all width (loaded) . . . . 114 in.
  Wheel tread . . . . 80 in.
  Wheelbase . . . . 240 in.

Ammunition
  Weight of projectile (H.E. shell, M114) . . . . 360 lb.
  Weight of projectile explosive charge . . . . 54 lb.
  Type of loading . . . . Separate
  Weight of propellant powder . . . . 78 lb., 8 oz.
  Weight of complete round . . . . 438 lb., 8 oz.

ARTILLERY FIRE CONTROL

All of the types of field artillery described required accurate fire-control instruments both "on carriage" and "off carriage," which would permit pinpoint accuracy of these pieces and their ammunition in the field. For the light and medium field artillery weapons, fire-control instruments were designed not only for the ordinary types of indirect laying, but also to permit all of these units to be directly fired should enemy tanks or armored fighting vehicles break through to artillery positions. Besides providing fire-control instruments for this purpose, the Ordnance Department also made it a policy to manufacture armor-piercing ammunition for all types of light and medium artillery which could be effectively used against such targets. In the "Battle of the Bulge," our artillery was very effective in destroying German tanks which broke through our front lines in critical periods of the fighting.

ANTIAIRCRAFT WEAPONS

The Ordnance Department had been working vigorously since 1925 on various types of antiaircraft weapons. Although this work was handicapped by lack of funds, still, by applying the funds available year after year, suitable types of antiaircraft weapons of the various calibers had been built or were being designed.

The Department assembled a completely automatic antiaircraft fire-control system in 1926. This system consisted of a range and height finder, a central computer, an electric transmission system, automatic fuze setter, and a follow-the-pointer system on the carriage. During this same period electronic power control, for moving the gun in azimuth and elevation, was also devised so that the gun movements could be controlled from the central director. In electronic control of antiaircraft gun carriages, this country was far in advance of all others. In fact, no enemy country devised a completely integrated power control system for antiaircraft weapons. Our experts, in checking after this war on the Germans' and Japanese progress in the development of electronic power control for gun carriages, found them years behind. Our efficient fire control for all types of artillery gave us a great advantage over both the Germans and Japanese.

37-mm A.A. gun, M1A2, on carriage, M3A1, in firing position at 45° elevation.

37-MM GUN, M1A2—CARRIAGE, M3A1

CHARACTERISTICS

Weight of gun and carriage, complete	6,124 lb.
Weight of carriage w/o gun and tube	5,759 lb.
Weight of gun, complete	365 lb.
Weight of tube	119 lb.
Type of breech block	Vertical sliding

37-MM GUN, M1A2—CARRIAGE, M3A1—Continued

Recoil mechanism	Hydrospring
Weight of complete round of H.E. ammunition, M54	2.62 lb.
Weight of projectile, H.E.	1.34 lb.
Weight of powder charge	8.00 oz.
Over-all length of vehicle (traveling position)	241 in.
Over-all height of gun (traveling position)	72 in.
Over-all width of vehicle (traveling position)	69.5 in.
Length of tube	78.2 in.
Diameter of bore	1.457 in.
Maximum length of recoil at 85° elevation	10.75 in.
Maximum length of recoil at 0° elevation	10.75 in.
Length of rifling, approximate	68.35 in.
Number of grooves in barrel	12
Maximum elevation	90°
Minimum elevation	—5°
Traverse	360°
Maximum vertical range (H.E. shell)	6,200 yd.
Maximum horizontal range (H.E. shell)	8,875 yd.
Muzzle velocity	2,800 ft./sec.
Rated maximum powder pressure	36,000 lb./sq. in.
Volume of powder chamber for M54 shell	18.56 cu. in.
Maximum rate of fire	120 rds./min.

A 37-mm automatic gun firing a 1¼-pound projectile at a muzzle velocity of 2,800 feet per second had been under development for several years before 1940. This gun, mounted on a towed carriage, was manufactured in considerable quantity. It was also mounted on a half-track vehicle for increased mobility. As the British desired to have the 40-mm Bofors antiaircraft gun manufactured in this country under lend-lease and since the facilities available for the manufacture of the 37-mm antiaircraft gun were required for the manufacture of the 37-mm aircraft cannon, the production of the 37-mm antiaircraft gun was later stopped and the production of the 40-mm Bofors undertaken.

One of the most effective antiaircraft weapons built during the war for use against low-flying airplanes consisted of one 37-mm automatic gun mounted on a special cradle with two caliber .50 machine guns. The whole unit was in turn mounted on the half-track vehicle and known as the 37-mm antiaircraft mount M15. These mounts were extensively used by our troops throughout the campaigns in Italy, France, and Germany. Fire was usually opened with a cali-ber .50 to get on the target, after which the 37-mm gun would open fire. This combination was found highly effective against enemy low-flying planes.

The following report was received from the North African Theater: "During recent operations in which this corps has been engaged, the value of antiaircraft artillery automatic weapons of highly movable self-propelled mounts has been established. Of 69 enemy aircraft known to have been shot down by antiaircraft artillery units of this corps, 49 were shot down by the 443rd Separate Coast Artillery Battalion (A.A.) equipped with 37-mm guns and .50 caliber machine guns on self-propelled mount (M15) T28E1." "The proficiency of this mobile weapon can be attributed to three characteristics: its mobility enabling it to work well in close support of combat troops in forward areas and also to effectively patrol roads over which heavy traffic must travel under constant threat of bombing and strafing; its flexible firepower combining the volume of caliber .50 with the knocking power of the 37-mm; and the facility with which its fire is controlled by using the tracer stream of one caliber .50 to bring it on the target before opening with the full volume of its armament. Numerous cases are cited where a 'mouse trap' effect has been obtained when enemy planes came in much closer on the initial caliber .50 fire than they would on light cannon and are caught by the 37-mm."

This is one of the many antiaircraft gun positions protecting the harbor of Cherbourg from possible Luftwaffe attacks. Two caliber .50 machine guns and one 37-mm A.A. automatic gun constitute one of these self-propelled units. France, 13 July 1944.

Our lightest antiaircraft weapon was the single caliber .50 machine gun mounted on a suitable tripod. This caliber .50 machine gun was also mounted on jeeps and trucks, and our tanks carried similar guns. In the early days of the African campaign, the Germans flew low over our positions until a large number had been shot down by the caliber .50 machine-gun fire. Thereafter the German fliers were less eager to engage directly our ground troops.

(See other illustration of caliber .50 machine gun under Chapter I, "Small Arms.")

Multiple Cal. .50 machine gun carriage, M51 (Multiple Cal. .50 machine gun mount, M45, on trailer mount, M17). Three-quarter left front view, in firing position.

MULTIPLE CALIBER .50 MACHINE GUN MOUNT, M45

CHARACTERISTICS

Weight, without armor, guns, ammunition chests, fuel, and operator . . . . 1,468 lb.
Weight, full equipped, including gunner (approx.) . . . . 2,396 lb.
Weight of armor . . . . 132 lb.
Over-all width . . . . 79½ in.
Overall height (guns level) . . . . 4 ft., 7 in.
Power drive . . . Maxson Var. Speed Drive, Model 120A with 1-hp., 12-volt, 90-amp. electric motor
Weight of power drive . . . . 139 lb.
Power charger . . Briggs & Stratton, Model 304, type 25592 driven by a 1-cylinder, 4-cycle gasoline motor
Charger output . . . . 300 watts, 15 volts
Weight of power charger . . . . 75 lb.
Batteries, storage, lead, acid, 3-cell, 17 plates per cell (6 volts each) 2
Armament, cal. .50, H.B., M2, fixed Browning machine guns, mounted outboard on right and left trunnions 4
Ammunition . Cal. .50, 800 rds. (200 rds. each in cal. .50 ammunition chests, M2, mounted outboard on guns)
Azimuth speed . . . . 0° to 60° per sec.
Elevation speed . . . . 0° to 60° per sec.

The Ordnance Department had been working for several years on a carriage for mounting four caliber .50 machine guns, to give increased firepower against low-flying targets. The four-gun caliber .50 Maxson turret proved to be one of the most effective units of this type. Thousands of these were used by our troops in all theaters. The mount was so arranged that the gunner sat between pairs of caliber .50 machine guns which were moved in azimuth and elevation as desired by power control. The electric motor for this purpose was driven by a storage battery, which, in turn, was kept charged by a small gasoline engine mounted on the unit. This small self-contained turret, mounted on half-track vehicles and on light trailers, was one of the important antiaircraft weapons.

Twin 40-mm Gun Motor Carriage, M19.

TWIN 40-MM GUN MOTOR CARRIAGE, M19

CHARACTERISTICS

Armament

Twin 40-mm guns	336 rds.
4 cal. .30 carbines	480 rds.
Grenades, smoke	6 rds.
Grenades, frag.	6 rds.

Armor

Average frontal	$\frac{1}{2}$ in.
" side	$\frac{1}{2}$ in.
" top	$\frac{3}{8}$ in.
" rear	$\frac{3}{8}$ in.
" turret, front	$\frac{1}{2}$ in.
" " sides	$\frac{5}{16}$ in.
" " rear	$\frac{5}{16}$ in.

General Data

Crew	6
Combat weight	38,500 lb.

TWIN 40-MM GUN MOTOR CARRIAGE, M19—Continued

Height, over-all	118 in.
Length, "	215 in.
Width, "	112 in.
Ground clearance	17 in.
Ground pressure	9.7 p.s.i.
Track width	16 in.
Electrical system	24 volts
Type steering	Controlled differential
Power train	Hydramatic transmission, transfer case
Suspension	Individual torsion bar
Fuel capacity	115 gal.
H.P. per ton (vehicle)	11.4

Performance

Maximum gradability	60%
Minimum turning radius	20 ft.
Maximum speed	35 m.p.h.
Cruising range	150 mi.
Fording depth	42 in.
Trench crossing	84 in.

Engine

Manufacturer and type	Cadillac Model 42; Dual V-8 liquid cooled
Displacement, total	692 cu. in.
Net H.P. at 3,400 RPM	Total 220 H.P.
Governed speed	Not governed

The 40-mm antiaircraft guns were frequently mounted on four-wheel vehicles to be towed behind suitable trucks or tractors. Upon arriving at the firing point the mount was dropped to the ground and the gun was then used from a fixed position.

To provide a more mobile antiaircraft weapon, two of the 40-mm guns were mounted on the chassis of the light tank, M24, to form the twin 40-mm gun motor carriage, M19. This proved itself an effective self-propelled antiaircraft weapon.

40-mm automatic antiaircraft gun, M1, on carriage, M2, in firing position at 50° elevation.

40-MM AUTOMATIC ANTIAIRCRAFT GUN, M1 (BOFORS)

CHARACTERISTICS

Weight of carriage	4,498 lb.
Weight of tipping parts	1,051 lb.
Weight of gun and carriage	5,549 lb.
Weight of barrel assembly	295.81 lb.
Length of bore	88.58 in.
Muzzle velocity	2,870 f./s.
Volume of chamber (A.P. M81)	29.90 cu. in.
Weight of projectile (A.P. M81)	1.96 lb.
Maximum pressure	40,000 lb./sq. in.
Time of flight at 1,500 yd.	2.0 sec.
Maximum elevation	90°
Maximum depression, carriage level	—6°
with jacks	—11°
Traverse	360°
Maximum recoil, permissible	8.3 in.
Range (maximum effective—limited by director)	3,000 yd.
Wheelbase	126 in.

40-MM AUTOMATIC ANTIAIRCRAFT GUN, M1 (BOFORS)—Continued

Wheel tread	55⅜ in.
Over-all length (traveling)	18 ft., 9½ in.
Over-all width (traveling)	6 ft.
Over-all height (traveling)	6 ft., 7½ in.
Road clearance	14⅛ in.

The 40-mm Bofors was one of the few foreign guns manufactured in this country during the war. First placed under production in the United States as a lend-lease weapon for the British, it was later manufactured in large quantities for our own troops. The Bofors gun was mounted on a four-wheeled carriage which provided satisfactory mobility. It was useful against low-flying targets at ranges of not more than one mile. Armor-piercing ammunition was also provided so that this automatic gun could be used against lightly armored vehicles at the shorter ranges. The Navy Bureau of Ordnance likewise used the 40-mm Bofors gun as one of its important antiaircraft naval weapons, and the two Departments cooperated in making as many of the parts alike as possible, although the Navy gun was water-cooled and the Army gun was air-cooled, so that the guns were therefore dissimilar in most respects.

Members of a U. S. Ninth Army antiaircraft unit on the alert for enemy aircraft. Dragons teeth of the Siegfried Line are seen in the background. (531st AAA Battalion, 30th Division.) Dec. 16, 1944.

3-Inch antiaircraft gun, M3, on mount, M2A2, in firing position.

3-INCH GUN, M3 (ANTIAIRCRAFT) MOUNT, M2A2

CHARACTERISTICS

Weight of gun, M3, and mount, M2A2, total .	16,800 lb.
Weight of gun, complete .	2,302 lb.
Weight of liner .	538 lb.
Weight of complete round of ammunition (M42A1 H.E.)	24.6 lb.
Weight of projectile (M42A1 H.E.) .	12.8 lb.
Over-all length of vehicle .	300 in.
Over-all height of vehicle, with gun in traveling position	120 in.
Over-all width of vehicle .	83 in.
Over-all length of gun, muzzle to rear face of breech ring	158.2 in.
Caliber of bore .	3 in.
Length of bore .	50 cal.
Maximum length of recoil at 85° elevation	32 in.
Maximum length of recoil at 0° elevation .	23.5 in.
Length of rifling .	125.83 in.
Number of grooves in barrel .	28
Rifling, uniform, R.H., one turn in .	40 cals.
Travel of projectile in bore of gun (M42A1 H.E.) .	127.73 in.
Maximum elevation .	80°
Maximum depression .	—1°

3-Inch antiaircraft gun, M3, on mount, M2A2, in traveling position.

3-INCH GUN, M3 (ANTIAIRCRAFT) MOUNT, M2A2—Continued

Traverse .	360
Maximum range, at 85° elevation	10,400 yd.
Maximum range, at 45° elevation (M42A1 H.E.)	14,780 yd.
Muzzle velocity (M42A1 H.E.) .	2,800 f./s.
Maximum powder pressure (M42A1 H.E.)	36,000 lb./sq. in.
(M62 A.P.C.)	38,000 lb./sq. in.
Volume of powder chamber (M42A1 H.E.)	2,035 cu. in.
Maximum rate of fire .	25 to 30 rds./min.

The first large-caliber army antiaircraft gun placed in production in this war was the 3-inch mobile gun, which had been standardized in 1926. This gun fired a 13-pound projectile to a vertical range of approximately 27,000 feet. The design and manufacture of these weapons gave the Ordnance Department much valuable experience which aided in the design and manufacture of the more powerful 90- and 120-mm guns. The 3-inch gun was a deadly antiaircraft weapon up to altitudes of 15,000 feet. Although it had been expected that the Germans would fly at high altitudes, it did not turn out that way, and most antiaircraft fire proved to average about 6,000 feet altitude.

The 3-inch antiaircraft gun was present in small numbers in the trying days of the Japanese attacks upon Corregidor and was effective in nullifying their bombing raids. As a result, the Japanese bombing of Corregidor did very little damage to artillery guns and other important installations; instead, the effective damage was inflicted by Japanese land artillery fired from Bataan.

3-inch Antiaircraft Gun, M3—Left side view, 80° elevation.

90-mm antiaircraft gun, M1A1, on mount, M1A1, in firing position.

90-MM GUNS, M1 AND M1A1 (ANTIAIRCRAFT) MOUNT, M1A1

CHARACTERISTICS

Gun, M1, M1A1

Total weight of gun and mount, M1A1	19,000 lb.
Weight of gun, complete	2,445 lb.
Weight of gun tube	1,465 lb.
Weight of recoil mechanism	1,740 lb.
Caliber	90-mm
Length of bore	50 cals.
Length (muzzle to rear face of breech ring)	186.51 in.
Muzzle velocity (M71 H.E., M77 A.P.)	2,700 f./s.
Weight of complete round (M71 H.E., M77 A.P.)	42.04 lb.
Weight of projectile (M71 H.E., M77 A.P.)	23.4 lb.
Chamber capacity (cartridge case) (M71 H.E.)	298.04 cu. in.
Maximum powder pressure	38,000 lb./sq. in.
Length over-all, (traveling position)	250 in.
Height over-all (traveling position)	112 in.
Width over-all (traveling position)	100⅞ in.
Weight of rammer	800 lb. (approx.)
Elevation	
Maximum	80°
Minimum (without depression stops)	0°
Minimum (with depression stops)	22½°
Traverse	360° cont.
Maximum slope on which mount can be leveled	4
Diameter of circle of emplacement	35 ft.
Distance from c. to c. of outside wheel treads	87½ in.
Tire size and type	10.00 x 22, combat or bus balloon
Type of brakes	Electric

90-MM GUNS, M1 AND M1A1 (ANTIAIRCRAFT)

The design of the 90-mm antiaircraft gun was rushed to completion during 1940 and manufacture was expedited. This gun fired a 24-pound projectile to an effective vertical range of 33,000 feet. The first 90-mm gun manufactured provided for hand-ramming, but later a spring-operated mechanical loading device was attached to the gun. With this apparatus, the unit could give rates of fire of 15 to 20 rounds per minute.

As the war progressed, thousands of these units were manufactured, and by the time our troops landed in North Africa, some 2,000 90-mm guns had been completed. Besides the normal high-explosive ammunition, our batteries were provided with armor-piercing ammunition, so that the 90-mm gun was an important anti-tank weapon. Later in the war, a new carriage was provided, so arranged that the gun could be fired directly from the traveling position without pausing for emplacement. Thus a unit being transported along a road, if intercepted by an enemy tank could open fire immediately.

A well-known company in the shoe industry undertook the development of an automatic electric rammer and fuze setter, which was uncanny in its action. When a complete round of ammunition was presented to the breech, the mechanism seized the round from the gunner, paused

A battery of 90-mm antiaircraft guns in action in the Pacific Theater. These guns were automatically set in azimuth and elevation from the director. American antiaircraft weapons surpassed all others in electronic power control devices.

an instant to set the fuze, and then rammed it into the gun. The fuze was being continuously set at the proper reading by remote control from the director. This mechanism converted the 90-mm gun into an automatic loader, increasing the rate of fire and decreasing the time for fuze setting. Power control for setting the gun continuously in azimuth and elevation from the director was also provided.

This weapon was, by a wide margin, the most effective antiaircraft gun of all nations in the war. The 90-mm antiaircraft gun was also used extensively as a field artillery piece; its range, rate of fire, and accuracy won it the admiration of the Field Artillery and the nickname of "Baby Long Tom." It performed harassing, counter-battery, and neutralizing missions for the Field Artillery up to effective ranges of 18,000 yards, thus outranging the German 105-mm field howitzer. At the Anzio beachhead, it was shown conclusively that the 90-mm guns could so effectively neutralize enemy antiaircraft positions that our Air Forces could conduct special missions close to the front lines without damage from German antiaircraft fire. On many occasions the 90-mm gun played the important role of tank destroyer with great effectiveness. This fact gave the unit the additional nickname of the

"Triple Threat Gun," as it could deliver effective antiaircraft, field artillery, and tank-destroyer fire wherever required. In the Pacific Theater, the gun also individually built up its reputation not only as a triple-threat weapon but also earned another name, the "Sniper Gun," because it was used effectively as a direct-fire weapon for driving Japanese out of dug-in positions in caves and pillboxes. Although the gun's primary purpose was antiaircraft, its high velocity and flexibility in elevation and traverse made it the nearest approach to an all-purpose weapon.

The 90-mm gun became the outstanding weapon in combating the V-1 attacks on London and Antwerp. Its use in the protection of those cities has been well publicized. Of the 5,000 V-bombs aimed at the vital eight-mile circles of Antwerp, which was used to supply our European armies, only 211 were able to penetrate the 90-mm antiaircraft defense area. During the last six days of the buzz-bomb attacks, the 90-mm antiaircraft gun destroyed 89 of 91 buzz-bombs aimed at Antwerp.

Because the Germans did not fly at altitudes greater than 10,000 feet in their normal operations in Europe, the 90-mm gun was able to deal effectively with all types of German aerial attacks.

The triple treat 90-mm antiaircraft gun is shown here in a typical role as an antitank gun. The 90-mm antiaircraft gun has been set up at a road block in Germany and is ready to engage any oncoming German tanks.

120-mm gun, M1—120-mm antiaircraft mount, M1.

120-MM GUN, M1—MOUNT, M1

CHARACTERISTICS

Gun, M1
   Weight (complete) . . . . 10,675 lb.
     Weight of projectile . . . . 50 lb.
     Weight of powder charge . . . . 24 lb.
   Dimensions
     Length of bore . . . . 60 cals.
     Length (muzzle to rear face of breech ring) . . . . . . 291 in.
   Caliber . . . . 4.7 in.
     Travel of projectile in barrel . . . . 248.35 in.
   Chamber capacity . . . . 1,046 cu. in.
   Muzzle velocity . . . . 3,100 f./s.
   Maximum powder pressure . . . . 38,000 lb./sq. in.
   Rate of firing . . . . 10 rds./min.
   Type of breech block . . . . Vertical sliding
   Type of recoil mechanism . . . . Hydropneumatic with variable recoil
Mount, M1
   Type . . . . 2 bogie, 8 wheel trailer, portable in one load
   Weight (gun and mount complete)
     Traveling position . . . . 61,500 lb.
     Rear bogie . . . . 4,100 lb.
     Front bogie . . . . 3,850 lb.
     Mount in firing position . . . . 53,550 lb.
   Dimensions of mount, traveling
     Over-all length, lunette to rear muzzle . . . . 369 in.
     Maximum height . . . . 124 in.
     Maximum width . . . . 123.5 in.
     Wheelbase . . . . 186 in.
     Center road clearance under spade . . . . 15 in.
     Size of tires (duals) . . . . 13 x 24 in.

120-MM GUN, M1—MOUNT, M1—Continued

Dimensions of mount, emplaced
  Height of trunnions above ground . . . . 79 in.
  Height of platform above ground . . . . 36 in.
  Diagonal of spread outriggers . . . . 33 ft. (approx.)
Maneuvering Data
  Maximum elevation . . . . +80°
  Maximum depression . . . . −5°
  Leveling adjustment (each way) . . . . 4°
  Traverse . . . . 360°
  Capacity of hydraulic jacks . . . . 15 tons each

In 1940 Ordnance believed that the Germans would attack from great altitudes, and that it would be necessary to build a gun reaching such high altitudes that it would be impossible for the enemy to fly above its effective range. After careful ballistic studies, the 120-mm caliber, firing a 50-pound projectile at a velocity of 3,100 feet per second, was selected; this gave a maximum altitude of 56,000 feet. It was decided to put this unit on wheels so that it could accompany the armies in the field. The unit as finally designed weighed 61,500 pounds. It was built along the same structural lines as the 90-mm antiaircraft mount, M2. It could be readily emplaced for firing and prepared for traveling by means of a hydraulic jack on each outrigger. The gun was aimed automatically by means of a remote power control system which in turn was controlled by firing data furnished by the director or central computing instrument. The mount permitted a maximum elevation of 80° and a depression of 5° (for employment against ground targets). The carriage was also provided with an automatic rammer and fuze setter so that all that the gunner had to do was to place the round on a tray, after which the mechanism set the fuze and loaded the piece. Because of the heavy projectile, high muzzle velocity, and short time of flight, calculations indicated that this weapon would be twice as effective as the 90-mm gun at the same ranges. As German aircraft did not fly at the high altitudes expected, it was not necessary to send this gun to the European Theater, as the smaller and less bulky 90-mm fulfilled all requirements. The 120-mm gun placed this country well ahead of all others in the development of large-caliber mobile antiaircraft weapons.

Antiaircraft Artillery Fire Control

Thanks to its peacetime progress, the Ordnance Department had available at the beginning of the war a mechanical antiaircraft director which was immediately placed in production for this country and England. It formed an important part of the antiaircraft fire-control equipment of the British Army. In 1943 the development of the electric director was completed and adopted for heavy antiaircraft weapons, i.e., the 3-inch, 90-mm, and 120-mm guns. It gave greater accuracy and flexibility and had the added advantage of being built to receive radar data. Thus blind firing was immediately possible. The electric director gave this country a lead over all other countries in the field of antiaircraft fire-control instruments.

For the lighter antiaircraft weapons, such as the 37-mm and 40-mm automatic cannon, on-carriage computing sights were developed. These sights provided mechanisms to compute the necessary lead angles for both azimuth and elevation and for setting the telescopes to the proper angles. Power for operating these mechanisms was taken from that provided for the gun mount and manual settings were made by estimating target speed and course. Further adjustments were made from tracer observations as the firing continued.

120-mm antiaircraft gun in action, showing crew feeding ammunition into the automatic loader.

Illustration of Radar

Controlled antiaircraft artillery firing at an enemy plane, showing that when the radar is focused on the plane the fire control will automatically point the guns so that their shells will burst at the position reached by the plane.

Results of Antiaircraft Fire During the Period from 6 June, 1944 to 7 May, 1945

The 12th Army Group reported 14,776 sorties by piloted enemy aircraft over its area. Of this number, a total of 2,070 German planes were destroyed and by official count an additional 937 probably destroyed by antiaircraft fire. Thus antiaircraft artillery of the 12th Army Group destroyed or probably destroyed one of every five attacking enemy aircraft. These results were obtained against highly maneuverable planes which most of the time were more concerned with evasive action than pressing home the attack. The best hunting for the antiaircraft units was afforded the automatic weapon battalions providing protection with the armored column spearheads. One such battalion accounted for 34 enemy planes destroyed and 6 probably destroyed during a 34-hour period. The following tabulation gives the results obtained with the various types of weapons employed by the 1st United States Army from 6 June 1944 to 1 January 1945:

Weapons	Enemy Aircraft Destroyed and Probably Destroyed	Rnds per Enemy A/C Destroyed and Probably Destroyed	Per Cent of Total No. Destroyed and Probably Destroyed by Weapons
90-mm	262.5	225	6.74
40-mm	379	239	9.75
37-mm	135	286	3.42
.50 Cal	129	21,997	3.32
TOTAL	905.5		23.23

During this period 3,888 enemy aircraft were engaged in 1,701 raids.

In the Southwest Pacific Area, the 14th A.A. Command reported 658 raids involving a total of 1,361 enemy planes during the period from 1 January 1944 to 15 January 1945. Antiaircraft artillery weapons engaged the enemy in 588 of these raids, during which they destroyed or probably destroyed 37.2 per cent of the enemy planes.

Aircraft range and height finder for 90-mm and 120-mm antiaircraft guns. A complicated optical instrument required for determining altitude of an enemy plane.

MORTARS AND AMMUNITION

The progress of the war made increasingly apparent the necessity for supporting advancing infantry with increased firepower—intense and accurate. Close-support weapons were required to supplement the artillery coverage to prevent the enemy from manning his weapons in the interval between the lifting of the artillery barrage and attainment of the objective. Since hostile forces are normally entrenched in defensive positions, plunging fire is essential. The need was for weapons readily transportable, capable of immediate action, and suited to fire from defilade in front-line emplacements.

Mortars have the basic advantage of providing infantry with firepower comparable in effectiveness to artillery. Comparing weight of materiel to ammunition delivered at the target, they are the most efficient of weapons. High-trajectory fire, with the fin type of projectile, enables mortars to operate at extreme angles from protected positions and destroy the enemy behind his frontal protection.

To meet the requirements of modern warfare, the Ordnance Department developed a well-integrated mortar coverage, zone by zone and caliber by caliber. The mortars at the beginning of the war were the small 60-mm and the 81-mm. As the war progressed, the need for larger mortars was indicated, and weapons of medium caliber, the 105-mm and 155-mm, both portable by hand and transportable by wheel-carts, were provided to permit blasting the enemy from strong points and machine-gun bunkers. A still larger mobile mortar, the 250-mm, which could be emplaced in forward positions for demolition against heavy fortifications, was also designed.

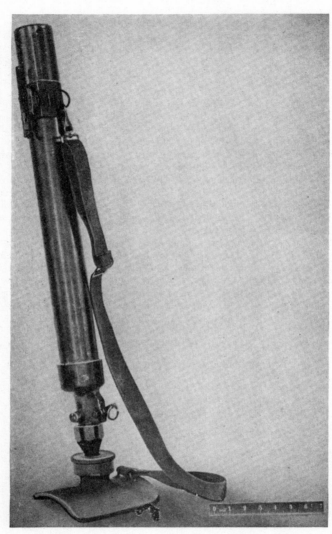

60-mm Mortar, M19, with base plate, sight bracket, and sight.

MORTAR, 60-MM, M19

CHARACTERISTICS

Weight (hand held) . . . .   20 lb.
Range . . . . 75 to 784 yd.
Weight (with mount) . . . .   42 lb.
Range . . . . 200 to 1,985 yd.

60-MM MORTARS

The 60-mm mortar as used in this war was a highly effective and versatile infantry weapon. Its principal value lay in the great firepower which it could produce for such a light weight. The complete mortar weighed 43 pounds and could be broken down into 12- to 16-pound manloads for carrying into the dense jungles. A great variety of ammunition was furnished, including high-explosive, illuminating, practice, and white phosphorus shells.

In their first battles with the Japanese our infantrymen had some doubt as to whether a mortar of this small size and weight was effective. These arguments continued until on one occasion the Japanese captured a number of 60-mm mortars and ammunition and used them against our troops. The fire was so deadly that the efficiency of the mortar and its ammunition was never again questioned throughout the war. This infantry mortar was universally used in all theaters.

The Japanese had developed a somewhat similar mortar with a much lighter and less effective projectile, known to us as the "knee mortar." It was thought at one time that the Japanese fired this mortar from the knee, because of the shape of the base plate. This designation was in error, for if used in this manner the mortar

60-mm mortar squad preparing to fire on German positions across the Rhine River from Strassbourg, France.

would have broken the firer's leg. Taking this idea from the Japanese, we changed the firing mechanism of the 60-mm mortar so that the base of the mortar could be placed on the ground and the round fired by pulling the lanyard. This per-mitted our mortar, like the Japanese, to be used for direct fire as well as plunging fire. This modification was found effective in jungle war-fare.

Gunner using 60-mm mortar, M19, from prone position.

American soldiers in France counting and checking 60-mm mortar ammunition at the supply dump, after containers were picked up by jeep and trailer.

Extension tube attached to 81-mm mortar, M1, ready to fire.

81-MM MORTAR, M1

CHARACTERISTICS

Extension Tube, T1
    Length   .   .   .   .   23 in.
    Weight .   .   .   .   27 lb.
81-mm Mortar, M1, with Extension Tube, T1
    Length, bore   .   .   .   .   68.55 in.
    Weight .   .   .   .   163 lb.

Ammunition	H.E. Shell M43A1 6 increments	H.E. Shell M56 4 increments
Muzzle velocity	744 f./s.	617 f./s.
Range	3,491 yd.	2,775 yd.

Extension Tube, T1, Showing Bolt for Clamping to 81-mm Mortar.

81-MM MORTAR, M1

This smooth-bore, muzzle-loading weapon was developed to supplant the British 3-inch Stokes trench mortar used by the U. S. Army during World War I. The basic design of our 81-mm mortar was taken from one developed by the Edgar Brant Company of France, and the Ordnance Department, before the war, had purchased the right to manufacture this mortar. During the war, development of the 81-mm mortar was rapid, and many notable improvements

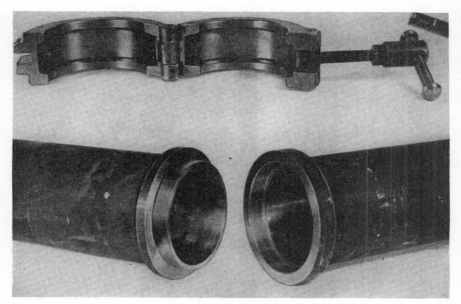

ABERDEEN PROVING GROUND
105-mm Mortar, T13E6, mfg'd, by A. B. Farquhar Co. Details of joint. TOP: Clamp. BOTTOM: (left) Bottom section joint, (right) Muzzle section joint.

were introduced. One of these was a barrel extension to increase the range to a maximum of 3,500 yards.

Near the end of the war a new 81-mm mortar was designed, called the universal mortar. In this the tube was shortened and the weight of the complete unit reduced to 66½ pounds. It was then suitable for accurate fire at moderate ranges. To obtain longer ranges, a muzzle extension could be added. The 81-mm mortar, with its several types of shell, was one of the most effective weapons in this war.

81-mm mortar being employed in the attack. A typical picture of mortar action in all theaters.

The 81-mm mortar throwing special projectile with wire cable attached. The projectile buries itself in the ground to form an anchor for the cable. There are many applications, such as throwing a line over a river for pulling men and supplies across, or throwing a line over a mine field to permit floats to be dragged across to explode the antipersonnel and antitank mines.

105-mm Mortar, T13, and Mount, T12.

105-MM MORTAR, T13—MOUNT, T12

CHARACTERISTICS

Mortar
    Caliber 105-mm
    Length . . . . 74 in.
    Weight . . . . 96.2 lb.
        Assembled to mount . . . . 190.3 lb.

105-MM MORTAR, T13—MOUNT, T12—Continued

Mount	
Type	Base plate and bipod
Weight, bipod	49.1 lb.
Base plate	45.0 lb.
Traverse	90 mils left, 90 mils right
Elevation	45° to 85°
Range	2,000 yd.
Rate of fire	3 rds./min.

During the war the Ordnance Department worked out a complete series of mortars to cover the entire field. An important item of this group was the 105-mm mortar. It weighed complete 200 pounds in the firing position and delivered a shell weighing 26 pounds to a maximum range of 2,000 yards. It was employed principally as an infantry weapon to accompany initial landing forces and to provide the equivalent of accurate artillery fire until the heavier field artillery weapons could be landed.

Covers for 105-mm mortar. (1) Cover, Muzzle, M334. (2) Cover, base, M535. (3) Cover, clamp, M534.

155-mm mortar, T25, with mount, T16E2, base plate, T2E2, and H.E. shell.

155-MM MORTAR, T25

CHARACTERISTICS

Mortar
Caliber 155-mm
Length . . . . 72 in.
Weight . . . . 164 lb.
   Assembled to mount . . . . 571 lb.
Mount
Type (T16E2) . . . . Base plate and bipod
Weight, bipod . . . . 75 lb.
   Base plate T2E2 (3 sections) . . . . 193 lb.
   Yoke . . . . 94 lb.
   Traversing mechanism . . . . 45 lb.
Traverse . . . . 60 mils left, 60 mils right
Elevation . . . . 45° to 85°
Range . . . . 200 to 2505 yd.
Rate of fire . . . . 1 to 3 rds./min.
Ammunition
Type . . . . H.E. Shell T26E1
Weight, complete round . . . . 63.5 lb.
Fuze . . . . Rocket, P.D. M4A1
Primer . . . . Standard, with ignition cartridge T2

155-MM MORTAR, T25

The 155-mm mortar was another weapon designed to provide increased firepower. The complete weapon weighed 600 pounds but could be broken down into loads not exceeding 150 pounds. This mortar reached a maximum range of 2,500 yards with a 60-pound projectile and was found to be very effective in destroying enemy resistance.

The 155-mm mortar was subjected to combat tests by the 37th Infantry Division during the advance from Sante Fe to Cagayan Valley in the Philippines. At Bagabag, for example, on Highway 4, six rounds were fired in the vicinity of a tank emplacement. The driving tank crew evacuated immediately. The range was 1,500 yards. Another combat experience by the same division was that during the preparation for the entry into Lantap on Highway 4, the mortar was emplaced 50 yards behind the front lines and various point targets were fired on at from 400 to 800 yards range. During this period, direct hits on five houses and a light tank were observed. All six targets were destroyed.

155-mm mortar in action in the Pacific Theater. This powerful weapon throws a 60-lb. high-explosive projectile with great accuracy.

"Little David" tube in traveling position. The world's most powerful mortar.

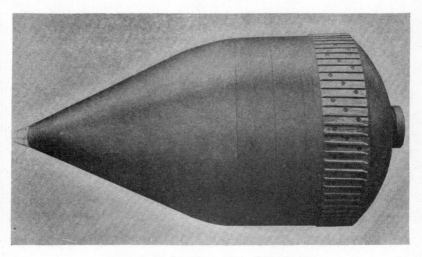

Projectile, T1, for 914-mm mortar (Little David).

"Little David" (914-mm mortar) in Firing Position.

914-MM MORTAR (Little David) AND AMMUNITION

By early 1944 it was apparent that unusually resistant enemy fortifications presented a problem which clearly required plunging fire with a projectile carrying the maximum practicable quantity of high explosive. Consideration of this type of target resulted in more and more emphasis on mortars, especially heavy mortars. None of the available mortars was suitable; the need was for a weapon able to deliver a projectile with far more destructive capacity than any previously conceived.

Engineering studies indicated that with present bridge and tire limitations the largest practicable weapon which could be transported over highways and cross-country would be a mortar of 914-mm (36-inch) bore.

The "Little David" (914-mm) mortar is the largest ever built. It is intended for the destruction of enemy subterranean fortifications, fortified cities, industrial targets, and important supply installations. This weapon, had the war lasted, would have given the land forces a powerful, mobile weapon with an accuracy and all-weather dependability comparable to those of artillery, with a far greater explosive effect. It fires a projectile weighing 3,700 pounds, with 1,600 pounds of high explosive.

Just before V-J Day, ammunition for "Little David" was being rapidly produced, and production facilities were in a position to expand if the need had arisen.

Crater caused by Little David projectile. Craters are roughly 13 feet deep and 39 feet in diameter.

Chapter V

ROCKETS AND LAUNCHERS

Chapter V

ROCKETS AND LAUNCHERS

Rockets were highly publicized throughout the war, principally because they were new weapons to the public. The rocket had been used in warfare for many years, but had not been used in World War I or developed in this country between the wars. The rocket was, at best, an auxiliary weapon for providing added firepower. Rockets in their present state cannot be used as a substitute for artillery because of their inaccuracy. The rocket is, however, a valuable ground weapon for laying down, quickly, a barrage over an area. Rockets can be fired from simple, light launching tubes at astonishing rates. In air warfare the rocket gave added firepower to fighter aircraft as it permitted the firing of a heavy missile with a large bursting charge from a light tube or rail.

The Navy improvised rocket ships which could lay down a heavy fire upon a beach at short ranges to assist in amphibious operations. The Navy's responsibility was to protect our troops until they had secured a beachhead, and rockets fitted admirably into this role.

It is probable that rockets will be developed into important weapons of the future and may supplant long-range artillery, since with radar the missile can be controlled and caused to fall accurately upon a desired target. Atomic explosives likewise will enhance the future value of rockets. Both the Army and Navy were engaged in rocket development throughout the war, though each worked in different fields. Most of the Navy rockets were built to be fired at very short ranges, for barrage purposes, while the Army rockets for land required much longer ranges.

ALUMINUM DISC   ALUMINUM CUP   MOTOR   IGNITER

BOOSTER   DETONATOR   SAFETY PIN   PROPELLANT   TRAP

SHELL   FIRING PIN SPRING   FIRING PIN·   SPACER   NOZZLE AND FIN ASSEMBLY

Rocket, H.E.A.T., 2.36-inch, M6A3, disassembled.

ROCKET, H.E.A.T., 2.36-INCH, M6A3

CHARACTERISTICS

Weight	3.4 lb.
Length	19.4 in.
Diameter	2.36 in.
Weight of H.E.	.5 lb.
Fuze	Base detonating
Weight of propellant	56 grams
Velocity (70° F.)	270 ft./ sec.
Range, Maximum	700 yd.
Ignition	Electric
Packing	In fiber containers and 20 containers per wooden box.

The practice rocket, M7A3, has the same characteristics as the M6A3 except, of course, for the H.E. charge. The practice rocket has an inert load in the head.

The active development of this small-caliber rocket, which was one of the most effective and widely used rockets in the war, began early in 1942. Some preliminary work in the rocket field had been carried out at Aberdeen Proving Ground from 1933 on. The earlier work pointed out the urgent need for intensive research work on propellants suitable for use in rocket motors.

Ballistite, a double base powder, was selected for this rocket and proved satisfactory. The Hercules Powder Company produced this propellant for the Army in large quantities. The rocket head was designed to use the deadly shaped-charge effect for penetration of enemy armor and pillboxes. The launcher was a tube,

60 inches long and open at each end. This launcher, dubbed the "bazooka" because of its appearance, is described in the small arms chapter because it is a shoulder-fired weapon.

This rocket was initially used in the landings in North Africa in November 1942. The bazooka rocket required no additional personnel and with a minimum of practice any rifleman could use it effectively. It proved valuable in providing security for support of field artillery batteries and for infantry combat units facing tank-led onslaughts. It quickly proved its versatility and found instant favor with the combat troops as an added defensive weapon in all theaters of operations.

Judged by artillery or traditional firearms standards, the bazooka's range is short, but from hidden positions it offered cover for the operator. It could pour death on light tanks, half-tracks, scout cars, and other enemy armored vehicles that unsuspectingly came within its range.

Interviews at random with returning veterans from both European and Pacific theaters indicated that this weapon was valued highly by the troops. One comment was: "I had a soldier in my company who was really an expert with the bazooka. When there was a Jap pillbox or tank that needed attention I called on him and he was always eager to get into the fight. On one occasion our advance had been halted by fire from two 75-mm cannon. I called for our own artillery to silence them, but that bazooka man couldn't wait. He worked his way up to within about 50 yards of one of the Jap cannon and let fly a rocket. The first round blasted the muzzle off the enemy weapon. He then started for the second cannon and quickly finished it."

The bazooka's versatility was increased with the development of a white-phosphorus shell for the rocket. Upon impact, the white phosphorus would burn and throw off dense white smoke. This rocket was particularly useful against bunkers and caves to produce enemy casualties and to screen advances of American troops.

Target rocket being fired for antiaircraft gun practice.

ROCKET, TARGET, 3.25-INCH, M2

CHARACTERISTICS

Weight . . . . 35.0 lb.
Length . . . . 59 in.
Diameter . . . . 3.25 in.
Weight of propellant . . . . 3.2 lb.
Velocity (70° F.) . . . . 530 f./s.
Range, Maximum . . . . 1,700 yd.
Ignition . . . . Electric
Packing . . . . One per wooden box, 3 fins assembled in the field

This rocket, referred to as the "target rocket," was developed to meet a specific requirement by the Antiaircraft Command. It provided a fast-moving target, of adequate size to be easily visible at speeds of 450 m.p.h., for the training of troops in the operation of antiaircraft guns. It was developed and placed in quantity production early in the war. A late improvement added a flare on the front of the round. The glow and smoke of the flare were visible throughout the entire flight and made the rocket trajectory more visible both for day and night training.

This rocket, as well as the bazooka and many other types, used solid fuel as its propellant. Solid propellant required less accessory equip- ment for ignition and for control of energy re- lease than other types of fuels, such as liquid.

PROJECTOR, ROCKET, 3.25-INCH, M1

Type	Two-wheel towed carriage
Rocket support	Two rails
Cable	100 ft.
Elevation	Manual with quadrant
Weight	800 lb.
Rate of fire	Single shot

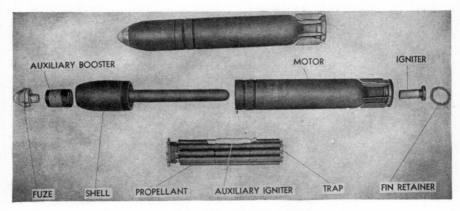

AUXILIARY BOOSTER   MOTOR   IGNITER

FUZE   SHELL   PROPELLANT   AUXILIARY IGNITER   TRAP   FIN RETAINER

Rocket, 4.5-inch, M8, Disassembled.

ROCKET, H.E., 4.5-INCH, M8 TYPE

CHARACTERISTICS

Weight, with fuze	38.5 lb.
Length, over-all	33.0 in.
Diameter	4.5 in.
Weight of H.E.	4.0 lb.
Fuze	M4A2 selective S.Q. and delay
Weight of propellant	M8A3—4.65 lb.; T22—4.75 lb.
Velocity (70° F.)	850 f./s.
Range, maximum	4,200 yd.
Packing	2 rounds in fiber container and wooden box
Ignition	Electric
Dispersion (P.E. from ground)	14 mils

This rocket can be fired from ground launchers of the T27 and T34 type. It can also be fired from aircraft using the M10 tube clusters.

With the addition of the T23 modification kit, the M8 rocket could be fired from the post type, low-drag aircraft launchers that were used by both Army and Navy planes. The kit consists of lug bands, large fixed fins, and igniter with long cable and plug. These parts were assembled to the rocket in the field.

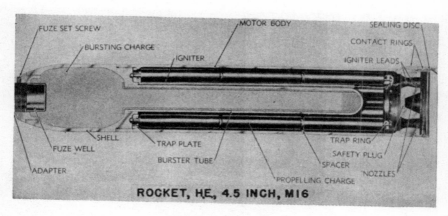

Rocket, H.E., 4.5-inch, M16.

ROCKET, H.E., 4.5-INCH, M16

CHARACTERISTICS

Weight, with fuze	42.5 lb.
Length	31 in.
Weight of bursting charge	5.2 lb. (T.N.T.)
Fuze	P.D. M48A2, with Booster, M21A1, or Fuze, P.D., M81
Weight of propelling charge	4.75 lb.
Maximum velocity (70°)	830 f./s.
Maximum range (45°)	5,250 yd.
Packing	1 rd. in metal container, T41
Ignition	Electric, 6 volts min.
Dispersion, P. E.	8 mils

The fuze can be set for superquick or 0.05-second delay action. The delay setting permits the round to penetrate ⅜-inch armor plate or 8 inches of wood and detonate 10 to 20 feet beyond the penetration. When superquick setting is used, only a small crater is obtained.

The rockets are issued unfuzed. The fuzes, staked together with the boosters, are assembled as units and shipped in separate containers.

4.5-inch T66 rocket launcher firing the 4.5-inch M16 H.E. rockets. Action taking place in early May 1945 near Wolfsham, Germany. Troops are part of 282nd Field Artillery Battalion, 8th Corps, 1st Army.

LAUNCHER, ROCKET, MULTIPLE 4.5-INCH, T66

CHARACTERISTICS

Weight, of launcher . . . . 1,200 lb.
    loaded with 24 rockets . . . . 2,220 lb.
Over-all length of launcher . . . . 10 ft.
Height of launcher (0° elevation) . . . . 43 in.
Number of tubes 24
Length of tubes . . . . 36 in.
Tire size . . . . 6.00 x 16
Tread . . . . 59 in.
Elevation . . . . 0° to 45°
Traverse . . . . 10° right to 10° left
Telescope mount T72E1
Elbow telescope M62
Instrument light M42
Rockets fired . . . . M16 and M17

The firing mechanism issued with each launcher is a 10-cap blasting machine with a 50-foot firing cord. The blasting machine is connected to a firing box which contains a solenoid-operated switch. This switch fires the rockets at a rate of two each second.

4.5-INCH H.E. ROCKET

To meet the need for a rocket for either ground-to-ground or air-to-ground firing, a 4.5-inch rocket, known at the M8, was developed. This rocket was characterized by folding stabilization fins, which allowed it to be fired from a tube. Upon emerging from the launcher tube, the fins opened under the accelerating force.

The tube launchers could be clustered and mounted on wheeled carriages or suspended from the wings of aircraft. A ground launcher, designated the T27, consisted of eight tubes on a framework which could be placed either on a truck or on the ground for firing. A three-tube cluster, designated the M10, was produced for

4.5-inch fin-stabilized rocket, M8, being prepared for firing by 5th Army troops.

suspension under the wings of fighter aircraft. Other types of launchers were also designed for firing this 4.5-inch rocket. One of the most widely used launchers was the T34, in a 60-tube cluster which was placed on the M4 medium tank. Launchers of this type and of the T27 type, with suitable quantities of M8 rockets, were sent to England before D-Day.

vantages were: Great firepower: 3 volleys fired in 18 minutes—approximately 1,800 rounds; effective fire en masse; morale effect on enemy troops of mass fire, terrific. The disadvantages were: Limited range: affected choice of position in placing weapons within range of counterbattery; short and erratic rounds; slowness in laying of launcher and reloading.

4.5-inch rocket launcher, T34, provides for 60 tubes on medium tank, M4.

A 105-mm field artillery battalion attached to the First U. S. Army was assigned to develop the tactical uses for this weapon. This was the 18th Field Artillery Battalion, which was taken out of the combat line late in October 1944 and issued T27 rocket launchers and 4.5-inch rockets. A tentative organization provided for 25 launchers per battery to be mounted, two each, on 2½-ton trucks.

Comments on the use of this weapon revealed certain advantages and disadvantages. The ad-

Rockets are at present viewed as merely supplementary to field artillery and are not yet sufficiently accurate to replace artillery. Rockets are generally employed to cover area targets and to obtain the benefit of surprising mass fire.

To improve the accuracy of the rocket, the spin-stabilized 4.5-inch M16 was developed and standardized. The Army Ground Forces Rocket Board, after test firings, reported that the spin-stabilized 4.5-inch rocket was far superior to the fin-stabilized rocket in range and accuracy and was of greater value as a supplement to artillery fire. With this favorable report, the Army Ground Forces requested that all 4.5-inch rockets should be of the spin-stabilized type.

Multiple-tube launchers were designed to fire this rocket. Firing tests showed that a short tube could be satisfactorily used and still obtain good accuracy. Launching tubes were muzzle-

approximately 12 seconds. A launcher can be reloaded in approximately a minute and a half. It is estimated that at least three volleys, or 2,892 rounds, can be fired before the batteries would have to shift position. These rockets gave great power with a minimum use of manpower.

An estimate of the value of the rocket for combat was obtained from several officers who had

Battery A, 18th Field Artillery Battalion, fires a volley from their rocket launchers in the Hurtgen Forest, Germany. V Corps, U. S. First Army, 11/26/44.

loaded, with permanently fixed backstops. Contacts were set in the wall of the tube so that it was only necessary to put the rocket in place to complete the electrical circuit for firing. Theater reports indicated that there was a place for these rockets as a supplement to artillery fire. Their use would be on such targets as an area to be saturated, to give a high rate of fire in a short period of time, and to search an area for concealed fire. A battalion can fire 964 rounds in

witnessed the use of the rocket on various occasions. From the First Infantry Division, the comment was: "Rockets are a coming weapon . . . there is a definite need and use for rockets . . . the drenching fire of the rocket is the thing we need," and, "We can use rockets very nicely for the initial softening-up in a break-through." An officer in the First Army stated: "Rockets have a definite place and use in a break-through; they will save a lot of guns if properly massed and handled; they are a form of artillery and should be treated and handled as such."

From aircraft, the folding-fin rocket was fired from tube clusters; later, a rocket with fixed fins was developed which could be fired from a very

1944, the expenditure of these 4.5-inch rockets was in excess of 1,000 per week. Limited use was made by the 7th Air Force based in the Pacific Ocean area. Their targets were mainly enemy personnel, vehicles, barracks, and radio

The Multiple Rocket Launcher T66 is shown being loaded with 4.5-inch M16 Rockets. The loading is being done by "B" Battery of the 282nd Field Artillery Battalion, VIII Corps, First Army.

simple type of launcher referred to as zero-rail launcher. Both types were used in combat. The 12th Air Force, operating in Florence, Italy, employed the M8 rocket for firing from P-47 fighter aircraft. They were used for attack on such targets as building and railroad rolling stock, and for the support of infantry. During the fall of

and radar stations. This last type of target was particularly suitable for rocket attack, as the fragmentation was good and the rocket had considerable incendiary effect.

The successful use of spin-stabilization for field artillery rockets led to its consideration for stabilization of aircraft rockets. Calculations of the stability factor for the rocket when launched forward from high-speed aircraft showed that a much greater rate of spin was necessary. This theoretical work was checked and found reliable by actual firing tests. The 4.5-inch T54 rocket was developed and a quantity was produced for experimental and proof tests at Aberdeen Proving

that could be developed further to provide more firepower.

For most of the various sizes and types of rocket, standard artillery or bomb fuzes may be used. The rocket heads were designed to accept the standard fuzes wherever possible. This was particularly true for the rotating rockets, which

M4 tank, mounting 60—4.5" Rockets, fires on enemy town.

Ground. Exhaustive tests were carried out with the cooperation of the Dover Air Base of the Army Air Forces. The results indicated that the rocket was stable up to aircraft speeds of over 600 miles per hour, and that reasonable accuracy could be obtained.

The smooth contours of this rocket made it particularly adaptable for firing from automatic launchers. One such launcher that was developed, the T47, had a cyclic rate of fire of 120 rounds per minute. The number of rounds which the launcher could hold was limited, however, to six rounds. The mechanism had certain features

could use certain of the artillery fuzes without change or modification. In the case, for the unrotated or fin-stabilized rockets, however, new fuzes had to be designed. Mortar fuzes which depend upon a high acceleration for arming could not be used, nor could bomb fuzes using propellers for arming. The rocket acceleration caused the blades of the latter to bend and fail, as they were designed for gravity dropping. Fuzes that would arm on rocket accelerations and still be safe to stand rough handling and transporting had to be designed, tested, and produced. One such fuze was the M4A2 that was used on the 4.5-inch M8 and T22 rockets. This fuze was selective for either superquick or delay functioning.

The unrotated rocket was the first application for the V.T. fuze development. The rocket development and the V.T. fuze development were kept in step so that a V.T. fuze would be ready for all of the sizes and types of rockets that would be employed. The good fragmentation of the rocket head made the use of the V.T. fuzes especially desirable. The V.T. fuze for use with the 4.5-inch M16 rocket is the T31E1.

A 4.5-inch multi-barreled rocket launcher fires at German-held Reinheim, France. The launcher, mounted on a jeep, is driven into position, fired, and then moved to avoid counter-battery fire.

S/Sgt. Henry Yoder of Sotherton, Pa. and Sgt. Lloyd Dunker of Portland, Ore. handle with the greatest of respect the rockets they are inserting into the launching tubes of an 8th Fighter Command. The rockets demand respect because of the great explosive power they contain, a power which German tanks, locomotives, and armored installations fear.

Loading T37, 7.2-inch, rockets in an M17 launcher mounted on an M4A1 tank. Rockets weigh 61 lbs. each. Launcher holds 20 rockets, which can be fired individually or in barrage.

LAUNCHER, ROCKET, MULTIPLE 7.2-INCH, M17

DATA

Weight of empty launcher . . . . 4,615 lb.
Length of launcher . . . . 105 in.
Width of launcher . . . . 105 in.
Limits of elevation:
   Maximum . . . . +25°
   Depression . . . . −5°
Limits of traverse in degrees right or left . . . . 360°

The M17 is designed to be mounted on the medium tanks M4, M4A1, M4A2, M4A3, M4A4, and M4A6. It has a capacity of 20 rockets which can be fired electrically either in single or automatic fire. The launcher is controlled in azimuth and elevation with the same controls as those used for the 75-mm gun mounted in the tank turret. It can be jettisoned by the tank crew by means of hydraulic controls operated from within the turret of the tank.

CHARACTERISTICS

Rocket, H.E., T37
   Weight . . . . 61 lb.
   Length . . . . 35 in.
   Maximum velocity . . . . 160 f./s.
   Maximum range . . . . 230 yd.

LAUNCHER, ROCKET, MULTIPLE 7.2-INCH, M17—Continued

Rocket, Chemical, M25 (T21)

Weight	51.8 lb.
Length	50 in.
Maximum velocity	680 f./s.
Maximum range	3,430 yd. (at 43″ elevation)

A demolition rocket using the newly developed plastic explosive was designed and constructed for use in clearing obstacles for beach landings and similar operations. This rocket had a 7.2-inch diameter head and carried a large amount of the explosive. Its motor was smaller in diameter (2¼ inches) and its velocity was relatively low as it was not originally intended for use except at very close ranges. Later the 4.5-inch T22 rocket motor was assembled to this same 7.2-inch head. This round, the T57, could be used at ranges up to 1,200 yards with good accuracy and effectiveness.

The launcher, M17 (T40), for these 7.2-inch rockets contained 20 sets of rails enclosed within armor plate, which protected the rockets from small-arms fire. The launcher was mounted over the turret of a medium tank and was equipped with a jettisoning mechanism controlled from within the tank. This equipment was used in the landings on the southern coast of France and for some operations in Italy.

A later development in launchers for this caliber of rocket, when used for demolition purposes, was the single launcher mounted in the gun position of a Sherman tank. The launcher had a sliding breech and was loaded from within the tank. The crew and the rockets were then completely protected by the tank armor.

The rocket has inherent characteristics that make it a particularly suitable weapon for the projection of chemical gases and smoke. The low acceleration and thin wall casing permitted for the head allows the rocket a higher percentcentage of chemical filler than is found in conventional ammunition. The lightweight multiple-type launchers, than can be employed in large numbers, make a high rate of fire possible. It is thus possible to saturate a large area in a matter of seconds.

The 7.2-inch M25 (T21) rocket could be filled with any one of several chemicals and the head would hold approximately 20 pounds. The maximum range for the employment of this round was 3,430 yards. This round was fin-stabilized; the circular portion of the fin also served as the contact ring.

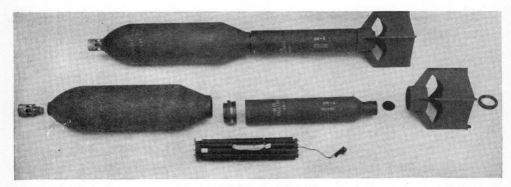

Rocket, H.E., 8-inch, T25.

ROCKET PROPULSION UNITS

To provide close support of infantry with a heavy caliber rocket, propulsion units were developed for firing 100-, 250-, and 500-pound G.P. bombs. One 4.5-inch T22 rocket motor was assembled to the base of the 100-pound bomb and the standard bomb fin was fastened to the rear portion of the rocket motor for stabilization. The 250-pound bomb used the T13 propulsion unit, which consisted of three 4.5-inch T22 rocket motors connected by a manifold. A special fin

had to be used. Limited quantities of both sizes of these rocket-propelled bombs were furnished to the Pacific Theater.

The launcher for the 100-pound rocket bomb was a simple steel framework which also served as the packing and shipping container. Elevation was adjusted by two legs which were fastened to the front end of the container.

The launcher for the 250-pound rocket bomb was a modification of the 105-mm howitzer. A V-shaped trough was mounted on the cradle in place of the gun. Elevation and azimuth change were accomplished in standard artillery manner. Very good accuracy was obtained with this weapon, and it proved effective to defoliate an area and to close and destroy caves.

The bombs propelled by these rockets could be filled with an incendiary mixture in place of the high explosive. Several types of a new incendiary mix, developed by the Chemical Warfare Service, were proof-tested with satisfactory results. Napalm, which was used in many of the incendiaries dropped by B-29's on Japan, was the filler for many of these rounds.

Samples of captured enemy material were sent to this country by the Ordnance Intelligence Teams operating in the combat zones. Among the ammunition returned from North Africa was

8-inch Rocket Launcher T53 Emplaced for Firing.

the 21-cm. German rocket. An American design was based on the caliber of the German rocket and was designated 210-mm T36. It was found desirable to formulate a new propellent composition to obtain a wider safe temperature range and to change the igniter to decrease the long hangfires which occurred at low temperatures with the German type. This rocket, which had a payload of over 100 pounds, had a range of nearly 10,000 yards.

Several proof launchers with both single and multiple tubes were constructed for testing this rocket. The rocket and the launchers were useful weapons for gaining experience on heavy rockets and for determining military characteristics for new field artillery type rockets.

The rocket-propelled 250-pound bomb with propulsion unit, jet, T13, is loaded on the T103 launcher preparatory to firing. The standard sight for the 75-mm pack howitzer is used for sighting on the target with this weapon. Firing is electric, by remote control. This action took place at the Marikina Watershed, Rizal Province, Luzon, P.I., August 8 1945.

Chapter VI

TANKS, GUN MOTOR CARRIAGES,
AND MOTOR TRANSPORT

Chapter VI

TANKS, GUN MOTOR CARRIAGES, AND MOTOR TRANSPORT

Between the wars, the Ordnance Department had continually worked on the design of tanks (both light and medium, combat cars, and other types of armored fighting vehicles, although funds for these, as for items in other fields, were limited. The Department made, nevertheless, considerable progress in keeping our designs in step with improvements being made abroad. This progress was attributable in part to the patriotic assistance of a number of concerns and individuals who worked closely with the Ordnance Department.

The Ordnance Automotive Advisory Committee, under the auspices of the American Society of Automotive Engineers, remained in continual session from 1920 until the war, meeting once a year, or more. This committee kept the Department advised as to the important developments in the automotive field which might be applicable to tank and combat-vehicle design.

When the emergency threatened in 1938, the Department already had a well-designed light tank and a medium tank which satisfied the requirements of the Infantry for a vehicle to accompany them into battle. When increased funds were obtained in 1939, the manufacture of limited numbers of light tanks (M-2A4) and medium tanks (M-2A1) was undertaken. This medium tank weighed about 20 tons and mounted a 37-mm gun and eight caliber .30 machine guns—four in sponson mounts, two forward, and two in rear hulls. The maximum armor carried was 1¼ inches thick.

MEDIUM TANK, M3 (General Grant) SERIES

TYPICAL CHARACTERISTICS

	M3 (riveted)	M3A1 (cast)	M3A2 (welded)	M3A3 (welded)	M3A4 (riveted)	M3A5 (riveted)
Crew	6	6	6	6	6	6
Physical Characteristics						
Weight (gross) . .	60,000 lb.	60,000 lb.	60,000 lb.	63,000 lb.	64,000 lb.	64,000 lb.
Length	18 ft., 6 in.	18 ft., 6 in.	18 ft., 6 in.	18 ft., 6 in.	19 ft., 8 in.	18 ft., 6 in.
Width	8 ft., 11 in.	8 ft., 11 in.	8 ft., 11 in.	8 ft., 11 in.	8 ft., 11 in.	8 ft., 11 in.
Height	10 ft., 3 in.	10 ft., 3 in.	10 ft., 3 in.	10 ft., 3 in.	10 ft., 3 in.	10 ft., 3 in.
Turret ring diameter (inside)	57 in.	57 in.	57 in.	57 in.	57 in.	57 in.
Ground clearance . .	17⅛ in.	17⅛ in.	17⅛ in.	17⅛ in.	17⅛ in.	17⅛ in.
Tread (center to center of track) . . .	83 in.	83 in.	83 in.	83 in.	83 in.	83 in.
Ground contact length at 0 penetration . . .	147 in.	147 in.	147 in.	147 in.	160 in	147 in.
Ground pressure per sq. in.	13.36 lb.	13.36 lb.	13.36 lb.	13.36 lb.	12.9 lb.	13.36 lb.
Performance						
Maximum speed .	26 m.p.h.	26 m.p.h.	26 m.p.h.	29 m.p.h.	26 m.p.h.	29 m.p.h.
Maximum grade ability .	60%	60%	60%	60%	60%	60%
Trench crossing ability .	6.2 ft.	6.2 ft.	6.2 ft.	6.2 ft.	6.2 ft.	6.2 ft.
Vertical obstacle ability .	24 in.	24 in.	24 in.	24 in.	24 in.	24 in.
Fording depth (slowest forward speed) . . .	40 in.	40 in.	40 in.	36 in.	40 in.	40 in.
Fuel capacity . .	175 gal.	175 gal.	175 gal.	150 gal.	160 gal.	175 gal.
Cruising range . .	120 miles	120 miles	120 miles	160 miles	120 miles	160 miles
Turning radius . .	37 ft.	37 ft.	37 ft.	37 ft.	39 ft.	37 ft.
Engine, Make . .	Continental	Continental	Continental	G.M. 6-71	Chrysler	G.M. 6-71
Model . . .	R-975-EC2 or C1	R-975-EC2 or C1	R-975-EC2 or C1	6046	A-57	6046
Type	Radial A.C.	Radial A.C.	Radial A.C.	Twin, In-Line, L.C.	Multibank, L.C.	Twin, In-Line, L.C.
No. of cylinders .	9	9	9	12	30	12
Fuel, octane or cetane .	92 or 80	92 or 80	92 or 80	50	80	50
Type .	Gasoline	Gasoline	Gasoline	Diesel	Gasoline	Diesel
Max. governed speed .	2,400 r.p.m.	2,400 r.p.m.	2,400 r.p.m.	2,100 r.p.m.	2,400 r.p.m.	2,100 r.p.m.
Net h.p. at r.p.m. . .	340 at 2,400	340 at 2,400	340 at 2,400	375 at 2,100	370 at 2,400	375 at 2,100
Max. torque, lb.-ft. at r.p.m. .	800 at 1,800	800 at 1,800	800 at 1,800	1,000 at 1,400	1,020 at 1,200	1,000 at 1,400

Armament
1 75-mm gun M2 or M3 . . . . In mount M1
1 37-mm gun M5 or M6 and 1 cal. .30 Browning machine gun M1919A4 (flexible) . . . . In combination mount M24 in turret
1 cal. .30 Browning machine gun M1919A4 (flexible) . . . . . On cupola, antiaircraft
1 cal. .30 Browning machine gun M1919A4 . . . . In bow
Provision for:
1 cal. .45 submachine gun . . . . Equipment of crew

Ammunition, Stowage
75-mm . . . . 46 rounds
37-mm . . . . 178 rounds
Cal. .45 . . . . 1,200 rounds
Cal. .30 . . . . 9,200 rounds
Hand grenades 12

MEDIUM TANK, M3 (General Grant) SERIES—Continued

	Actual	Basis
Armor		
Hull, front, upper	2 in.	4⅜ in.
lower	1½ in.	2¾ in.
Sides	1½ in.	1½ in.
Rear	1½ in.	1⅝ in.
Top	½ in.	
Bottom	½ in.–1 in.	
Turret, front	2¼ in.	6½ in.
Sides and rear	2¼ in.	2 in.
Top	⅞ in.	
Vision and Fire Control		
Periscope M1		
Periscope M3		1
Protectoscopes		1
Communications		7
Radio (with interphone)		
Command tank		SCR-508
Battery, voltage, total		SCR-506
Fire Protection		24
Fire extinguisher, CO₂–10 lb. (fixed)		
CO₂—4 lb. (hand)		2
Transmission, type		2
Gear ratios		Synchromesh
First speed		
Second speed		7.56:1
Third speed		3.11:1
Fourth speed		1.78:1
Fifth speed		1.11:1
Reverse		0.73:1
Differential, Controlled, gear ratio		5.65:1
Steering ratio		3.53:1
Final Drive, type		1.515:1
Gear ratio		Herringbone
Sprocket, no. of teeth		2.84:1
Pitch diameter		13
Suspension, type		25.038
Wheel or tire size		Volute spring
Idler, type		20 x 9
Wheel or tire size		Adjustable eccentric
Track, type		22 x 9
Width		Rubber block
Pitch		16 9/16 in.
No. of shoes per tank		6 in.
		158 (166 on M3A4)

Note: Fire extinguisher CO₂ entries use CO_2.

MEDIUM TANK, M3 (General Grant)

When money became available for quantity production of tanks, the Ordnance Department realized that the medium tank, M-2A1, would not be suitable for use against the Germans. It was necessary, therefore, to take time to redesign this tank completely to give it adequate firepower and armor protection. It was decided to place a 75-mm gun in the turret of the redesigned tank, but the Infantry, then the principal user of tanks, preferred the 37-mm gun; they were willing, however, to have the 75-mm gun placed in the tank hull. This tank was known as the M-3, or General Grant. The five manufacturers originally engaged in the manufacture of the M-3 tank pooled their resources for its rapid production—a most fortunate move, as it permitted early shipment of these tanks to the British in Africa.

Medium tank, M3 (General Grant), in Africa. This tank was important because it mounted a powerful 75-mm gun and was a reliable track-laying vehicle.

Medium Tank, M4, (General Sherman), showing welded hull. Medium tanks, M4A2 and M4A3, are generally similar in appearance.

Medium tank, M4A1—Left front view. Note elimination of direct vision. Cast armor plate hull.

Overhead view of medium tank, M4A1, showing entrance hatches.

MEDIUM TANK, M4 (General Sherman) SERIES

CHARACTERISTICS

	M4	M4A1	M4A2	M4A3	M4A4	M4A6
Crew	5	5	5	5	5	5
Physical Characteristics						
Weight (gross) . . .	66,500 lb.	66,500 lb.	69,000 lb.	68,500 lb.	71,000 lb.	71,000 lb.
Length . . .	19 ft., 4 in.	19 ft. 2 in.	19 ft., 5 in.	19 ft. 4½ in.	19 ft., 10½ in.	19 ft., 10½ in.
Width . . .	8 ft., 7 in.	8 ft., 7 in.	8 ft., 7 in.	8 ft., 7 in.	8 ft., 7 in.	8 ft., 7 in.
Height . . .	9 ft.	9 ft.	9 ft.	9 ft.	9 ft.	9 ft.
Ground clearance .	17⅛ in.	17⅛ in.	17⅛ in.	17⅛ in.	15¾ in.	15¾ in.
Tread (center to center of tracks) . .	83 in.	83 in.	83 in.	83 in.	83 in.	83 in.
Ground pressure, per sq. in.	13.7 lb.	13.7 lb.	14.2 lb.	14.1 lb.	13.4 lb.	13.4 lb.
Ground contact length at 0° pentration .	147 in.	147 in.	147 in.	147 in.	160 in.	160 in.
Performance						
Sustained speed on level .	24 m.p.h.	24 m.p.h.	29 m.p.h.	26 m.p.h.	25 m.p.h.	25 m.p.h.
Maximum grade ability .	60%	60%	60%	60%	60%	60%
Trench crossing ability .	7 ft., 5 in.	7 ft., 5 in.	7 ft., 5 in.	7 ft., 5 in.	8 ft.	8 ft.
Vertical obstacle ability .	24 in.	24 in.	24 in.	24 in.	24 in.	24 in.
Fording depth (slowest forward speed) .	36 in.	36 in.	40 in.	36 in.	42 in.	42 in.
Fuel capacity . .	175 gals.	175 gal.	148 gals.	174 gals.	150 gals.	150 gals.
Cruising range . .	120 miles	120 miles	150 miles	130 miles	100 miles	100 miles
Maximum drawbar pull .	42,350 lb.	42,350 lb.	44,800 lb.	43,050 lb.	47,600 lb.	47,600 lb.

MEDIUM TANK, M4 (General Sherman) SERIES—Continued

Engine, Make	Continental	Continental	G.M. 6-71	GAA-III	Chrysler	Caterpillar
Model	R975-C1	R975-C1	6046	V-W.C.	5-line W.C.	RD-1820
Fuel (gasoline)	80	80	—	80	80	—
(Diesel)	—	—	50	—	—	45
Max. governed speed	2,400 r.p.m.	2,400 r.p.m.	2,100 r.p.m.	2,600 r.p.m.	2,400 r.p.m.	2,000 r.p.m.
Net h.p. at r.p.m.	353 at 2,400	353 at 2,400	375 at 2,100	450 at 2,600	370 at 2,850	450 at 2,000
Max. torque (lb.-ft. at r.p.m.)	800 at 1,800	800 at 1,800	1,000 at 1,400	950 at 2,100	1,025 at 1,200	1,470 at 1,200

Armament
75-mm gun, M3, and
1 cal. .30 Browning machine gun, M1919A4 (flexible) . . . In combination gun mount, M34A1, in turret
1 cal. .30 Browning machine gun, M1919A4 (flexible) . . . . In bow
1 cal. .50 machine gun, M2, H.B. (flexible) . . . . On turret (antiaircraft)
1 mortar, 2-Inch, M3
1 tripod mount, M2, cal. .30
Provision for:
1 cal. .45 submachine gun . . . . Equipment of crew

Ammunition, Stowage	M4, M4A2, M4A3, M4A4, M4A6	M4A1
75-mm (H.E., M48, A.P., M72; A.P.C., M61)	97	90
Cal. .30 (A.P. and tracer)	4,750	4,750
Cal. .45	600	600
Cal. .50 (A.P. and tracer)	300	300
Grenades, hand (fragmentation, Mk. III, 4; smoke, H.C., M8, 4; offensive, Mk. III, w/fuze, detonating, M2; thermite, incendiary, 2)	12	12
Smoke ammunition (minimum)	12	12

Armor	Actual	Basis
Hull, front, upper	2 in.	2-4 in.
Lower	1½-2 in.	2-2½ in.
Sides	1½-2 in.	1½-2 in.
Rear	1½ in.	
Top	1 in.	
Bottom	½-1 in.	
Turret, front	3 in.	3¾ in.
Sides	2 in.	2 in.
Top	1 in.	

Vision and Fire Control
Periscope, M4 (w/telescope, M38)	1
Periscope, M6	6
Gunner's quadrant, M1	1
Bore sight	1
Telescope, M70F	1
Azimuth indicator, M19	1
Elevation quadrant, M9	1

Communications
Radio	SCR-508
Command tank	SCR-506
Flag set, M238	5
Battery, voltage total	24

Fire Protection and Decontamination
Fire extinguisher—CO_2-10 lb. (fixed)	24
CO_2-4 lb. (hand)	2
Decontaminating apparatus, M2, 1½ qts.	2

MEDIUM TANK, M4 (General Sherman) SERIES—Continued

Track, type . . . . Rubber block
   Width . . . . 16½ in.
   Pitch . . . . 6 in.
   No. of shoes per vehicle 158 (Medium Tank, M4A4, uses 166 shoes)
Suspension, type . . . . Volute spring
   Wheel or tire size 20x9
Idler, type . . . . Fixed
   Wheel or tire size 28⅛x9
Final Drive, type . . . . Herringbone
   Gear ratio 2.84:1
   Sprocket, no. of teeth 13
   Pitch diameter 25.038
Differential, controlled, gear ratio 3.53:1
   Ring gear, no. of teeth 60
   Pinion, no. of teeth 17
   Steering ratio 1.515:1
Transmission, type . . . . Mechanical synchromesh
   Gear, ratios, first speed 7.56:1
     Second speed 3.11:1
     Third speed 1.78:1
     Fourth speed 1.11:1
     Fifth speed 73:1
     Reverse 5.65:1

Medium tank, M4 (General Sherman), in action. The best all-around tank in World War II. German prisoners said if they had had the M4 tank, they could have gone to Paris in the Battle of the Bulge.

MEDIUM TANK M4 (General Sherman)

As soon as production of the M3 was well under way, the tank was redesigned to place the 75-mm gun in the turret, dispense with the 37-mm gun, and add additional armor plate. This tank became known as the M4, or "General Sherman." The design of the tank was started in May 1941, and by October of the same year it had been standardized and placed in quantity production.

The receipt of M3 and M4 tanks in Egypt probably secured Africa for the Allies. The British were about to make their final stand at El Alamein. M3 and M4 tanks were taken away from troops in training in the United States and every available tank was shipped to Egypt. The British High Command cleverly kept secret the arrival of these tanks in Africa and sent them to the front covered with canvas so arranged that a tank on the road appeared to be a truck. A secret concentration of these tanks was made in this manner. When the Germans attacked, these American tanks were uncovered and the German Armored Corps found themselves in the presence of American 75-mm gun tanks instead of facing, as they expected, the British medium tanks mounting 2-pounder guns (39-mm). The German tank corps were caught in the deadly fire of these 75-mm guns and completely demoralized. The resulting flight of Rommel and his army across Africa is now history.

Medium tanks, M4 (General Sherman), advancing into Germany. A typical tank battle scene.

The M4 tank series was under continual development throughout the war; it became the most universally used tank of the United Nations. A total of 49,234 of these versatile vehicles were produced for all purposes in the war. Through thousands of miles of testing, under conditions of extreme cold as experienced in Russia, and under high temperatures and difficult terrain conditions as they existed in desert country, this tank gradually was developed into one of the most reliable track-laying tanks in the world's history.

The power plant originally used was unique for a track-laying vehicle in that a radial airplane type of motor modified for tank use was employed. As the requirements for tanks grew rapidly, it was necessary also to use several other engines, such as a commercial Diesel engine, a composite engine formed by combining five large truck engines into a unit power plant, and, finally, a highly developed V-8 engine. The suspension was of the volute spring, bogie type. This suspension was simple, rugged, and highly reliable.

The U. S. Ordnance Department was the only designer of tanks in this war to employ the rubber-block track and the rubber-jointed steel track. In both types of tracks, the track pin was protected from abrasion by being encased in rubber which provided the necessary track flexibility. The Germans and the Japanese employed the usual metal pin-jointed type. Their problem of keeping tanks equipped with tracks in all theaters was of great proportions; the life of these enemy tracks was approximately 600 miles as compared with 3,000 miles for American rubber-jointed tracks. In some theaters, our soldiers much preferred the rubber-block track, while in others, such as Italy, because of the rocky terrain, they considered the steel type of track nec-

A medium tank, M4 (76-mm), goes through a Normandy hedgerow that had been previously cut through by a bulldozer. Note special equipment in front of the tank, now released for first time. France, July 26 1944.

essary. As a result of the global employment of the M4 tank, it was necessary for the Ordnance Department to supply both the steel and rubber-block types, to be used as conditions demanded.

In addition to its universal use as a tank, the M4 reliable chassis was extensively employed, as hereinafter pointed out, as the basis for gun motor carriages. Praise of the M4 medium tank was universal in all theaters and it would take many pages to record adequately the performance of this important weapon in the war. Concerning its use in Europe, General Patton wrote (26 January 1945): "Our machine guns, mortars, artillery, and tanks are without equal on the battlefields of the world. In the hands of the unconquerable veterans now composing our armies, the utter destruction of the armed forces of our enemies is certain."

Heavy tank, M6, has cast hull and double tracks. Turret mounts 3-inch and 37-mm guns.

HEAVY TANK M6, M6A1

TYPICAL CHARACTERISTICS

Physical Characteristics
Weight (gross) . . . . 126,500 lb.
Length, gun forward . . . . 27 ft., 8 in.
Hull only . . . . 24 ft., 9 in.
Width (over-all) . . . . 10 ft., 2½ in.
Height, top of turret . . . . 9 ft., 10 in.
Top of machine-gun mount . . . . 10 ft., 7 in.
Turret ring diameter (inside) . . . . 69 in.
Ground clearance . . . . 20½ in.
Tread (c. to c. of tracks) . . . . 93 in.
Ground contact length . . . . 186 in.
Ground pressure . . . . 12.3 lb./sq. in.
Armament
3-in. gun M7 and 37-mm Gun M6 . . . In combination gun mount T49, in turret
1 cal. .30 machine gun M1919A4 (flexible) . . . . In bow
1 cal. .30 machine gun M1919A4 (flexible) . . . . On turret
2 cal. .50 machine guns M2 H.B. (fixed) . . . . . In twin mount in bow
1 cal. .30 machine gun tripod mount M2
Provision for:
2 cal. .45 submachine guns M3
Ammunition, stowage
3-in. 75 rds.
37-mm . . . . 202 rds.
Cal. .50 . . . . 5,700 rds.
Cal. .45 . . . . 1,200 rds.
Cal. .30 . . . . 7,500 rds.
Hand grenades 12

HEAVY TANK M6, M6A1—Continued

Armor	Actual	Basis
Hull, front, upper	3¼ in.	4 in.
lower	2¾–4 in.	4 in.
Sides	1¾ in.	1¾ in.
Rear	1⅝ in.	2 in.
Top	1 in.	
Bottom	1 in.	
Turret, front	3¼ in.	3¼ in.
Sides and rear	3¼ in.	3¼ in.
Top	1 in.	

Performance	
Maximum speed on level	22 m.p.h.
Maximum grade ability	60%
Trench crossing ability	11 ft.
Vertical obstacle ability	36 in.
Fording depth (slowest forward speed)	48 in.
Angle of approach	32°
Turning diameter	74 ft.
Fuel capacity	464 gals.
Cruising range (approx.)	100 miles
Vision and Fire Control	
Periscope M6	5
Periscope M8, w/Telescope M39	1
Gunner's Quadrant M1, w/case	1
Bore sight, 3-inch gun	1
Telescope M15	1
Communications	
Radio	SCR-508, 528, or 538
Command tank	SCR-506
Interphone stations	6
Battery, voltage, total	24
Fire Protection and Decontamination	
Fire extinguisher	
CO_2–10 lb. (fixed)	6
CO_2–4 lb. (hand)	2
Decontaminating apparatus M2, 1½ qt.	4
Engine, make and model	Wright G-200
Type	Radial, A.C.
No. of cylinders	9
Fuel (gasoline)	80 octane
Max. governed speed	2,300 r.p.m.
Gross hp	800 at 2,300 r.p.m.
Max. torque	1,850 lb.-ft. at 2,300 r.p.m.
Transmission, type	Torque converter
Gear ratios	
First speed	1.61:1
Second speed	0.22:1
Reverse	1.61:1
Gear Reduction Case, type	Twin Disc Clutch Co.
Torque Converter, type	Twin Disc Clutch Co.
Differential, type	Controlled
Gear ratio	0.62:1
Steering ratio	1.62:1

HEAVY TANK M6, M6A1—Continued

Final drive, gear ratio	5:1
Sprocket, no. of teeth	14
Pitch diameter	26.806
Suspension, type	Horizontal volute spring
Wheel or tire size	18 x 7 x 15
Idler, type	Adjustable
Track, steel bottom, rubber top, rubber bushed	
Width	25¾ in.
Pitch	6 in.
No. of blocks per vehicle	198

In 1940, the Ordnance Department believed that a far heavier tank than the M3 or M4 would be required during the war. The development of a super-tank, weighing approximately 65 tons with very heavy armor and mounting a powerful 3-inch gun, was then undertaken. This tank was rapidly developed and the first pilot model was accepted the day after Pearl Harbor—8 December 1941. It was known as the heavy tank, M6. This was the first tank ever built in any country with a one-thousand horsepower engine. This large engine gave a mobility comparable

Heavy tank, M6, the American 65-ton tank developed one year ahead of the German Tiger tank, but never used in battle.

with that of the M4 tank, permitting these tanks to be used together as a team. This tank was completed one year ahead of the German "Tiger" (Mark VI) tank.

The S.A.E. Ordnance Advisory Committee assisted in the design of this secret tank, especially with regard to the transmission, since no transmission had been built up to that time for an automotive vehicle of this great size, weight, and horsepower. The gun selected was the high-powered 3-inch, which at that time was the most powerful gun ever mounted in a tank. A year later, a 90-mm high-velocity gun was designed which would fit into the turret provided for the 3-inch gun. After the successful trials of the M6 tank, orders were placed for a large quantity.

At that time and, in fact, throughout the war, the problem of getting heavy equipment overseas was difficult, in view of the vast demands of our armies. The General Staff decided that they preferred to ship two medium tanks, each weighing 35 tons, rather than one heavy tank, M6, weighing 65 tons. The Engineer Corps had not yet provided suitable portable bridges for equipment of this great weight. The War Department therefore directed the Ordnance Department to discontinue the production of these heavy tanks after some 40 had been completed.

Heavy tank, M26 (General Pershing), with 90-mm high-power gun. The best American tank in the war, it could outmaneuver and outshoot the German Tiger (Mark VI).

HEAVY TANK, M26

CHARACTERISTICS

Crew	5
Physical Characteristics	
Weight (gross)	92,000 lb.
Length, gun forward	28 ft., 8 3/16 in.
Gun to rear	24 ft., 1 9/16 in.
Hull only	20 ft., 9⅛ in.
Width (over-all)	11 ft., 6¼ in.
Reducible to	10 ft., 4 in.
Height	9 ft., 1⅜ in.
Turret ring diameter (inside)	69 in.
Ground clearance	17 3/16 in.
Tread (center to center of tracks)	110 in.
Ground contact length, right side	152 7/16 in.
Left side	148 7/16 in.
Ground pressure	12.7 lb./sq. in
Armament	
1 90-mm gun M3 and 1 cal. .30 machine gun M1919A4	
(flexible)	In combination gun mount M67
Elevation	−10° to +20°
Traverse	360°
1 cal. .30 machine gun M1919A4 (flexible)	In bow
1 cal. .50 machine gun M2 H.B. (flexible)	On turret
1 cal. .30 machine gun tripod mount M2	
Provision for:	
5 cal. .45 submachine guns M3	
1 cal. .30 carbine M2 and grenade launcher M8	
Ammunition, Stowage	
90-mm	70 rds.
Cal. .50	550 rds.
Cal. .45	900 rds.
Cal. .30	5,000 rds.
Hand grenades	12
Signal flares	12

	Actual	Basis
Armor		
Hull, front, upper	4 in.	6.9 in.
Lower	3 in.	6.4 in.

HEAVY TANK M26—Continued

Sides, forward . . . . 3 in.   3 in.
    Engine compartment . . . . 2 in.   2 in.
Rear . . . . 2 in.   2 in.
Top . . . . ⅞ in.
Bottom . . . . 1 in. and ½ in.
Turret, front . . . . 4 in.   4.4 in.
    Sides and rear . . . . 3 in.   3 in.
    Top . . . . 1 in.
Gun mount shield . . . . 4½ in.
Performance
    Maximum speed on level . . . . 20 m.p.h.
    Maximum grade ability 60%
    Trench crossing ability . . . . 7 ft., 11 in.
    Vertical obstacle ability . . . . 46 in.
    Fording depth (slowest forward speed) . . . . 48 in.
    Turning diameter . . . . 60 ft.
    Fuel capacity . . . . 186 gals.
    Cruising range (approx.) . . . . 75 miles
Vision and Fire Control
    Commander's vision cupola 1
    Periscope M6 6
    Periscope M10F, w/instrument light M30 1
       1 periscope M4A1, w/telescope M77F as spare) .
    Telescope mount T90 1
    Elevation quadrant M9, w/instrument light M30 1
    Gunner's quadrant M1 1
    Azimuth indicator M20 1
    Aiming post M1, w/aiming post light M14 2
    Fuze setter M22 1
    Pistol port 1
Communications
    Radio . . . . SCR–508, 528, 608B or British No. 19; AN/VRC–3
    Interphone stations 5
Battery, voltage, total 24
Fire Protection and Decontamination
    Fire extinguisher, CO_2-10 lb. (fixed) 2
       CO_2-4 lb. (hand) 2
    Decontaminating apparatus M2, 1½ qt. 2

Overhead view of M26 heavy tank, showing commander's cupola and loader's hatch on turret. Turret is turned to rear during travel.

HEAVY TANK M26—Continued

Engine, make and model	Ford GAF
Type	V–8, LC
No. of cylinders	8
Fuel (gasoline)	80 octane
Max. governed speed	2,600 r.p.m.
Gross hp.	500 at 2,600 r.p.m.
Max. torque	1,040 lb.-ft. at 2,200 r.p.m.
Transmission, type	Torqmatic
Gear ratios	
First speed	1:1
Second speed	1:2.337
Third speed	1:4.105 } overdrive
Reverse	1:1.322
Transfer Case	
Gear ratio, engine to transmission	1.38:1
Torque Converter, Ratio	Varies from 1:1 to 4.8:1
Differential, type	Controlled
Steering ratio	1.78:1
Final Drive	
Sprocket, no. of teeth	13
Pitch diameter	25.068
Gear ratio	3.82:1
Suspension, type	Torsion bar
Wheel or tire size	26x6
Idler, type	Compensating
Wheel or tire size	26x6
Track, type	T80E1 or T81
Width	23 or 24 in.
Pitch	6 in.
No. of shoes per vehicle	164
Radiator, type	Fin and tube
Brakes, type	External-contracting
Operation	Manual lever

HEAVY TANK, M26 (General Pershing)

Although the heavy tank, M6, had not met with favor from the War Department General Staff, the Ordnance Department set to work to design a tank which would be smaller and lighter and thus easier to ship, but which would, nevertheless, have the superior armor protection and the firepower of the M6. Development of the so-called T20 series of tanks was started in September 1942. The design of these tanks was based upon use of the newly designed V-8 engine—an engine of low silhouette of approximately 500 horsepower. This permitted the development of a low-silhouette tank, with the best possible slope of the armor plate. Although the Armored Force preferred the new high-powered 76-mm gun, the Ordnance Department felt that the high-velocity 90-mm gun would be necessary. Tanks mounting both guns were designed and built with the greatest possible speed. As a result of tests, the T26 tank, mounting the 90-mm high-powered gun, was selected. This tank had many features not found in any foreign tank—such as the torquematic transmission, a combination of the hydramatic transmission and a torque-converter. The tank used torsion-bar suspension which gave easy riding and a stable

One of a convoy of General Pershing tanks, M26, moving through a blasted German village on its way to a bridge across the Rhine. Only four days previously the tanks were being unloaded from a ship in a Belgian harbor. Near Wessel, Germany.

gun platform. It weighed only 46 tons and yet carried heavier armor and a more powerful gun than either the German Panther (Mark V) or Tiger (Mark VI) tanks.

The T26 was adopted by the Army as the M26 and was used in the final attack in the spring of 1945 upon the German armies. The M26 tanks were among the first to cross the Rhine at the Remagen bridgehead. By the time the war ended, this tank was in heavy production in the United States and was being sent in ever-increasing quantities to Europe and the Pacific. As the tanks arrived, they were distributed to Armored Divisions so that at least a portion of the tanks in those divisions would be of this superior heavy type. During the latter months of the war, the production of the M4 tank was stopped altogether in favor of the M26.

Comments by the using services on the M26 tank were all favorable. For example, here is part of a report made by Company "I," 32nd Armored Regiment: "One M26 was fired upon by the German 75-mm tank guns at approximately 1,200 yards range. The M26 was struck on both the upper and lower glacis plates, in front of gun shields, and on the sides of the turret. A total of 13 hits were made on the tank but no complete penetration. The tank was repaired by welding and went back into action." And this report by Headquarters, 3rd Armored Division: "One M26 shot an enemy half-track at approximately 2,000 yards with hypervelocity ammunition. The half-track burst into flames; the shot went completely through. A German Mark IV tank was shot at the same range and hit at the left side plate which penetrated and the tank burned immediately. One M26 tank successfully attacked and destroyed a German Tiger tank and two German Mark IV tanks. All tanks were burned and the fleeing personnel were destroyed by H.E. fire."

Heavy tank, M26 (General Pershing), in Germany.

LIGHT TANK, M3

TYPICAL CHARACTERISTICS

Crew 4
Physical Characteristics
  Weight (gross) . . . . 27,400 lb
  Length (hull) . . . . 14 ft., 10⅜ in.
  Width . . . . 7 ft., 4 in.
  Height . . . . 8 ft., 3 in.
  Turret ring diameter . . . . 46¾ in.
  Ground clearance . . . . 16½ in.
  Tread (c. to c. of tracks) . . . . 73 in.
  Ground contact length . . . . 117 in.
  Ground pressure . . . . 10.47 lb./sq. in.

Armor

	Actual	Basis
Hull, front, upper .	1½ in.	1¾ in.
lower .	⅝–1¾ in.	1¾–3 in.
Sides and rear .	1 in.	1 in.
Top .	⅜ in.	
Bottom .	⅜–½ in.	
Turret, front .	1½ in.	1¾ in.
Sides and rear .	1¼ in.	1¼ in.
Top .	½ in.	

Performance
  Maximum speed on level . . . . 36 m.p.h.
  Maximum grade ability 60%
  Trench crossing ability . . . . 6 ft.
  Vertical obstacle ability . . . . 24 in.
  Fording depth (slowest forward speed) . . . . . 36 in.
  Turning radius . . . . 21 ft.
  Fuel capacity—without jettison tanks . . . . . 55 gal.
    with jettison tanks . . . . 106 gal.
  Maximum drawbar pull . . . . 14,800 lb.
  Cruising range (approx.) . . . . 70 miles

Engine,

Make .	Continental	Guiberson
Model .	W670–9A	T1020–4
Type .	Radial A.C.	Radial A.C.
Cylinders .	7	9
Fuel .	Gasoline (80 octane)	Diesel (50 cetane)
Maximum governed speed	2,400 r.p.m.	2,200 r.p.m.
Rated h.p. .	250 at 2,400 r.p.m.;	220 at 2,200 r.p.m.
Maximum torque	584 lb.–ft.	580 lb.-ft.
	at 1,800 r.p.m.	at 1,400 r.p.m.

Vision and Fire Control
  Protectoscopes 2
  Direct vision slots 2
Communications—Radio SCR–245
  Battery, voltage, total 12
Fire Protection and Decontamination
  Fire extinguisher, CO_2–10 lb. (fixed) 1
    CO_2–4 lb. (hand) 1
  Decontaminating apparatus, M2, 1½ qts. 1
Transmission, type . . . . Manual shift
  Gear ratios
    First speed . . . . 5.37 : 1
    Second speed . . . . 2.82 : 1
    Third speed . . . . 1.72 : 1
    Fourth speed . . . . 1.09 : 1
    Fifth speed . . . . .738 : 1
    Reverse speed . . . . 6.19 : 1

LIGHT TANK, M3—Continued

Differential, Controlled, gear ratio 2.62:1
  Steering ratio 1.845:1
Final Drive, type . . . . Herringbone
  Gear ratio 2.41:1
  Sprocket, no. of teeth 14
  Pitch diameter 24.56
Suspension, type . . . . Volute spring
  Wheel or tire size 20x6
  Wheel construction . . . . Welded
Idler, Trailing, type . . . . Ind. vol. spring
  Wheel or tire size 30x6
  Wheel construction . . . . Welded
Track, type . . . . Rubber block
  Width . . . . 11⅝ in.
  Pitch . . . . 5½ in.
  No. of shoes per vehicle . . . . 132 or 134

LIGHT TANK, M3A1

Light tank, M3A1, has streamlined turret and omits sponson guns.

LIGHT TANK, M3A1

Characteristics same as for Light Tank, M3, except as noted:
Physical Characteristics

Weight	. 28,500 lb.
Height	. 7 ft. 6½ in.
Ground pressure	10.56 lb./sq. in.
Vision—Protectoscopes	5
Periscopes	2
Direct vision slots	2
Communications—radio	. SCR–508
Interphone stations	4

LIGHT TANK, M3A3

Characteristics same as Light Tank, M3A1, except as noted:
Physical Characteristics

Weight (gross) (with track, T16)	. 31,752 lb.
Length (with bustle box)	. 16 ft., 6 in.
Width	. 8 ft., 3 in.
Height	. 7 ft., 6½ in.
Fuel Capacity	. 102 gals.
Vision and Fire Control	
Periscopes	5
Protectoscopes	. Omitted
Direct vision slots	. Omitted
Telescope, M54	1

ARMAMENT—LIGHT TANKS, M3, M3A1, M3A3

37-mm gun, M5 or M6, and . . . .⎱	
1 cal. .30 Browning machine gun . . . .⎰	In combination mount, M22, M23 or M44, in turret
1 cal. .30 Browning machine gun	. In ball mount in bow
1 cal. .30 Browning machine gun	. On turret, antiaircraft
2 cal. .30 Browning machine guns	. Sponsons: on M3 only
1 tripod mount, cal. .30, M2	
Provision for 1 cal. .45 submachine gun	

AMMUNITION STOWAGE

	M3	M3A1	M3A3
37-mm (A.P.C., M51B1; A.P.C., M51B2; H.E., M63;			
Can., M2)	. 103 rds.	116 rds.	174 rds.
Cal. .30	. 8,270 rds.	6,400 rds.	7,500 rds.
Cal. .45	. 500 rds.	510 rds.	540 rds.
Grenades, hand (fragmentation, Mk. II, 4; Offensive,			
Mk. IIIA2, w/fuze, detonating, M6, 2; smoke, W.P.,			
M15, 4; thermite, incendiary, 2)	. 12	12	12

Light tank, M5—Three-quarter right front view.

LIGHT TANK, M5

CHARACTERISTICS

Crew 4

Physical Characteristics
Weight (gross) . . . . 15½ tons
Length . . . . 14 ft., 2⅜ in.
Width . . . . 7 ft., 4¼ in.
Height . . . . 7 ft., 6½ in.
Ground clearance . . . . 16½ in.
Center of gravity—above ground . . . . 33½ in.
     rear of sprocket . . . . 79½ in.
Tread (center to center of tracks) . . . . 73 in.
Ground pressure per sq. in. . . . . 11.59 lb.
Ground contact . . . . 9 ft., 7 in.

Armor		Actual	Basis
Hull, front, upper		1⅛ in.	2 in.
	lower	1¾ in.	2 in.
Sides		1 in.	1 in.
Rear		1 in.	1 in.
Top		½ in.	—
Bottom		⅜-½ in.	⅜-½ in.
Turret—front		1¾ in.	1¾ in.
Sides		1¼ in.	1¼ in.
Top		½ in.	—

LIGHT TANK, M5—Continued

Performance
Road speed (maximum) . . . . 40 m.p.h.
Allowable engine speed
  short periods . . . . 4,250 r.p.m.
  sustained . . . . 3,500 r.p.m.
Grade ascending ability 60%
Grade descending ability 60%
Ditch crossing ability . . . . 5 ft., 5 in.
Vertical obstacle ability . . . . 24 in.
Fording depth (slowest forward speed) . . . . 3 ft.
Fuel capacity . . . . 89 gals.

Vision
Periscopes 4
Protectoscopes 3

Communication
Radio .
  Command tank SCR/508
Intratank SCR/506
Battery, voltage . . . . Telephone
 12

Engine, make and model . . . . Cadillac, Series, 42
Type . . . . Dual, V-8, W.C.
No. of cylinders 16
Cycle 4
Fuel (gasoline) . . . . 80 octane
Bore and stroke 3½x4½
Displacement 692
Compression 7.2:1
Net H.P. at R.P.M. . . . . 242 at 3,200
Max. torque at R.P.M. . . . . 536 lb.-ft. at 1,100
Crankshaft rotation . . . . C'clockwise
Length . . . . 35¾ in.
Width . . . . 50 in.
Height . . . . 34½ in.
Ignition . . . . Battery
Weight dry . . . . 1,435 lb.
Weight installed . . . . 3,500 lb.

Transmission . . . . Hydramatic

Differential, controlled
Gear ratio . . . . 2.62 to 1
Ring gear, no. of teeth 42
Pinion, no. of teeth 16
Steering ratio . . . . 1.845 to 1

Final Drive, gear ratio . . . . 2.41 to 1
Sprocket, no. of teeth 14
Pitch diameter 24.56

Track, type . . . . Steel, rubber bushed
Width . . . . 11⅝ in.
Pitch 5½
No. of shoes per tank 134

Suspension, type . . . . Volute spring
Wheel or tire size 20x6
Wheel construction . . . . Welded

Idler, trailing, type . . . . Ind. vol. spring

LIGHT TANK, M5A1

Characteristics same as for Light Tank, M5, except as noted:

Weight, with rubber tracks . . . . 16 tons
    with steel tracks . . . . 16½ tons
Track type . . . . Rubber or steel
Vision
    Periscopes 5
    Protectoscopes . . . . Omitted

ARMAMENT—LIGHT TANKS, M5 AND M5A1

1 37-mm gun, M6, and . . . . ⎱ In combination mount, M23, in turret;
1 cal. .30 Browning machine gun, M1919A5 (fixed) . . . . ⎰ (Mount, M44, in Light Tank, M5A1)
1 cal. .30 Browning machine gun, M1919A4 (flexible) . . . . In bow
1 cal. .30 Browning machine gun, M1919A4 (flexible) . . . . Turret (Antiaircraft)
1 tripod mount, M2
Provision for:
1 cal. .45 Thompson submachine gun, M1928A1 . . . . Equipment of crew

AMMUNITION, STOWAGE

	M5	M5A1
37 mm (A.P.C. M51B1, A.P.C. M51B2, A.P. M74, H.E. M63, Can. M2)	123 rounds	123 rounds
Cal. .30	6,250 rounds	6,500 rounds
Cal. .45	420 rounds	720 rounds
Hand grenades	12	12

Light Tank, M24.

LIGHT TANK, M24

CHARACTERISTICS

Crew 4

Physical Characteristics
Weight (gross, approx.) . . . . 38,750 lb.
Length—hull . . . . 16 ft., 3 in.
over-all, with armament . . . . 18 ft.
Width . . . . 9 ft., 4 in.
Height—top of cupola . . . . 8 ft., 1 in.
top of A.A. mount . . . . 8 ft., 4 in.
Turret ring diameter (inside) . . . . 60 in.
Ground clearance . . . . 17 in.
Tread (center to center of tracks) . . . . 96 in.
Ground contact length . . . . 112 in.
Ground pressure . . . . 10.7 lb./sq. in.

Armament
1 75-mm gun, M6 and
1 cal. .30 machine gun, M1919A4 (flexible) . . . In combination gun mount, M64, in turret
Elevation . . . . −10° to +15°
Traverse . . . . 360°
1 cal. .50 machine gun, M2, HB (flexible) . . . . . On turret, antiaircraft
1 cal. .30 machine gun, M1919A4 (flexible) . . . . In bow mount
1 2-inch mortar, M3 . . . . In turret
1 cal. .30 tripod mount, M2

LIGHT TANK, M24—Continued

Provision for:
4 cal. .45 submachine guns, M3, or
   3 cal. .45 submachine guns, M3, and
   1 cal. .30 Carbine, M1, with grenade launcher, M8 .

Ammunition, Stowage
75-mm . . . . 48 rounds
Cal. .50 . . . . 440 rounds
Cal. .30 . . . . 3,750 rounds
Cal. .45 . . . . 720 rounds
2-inch smoke bombs, Mk. I/L (British) . . . . 14 rounds
Grenades (smoke, 2; fragmentation, 6) 8

Armor	Actual	Basis
Hull, front, upper	1 in.	2½ in.
lower	1 in.	1½ in.
Sides, forward	1 in.	1 in.
rear	¾ in.	¾ in.
Rear, upper	¾ in.	¾ in.
lower	¾ in.	1¼ in.
Top	½ in.	
Bottom (first 36 ins.)	½ in.	
(remainder)	⅜ in	
Turret, front and sides	1 in.	1¼ in.
rear	1 in.	1 in.
roof	½ in.	
Gun shield, upper	1½ in.	2 in.
lower	1½ in.	2¼ in.

Performance
Maximum speed on level . . . . 35 m.p.h.
   3% grade . . . . 17 m.p.h.
   10% grade . . . . 11 m.p.h.
Maximum grade ability 60%
Trench crossing ability . . . . 6½ ft.
Vertical obstacle ability . . . . 36 in.
Fording depth (slowest forward speed) . . . . 40 in.
Turning radius . . . . 20 ft.
Fuel capacity . . . . 110 gals.
Cruising range (approx.) highway . . . . 175 miles
   cross country . . . . 100 miles
Maximum drawbar pull . . . . 22,000 lb.

Vision and Fire Control
Periscope, M6 3
Telescope, M71G, with instrument light, M33 (or tele-
   scope, M70N, with instrument light, M39C) in tel-
   escope mount, M65, with headrest 1
Periscope, M10C, in periscope mount, M66 (or
   periscope, M4A1) 2
Azimuth indicator, M21 1
Elevation quadrant, M9, with instrument light, M30 1
Gunner's quadrant, M1 1
Vision blocks (in cupola) 6

Communications
Radio . . . . SCR–508, 528, 538, or British No. 19
   Command tank SCR–506
Interphone stations 5
Flag set, M238 1

Battery, voltage, total 24

Fire Protection and Decontamination
Fire extinguisher, CO₂–10 lb. (fixed) 1
   CO₂–4 lb. (hand) 1
Decontaminating apparatus, M2, 1½ qts. 2

LIGHT TANK, M24—Continued

Engine, make and model	Cadillac, Series 42
Type	Dual, V–8, L.C.
No. of cylinders	16
Fuel (gasoline)	80 octane
Max. governed speed	4,000 r.p.m.
Net hp.	220 at 3,400 r.p.m.
Max. torque	488 lb.-ft. at 1,200 r.p.m.
Transmission, type	Hydra-Matic, with transfer unit and synchronizer
Gear ratios (with transfer unit)	
Forward—First speed	9.19:1
Second speed	5.96:1
Third speed	3.62:1
Fourth speed	2.34:1
Fifth speed	4.05:1
Sixth speed	2.62:1
Seventh speed	1.59:1
Eighth speed	1.03:1
Reverse—First speed	9.57:1
Second speed	6.17:1
Third speed	3.78:1
Fourth speed	2.44:1
Transfer Case, type	Synchromesh
Gear ratios—forward	2.34:1; 1.03:1
reverse	2.44:1
Differential, controlled, gear ratio	2.625:1
Steering ratio	1.55:1
Final Drive, type	Herringbone
Gear ratio	2.571:1
Sprocket, no. of teeth	13
Pitch diameter	23.108
Suspension, type	Torsion bar
No. of wheels	10, dual
Wheel or tire size	$25\frac{1}{2}$x$4\frac{1}{2}$
Wheel construction	Stamped disk
Idler, type	Fixed
Wheel or tire size	$22\frac{1}{2}$x$4\frac{1}{2}$, dual
Wheel construction	Stamped disk
Track, type	Steel block, single pin, rubber bushed, with center guide
Width	16 in.
Pitch	$5\frac{1}{2}$ in.
No. of shoes per vehicle	150

LIGHT TANKS

The Ordnance Department had been experimenting long before the war with light tanks or, as they were called by the Cavalry before the war, combat cars. This was fortunate, as the Department was able to get into early production of light tanks which had received thorough tests by the using services. We entered the war with a light tank known as the M3. It was light and speedy and had been developed with the idea of using it as a fighting reconnaissance vehicle to serve as a cavalry screen. This tank, which was under constant improvement through-out the war, started as a riveted tank and was gradually converted to an all-welded hull. It mounted the 37-mm gun as the main armament. It was used extensively by the British in Africa and, with the M3 and M4 medium tanks, formed a valuable contribution to the fighting equipment of the British Army. The British called the light tank the "Honey" because it proved to be one of the most reliable vehicles on the African desert. Our first troops landing in Africa were likewise equipped with a suitable number of these excellent vehicles.

Light tanks, M3A1. These light, versatile tanks were the cavalry of World War II. They were noted for their ability to keep going under all conditions of terrain.

After the M3 light tanks had been placed in quantity production, the new design of light tank known as the M5 series was started. This tank provided more armor protection and an improved turret as well as many additional features. It was placed in production in 1942, and we manufactured large numbers for ourselves and our Allies. In 1945, the design of another light tank, later known as the M24, was begun. This tank was built around a light but powerful 75-mm gun. This gun had, in fact, been developed as an aircraft cannon; and both the gun and recoil mechanism were devised to occupy the smallest practicable space, at the least weight. Thus this aircraft gun, which had the same power as the 75-mm gun in the M4 tank, also was attractive as a tank weapon. The M24 light tank possessed many new features such as the torsion-bar suspension and an improved turret. Introduced on the battlefield in the spring of 1945, it immediately met with great success. By V-J Day, all armored units equipped with light tanks were being re-equipped with the new light tank, M24, as rapidly as possible.

A 1st Armored Division light tank crosses a road block, blasted-in ten minutes before by the Germans in an effort to delay troops from reaching Rome, Italy. Fifth Army, Rome area, June 4 1944.

Ready to blast at the remaining German resistance, this M24 light tank goes into action with the Infantry somewhere in Germany. The last light tanks of this war had the same fire-power as the medium tank, M3, used at the beginning of the war. This tank was built around the remarkable 75-mm aircraft gun, the lightest for its power in existence.

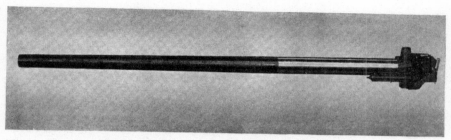

76-mm tank gun M1E4 for medium tank M4. This high-velocity gun, which is built of high strength steel for light weight, is typical of the guns used in American tanks.

TANK GUNS

All of the above-mentioned tanks, which were so successful in this war, were based upon special cannon designed solely for tank purposes. At the beginning of the war, the steel used in cannon had an elastic limit of approximately 60,000 pounds per square inch. By the end of the war, very light tank guns built to meet the special requirements of the battlefield were using metal of great strength and, in the 75-mm tank gun, the elastic limit of its steel was 160,000 pounds per square inch. This improvement in metallurgy made possible mounting of larger-caliber and higher-powered guns in lighter vehicles. The 76-mm tank gun, made of high-quality steel, was designed in 1942 as a replacement in the M4 tank for the lower-powered 75-mm gun. The 76-mm gun could be put into the same turret and into the same space as that formerly occupied by the relatively low-powered 75-mm gun. The 76-mm gun, with its special high-powered ammunition, had a muzzle velocity of 3,400 feet per second so that H.V.A.P. ammunition, described elsewhere, penetrated the heaviest German tank armor. Likewise the 90-mm gun used in the M26 tank was a thin gun made of steel of high strength. Thus it was possible to place a gun of this size and firepower in the relatively small space available in the M26 tank. The low silhouette, combined with this high-strength gun, made it possible for the M26 tank to carry heavier armor and a more powerful gun and yet weigh 15 tons less than the German Tiger tank.

Medium tank, M4A1, equipped with swimming device, M19. This development made it possible for a tank to be launched at sea from a ship and to swim inshore, firing on land targets as it progressed.

DEVICE M19, with M4 Series Medium Tank*

CHARACTERISTICS

Physical Characteristics

Weight, including medium tank M4 or M4A1	84,000 lb.
Including medium tank M4A2	86,000 lb.
Including medium tank M4A3	85,000 lb.
Including medium tank M4A4	88,000 lb.
Device M19 only	17,200 lb.
Weight-draft Ratio	2,570 lb./in.
Length, over-all	47 ft., 8 in.
Folded	32 ft.
Width	11 ft.
Height, to top of stacks	10 ft., 8 in.
Over-all, Folded	11 ft., 8 in.
Freeboard (to top of floats)	14 in.

Armament

1 75-mm gun M3 and	
1 cal. .30 machine gun M1919A4 (flexible)	In combination mount M34A1
Elevation	+1° to +25°
Traverse	310°
1 cal. .50 machine gun M2 H.B. (flexible)	On turret
1 cal. .30 machine gun M1919A4 (flexible)	In bow mount

Performance (in water)

Maximum speed	5½ m.p.h.
Draft (combat loaded)	60 in.
Angle of approach	10°
Angle of departure	8°
Turning diameter	120 ft.
Cruising range	5 hours

* Characteristics stated are for Medium Tank M4 series with 75-mm gun. Device M19 is equally applicable to M4 series tanks with 76-mm gun or 105-mm howitzer.

SWIMMING DEVICES (Tank)

During landing operations, troops and their equipment are particularly vulnerable to enemy fire until they have arrived on the beach and have been able to set up their weapons for defense. In England, a device was worked out whereby a tank could be taken off a ship at sea a few miles off the coast and swim ashore with its crew. Called the D.D. device, it consisted of a canvas framework attached to the top of a tank. When not in use, it folded down neatly on top of the tank; but when in use, it formed a boat above the tank, thereby giving it the necessary flotation. A propeller arrangement was attached to the tank engine so that the device could proceed under its own power to shore. The disadvantages were that the tank and its crew were submerged about 20 feet under the water and the canvas boat was very vulnerable to wave action. Furthermore, when in the water, the tank's gun could not be fired. A number of these devices were built in the United States and were employed in the invasion of France by British and American troops.

A new, less vulnerable type of swimming device was developed in this country. It consisted of metal boxes attached to the front, rear ends, and sides of the tank. These boxes, filled with a plastic foam, provided the necessary buoyancy. The advantages of this system were that the tank turret was above water and the turret guns could be fired in the usual manner. Thus as the tank approached a hostile shore, it could open fire on the enemy and help to destroy the guns which were holding up landing operations. Furthermore, the swimming devices converted the tank into a very seaworthy vessel which could withstand high seas and would not veer and capsize in landing through surf. The metal floats were attached to the tank in such a manner that the tank crew, without getting out, could set off charges in special explosive bolts which allowed the floats to be jettisoned. The tank, after landing, could be used normally. Another advantage was that the tank-swimming device propelled itself through the water at speeds up to 6 miles per hour by simply driving the tracks in normal manner. The device could also be steered quite well by slowing up one track and speeding up the other, just as in steering a tank on land. In addition, rudders were employed on the swimming device. These devices were designed for our light and medium tanks. Swimming devices attached to the M4 tank were successfully used in the Pacific. These would have proved of great value in the planned operations against the Japanese homeland.

GUN MOTOR CARRIAGES, SELF-PROPELLED

For many years before the war, the Department had strongly advocated the use of guns mounted on track-laying vehicles instead of the more common types of towed artillery. This self-propelled artillery had the advantage that the piece could be made ready to fire in a few minutes after arrival at any desired position, while with towed artillery, considerable time was lost in preparing the position for firing. Furthermore, the self-propelled gun could travel under its own power across difficult terrain and could go into places where it would be difficult or impossible for artillery to be pulled by motors or trucks.

105-MM HOWITZER MOTOR CARRIAGE, M7

105-mm howitzer motor carriage, M7—Left front view showing howitzer and caliber .50 machine gun.

105-MM HOWITZER MOTOR CARRIAGES M7, M7B1, M37

CHARACTERISTICS

	M7*, M7B1**		M37†	
Crew	7		7	
Physical Characteristics				
Weight	50,634 lb.		40,000 lb.	
Length	19 ft., 9 in.		18 ft., 2 in.	
Width	9 ft., 5 5/16 in.		9 ft., 11 in.	
Height	8 ft., 4 in.		7 ft., 4 in.	
Over A. A. gun	9 ft., 8 in.		8 ft., 8 in.	
Ground clearance	17⅞ in.		17 in.	
Tread (c. to c. of tracks)	83 in.		96 in.	
Ground contact length	147 in.		124 in.	
Ground pressure	10.4 lb./sq. in.		10.1 lb./sq. in.	
Armament				
105-mm howitzer	M2A1 in mount M4		M4 in mount M5	
Elevation	−5° to +35°		−10° to +45°	
Traverse	30° right, 15° left		22½° right, 22½° left	
1 cal. .50 machine gun M2 H.B. (flexible)	On ring mount		On ring mount	
Provision for:				
Cal. .45 submachine guns	3		1	
Cal. .30 carbines	0		6	
Ammunition, stowage				
105-mm	69 rds.		90 rds.	
Cal. .50	300 rds.		900 rds.	
Cal. .45	1,620 rds.		600 rds.	
Hand grenades	8		8	
Armor	Actual	Basis	Actual	Basis
Hull, front, upper	½ in.	½ in.	½ in.	1¼ in.
Lower	2–4¼ in.	2–4½ in.	½ in.	⅞ in.
Sides, upper	½ in.	½ in.	½ in.	½ in.
Lower	1½ in.***	1½ in.	½ in.	½ in.
Rear, upper	½ in.	½ in.	½ in.	½ in.
Lower	1½ in.***	1½ in.	½ in.	⅞ in.
Bottom, front	1 in.	1 in.	½ in.	½ in.
Rear	½ in.	½ in.	⅜ in.	⅜ in.
Top, forward			½ in.	
Gun mount shield			½ in.	½ in.
Performance				
Maximum speed on level	25 m.p.h.		35 m.p.h.	
Maximum grade ability	60%		60%	
Trench crossing ability	7 ft., 6 in.		7 ft.	
Vertical obstacle ability	24 in.		42 in.	
Fording depth (slowest forward speed)	48 in.		42 in.	
Turning diameter	62 ft.		40 ft.	
Fuel capacity	179 gals.		115 gals.	
Cruising range (approx.)	85–125 miles		110–150 miles	
Vision and Fire Control				
Periscope M6	0		2	
Protectoscope	1		0	

* Other characteristics same as for Medium Tank M3.
** Characteristics of M7B1 same as for M7 except: weight, 50,000 lb.; length, 20 ft., 3¾ in.; ground pressure, 10.3 lb./sq. in.; maximum speed, 26 m.p.h.; fording depth, 36 in.; fuel capacity, 168 gals.
***Soft plate, minimum ballistics of ½-inch armor.
† Other characteristics same as for light tank M24.
†† Displaces 18 rounds of 105-mm ammunition.

105-MM HOWITZER MOTOR CARRIAGES M7, M7B1, M37—Continued

Panoramic telescope M12-A2, w/instrument light M19 .	1	1
On mount M21A1, w/8-in. filler piece	1	0
On mount T96	0	1
Telescope M76G (3-power), on mount T95, w/instrument light M33	0	1
Elbow telescope M16 or M16A1C	1	0
Telescope mount M42	1	0
Instrument light M36 (for M16A1C)	1	0
Aiming post M1, w/aiming post light M14 . . .	2	2
Range quadrant M4	1	0
Range quadrant T14, w/instrument light M18 . .	0	1
Gunner's quadrant M1	1	1
Fuze setter M22	1	1
Communications		
Flag set M238	1	1
Panel set AP50A	0	1
Provision for:		
Telephone EE–8–( ) and Reel unit RL–39 . . .	0	1
Interphone RC–99	0	1
British wireless set No. 19	0	1††
Battery, voltage, total	24	24
Fire Protection and Decontamination		
Fire extinguisher		
CO_2–10 lb. (fixed)	2	2
CO_2–4 lb. (hand)	2	2
Decontaminating apparatus, 1½ qt.	3	2

105-MM HOWITZER MOTOR CARRIAGE, M7

One of the most important gun carriers used in this war was the 105-mm self-propelled mount, M-7. This materiel comprised the 105-mm field howitzer mounted upon the M3 and M4 tank chassis. A number of these vehicles were built in 1942 and sent to the British Army in Africa. This weapon played an important part in the battle of El Alamein and was known to the British as "The Priest." On several occasions these vehicles destroyed German tanks at ranges up to 12,000 yards. This important weapon was widely used in all theaters of this war.

105-mm howitzer motor carriage, M7, fires 105-mm shells into a woods from which the Germans have been counterattacking. The crew has just completed a fire mission consisting of 200 rounds. This weapon was used in combat in Africa by both American and British troops.

3-inch gun motor carriages, M10, M10A1.

3-INCH GUN MOTOR CARRIAGES, M10, M10A1

3-INCH GUN MOTOR CARRIAGE, M10

CHARACTERISTICS

Crew 5
Physical Characteristics
  Weight . . . . 65,000 lb.
  Length . . . . 19 ft., 7 in.
  Width . . . . 10 ft.
  Height . . . . 8 ft., 1½ in.
  Height of center line, 3-inch gun . . . . 82½ in.
  Turret ring diameter (inside) . . . . 69 in.
  Ground clearance . . . . 17⅛ in.
  Tread (center to center of tracks) . . . . 83 in.
  Ground contact length . . . . 147 in.
  Ground pressure . . . . 12.3 lb./sq. in.
Armament
  3-inch gun, M7, in mount, M5 . . . . In turret
    Elevation . . . . −10° to +19°
    Traverse . . . . 360°
  Cal. .50 machine gun, M2, H.B. (flexible) . . . . . . On turret (antiaircraft)
  1 tripod mount, cal. .50, M3
  Provision for:
  5 cal. .30 carbines, M1
Ammunition, stowage
  3-inch (A.P.C., M62, and H.E., M42A1) . . . . 54 rds.
  Cal. .50 (in 50 rd. boxes) . . . . 300 rds.
  Cal. .30 (carbine, M1) . . . . 450 rds.
  Grenades, hand (smoke, W.P., M15, 6; fragmentation,
    Mk., II, 6) 12
  Smoke pots, H.C., M1 4
Armor   Actual   Basis
  Hull, front . . . . ½–2 in.   3¼ in.
  Sides . . . . ¾–1 in.   1–1⅜ in.

3-INCH GUN MOTOR CARRIAGE, M10—Continued

Rear	1–1½ in.	
Top	⅜–¾ in.	
Bottom	¼ in.	
Turret, front	2½ in.	4½ in.
Sides and rear	1 in.	1⅛–1¾ in.
Top	¾ in.	
Performance		
Maximum speed on level		30 m.p.h.
Speed on 3% grade		20 m.p.h.
Maximum grade ability		60%
Trench crossing ability		7 ft., 6 in.
Vertical obstacle ability		24 in.
Fording depth (slowest forward speed)		36 in.
Turning radius		31 ft.
Fuel capacity		164 gals.
Cruising range (approx.)		200 miles
Vision and Fire Control		
Periscopes, M6		3
Telescope, M51		1
Bore sight		1
Gunner's quadrant, M1		1
Communication		
Radio		SCR–510 or 610 or British 19
Interphone stations		5
Flag set, M238		1
Battery, voltage, total		24
Fire Protection and Decontamination		
Fire extinguisher—CO_2–10 lb. (fixed)		2
CO_2–4 lb. (hand)		2
Decontaminating Apparatus, 1½ qts., M2		2
Engine, make and model		G.M. 6-71-6046

3-INCH GUN MOTOR CARRIAGE, M10A1

Characteristics same as for 3-inch gun motor carriage, M10, except as noted:

Weight (gross)	64,000 lb.
Fuel capacity	192 gals.
Cruising range	160 miles
Engine, made and model	Ford GAA

The 3-inch gun motor carriage was one of the important weapons of this war. Thousands of these powerful units, quickly produced, helped to turn the tide against the Germans in Africa, Italy, and France.

This gun motor carriage was made by mounting the 3-inch gun and recoil mechanism—initially designed for use on the heavy tank, M6—in a special turret on the M4 tank chassis. The design was completed and the vehicle standardized in July 1942. As mounted, the gun had a range of 16,000 yards, and with the armor-piercing ammunition available from the start, it could penetrate four inches the best armor plate at 1,000 yards.

Some battle experiences with this weapon are interesting: The 773rd Tank Destroyer Battalion, armed with 3-inch gun motor carriages, M10, destroyed four German Mark VI's (Tigers) and six Mark V's (Panthers) with a loss of three tank destroyers in one action. The 803rd Tank Destroyer Battalion, 2nd Platoon, Company "B," with the same equipment in the vicinity of Hescheid, fired eleven rounds of high-explosive and one round of armor-piercing ammunition, knocking out a Mark V and killing 30 enemy personnel. The 1st Platoon, Company "C," fired 205 rounds of A.P. ammunition, knocking out two Mark V's, three half-tracks, two antitank guns, and killing 90 enemy personnel.

Carriage, Gun, Motor, 90-mm, M36. Right front view.

CARRIAGE, GUN MOTOR, 90MM, M36

CHARACTERISTICS

Crew 5
Physical Characteristics:
  Weight (gross) . . . . 62,000 lb.
  Length . . . . 20 ft., 2 ins.
  Width . . . . 10 ft.
  Height—pedestal A.A. gun folded . . . . 8 ft., 11 in.
  Ground clearance . . . . 17⅛ in.
  Tread (center to center of tracks) . . . . 83 in.
  Ground contact length . . . . 147 in.
  Ground pressure . . . . 12.7 lb./sq. in.
Armament:
  90-mm gun, M3, in mount, M4A1 . . . . In turret
    Elevation . . . . −10° to +20°
    Traverse . . . . 360°
  Cal. .50 machine gun, M2, H.B. (flexible) . . . . On pedestal mount
  1 tripod mount, cal. .50, M3
  Provision for:
  5 cal. .30 carbines
Performance:
  Maximum speed on level . . . . 26 m.p.h.
  Maximum grade ability 60%
  Trench crossing ability . . . . 7 ft., 5 in.
  Vertical obstacle ability . . . . 24 in.
  Fording depth (slowest forward speed) . . . . . . 36 in.
  Fuel capacity . . . . 192 gal.
  Cruising range . . . . 150 miles

CARRIAGE, GUN MOTOR, 90MM, M36—Continued

Vision and Fire Control:		
Periscope, M6		4
Telescope, M70P, or M76D or M76F, w/instrument light, M33		1
Telescope mount, M64 (T92)		1
Elevation quadrant, M9, w/instrument light, M30		1
Gunner's quadrant, M1		1
Panoramic telescope M12, with telescope mount M69 and instrument light M31		1
Ammunition: Stowage:		
90-mm (H.E., M71; A.P.C, M82)		47 rds.
Cal. .50		1,000 rds.
Cal. 30 carbine		450 rds.
Grenades, hand (fragmentation, Mk. II, 6; smoke, M15, 6)		12
Smoke pots, H.C., M1		4
Armor:	Actual	Basis
Hull, front, upper	1½ in.	3¼ in.
lower	4 in.–2½ in.	4 in.
Sides, upper	¾ in.	1⅜ in.
lower	1 in.	
Rear, upper	¾ in.	1 in.
lower	1 in.	
Sides, lower	1 in.	
Top, forward	¾ in.	
rear	⅜ in.	
Bottom	½ in.	
Turret, front		3 in.
Sides		1¼ in.
Top		1⅛ in.
Rear		4 in.
Communications:		
Radio		SCR-510 or 610 (with reel assembly, RL-106/VI) or British No. 19
Interphone stations		5
Flag set, M238		1
Fire Protection and Decontamination:		
Fire extinguisher—10 lb.-CO_2 (fixed)		2
4 lb.-CO_2 (hand)		2
Decontaminating apparatus, M2, 1½ qts.		2
Engine: make and model		Ford, GAA
Type		V8 W.C.
Number of cylinders		8
Fuel (gasoline)		80 octane
Maximum governed speed		2,600 r.p.m.
Gross hp.		500 at 2,600 r.p.m.
Maximum torque		1,040 lb.-ft. at 2,200 r.p.m.
Transmission: Type		Constant mesh, synchronized
Suspension: Type		Vertical volute spring
Track: Type		Rubber or steel block
Width		16 9/16 in.
Pitch		6 in.
No. of shoes per vehicle		158

90-MM GUN MOTOR CARRIAGE, M36

As soon as the new light-weight, high-power 90-mm gun had been developed, it was then possible to mount this more powerful weapon on the same chassis as the gun motor carriage, M10, by providing a new turret. This work was undertaken in April 1943, and the vehicle, standardized in June 1944, was known as the 90-mm gun motor carriage, M36. The 90-mm, M3, gun used in this vehicle can penetrate more than six inches of armor with standard armor-piercing ammunition, and more than ten inches of armor

with the high-velocity, tungsten carbine ammunition, at a range of 1,000 yards. (Penetration at 1,000 yards' range is given because this was the range at which fire was opened in most tank engagements.)

One combat report describes an engagement by the 702nd Tank Destroyer Battalion which destroyed 27 vehicles including German Mark IV, V, and VI Tanks, six antitank guns, and one machine gun at the cost of eight M36 gun motor carriages. Another account, by the 776th Tank

90-mm gun motor carriage, M36. The design of a new 90-mm gun made possible the powerful weapon mounted on the chassis of the medium tank, M4. More than one thousand of these weapons were used in France and Germany.

Destroyer Battalion, includes a story of the destruction of a Tiger tank by one round fired at a range of 900 yards into its flank. The tank was apparently hit in the ammunition racks and immediately exploded. Another incident was reported by a platoon of the 803rd Tank Destroyer Battalion, which discovered two enemy tanks and a self-propelled gun moving down the road toward them. The platoon leader held his fire until they were within 900 yards and then knocked out the last tank, thus blocking the road.

The other tank and the self-propelled gun turned to retreat and were easy targets for the tank-destroyer guns. Still another report, by the artillery officer of the 9th Army, gave the following box score for one battalion of M36's: "Enemy materiel destroyed consisted of one German Mark III, eight Mark IV's, fifteen Mark V's, one Mark VI, two self-propelled guns, two antitank guns, two pillboxes, two armored vehicles, and one machine-gun nest against eight 90-mm gun motor carriage M36 lost."

76-mm gun motor carriage, M18, has sloping armor and uses torsion-bar independent suspension.

76-MM GUN MOTOR CARRIAGE, M18

CHARACTERISTICS

Crew 5

Physical Characteristics
Weight (gross, approx.) . . . . 40,000 lb.
Length—to end of gun . . . . 21 ft., 10 in.
    excluding gun . . . . 17 ft., 4 in.
Width . . . . 9 ft., 2 in.
Height . . . . 8 ft., 5 in. over A.A. gun
Ground clearance . . . . 14 in.
Tread (c. to c. of tracks) . . . . 95 in.
Ground contact length . . . . 116 in.
Ground pressure . . . . 12.5 lb./sq. in.

Armament
76-mm gun, M1A1 or M1A2, in open top turret (with partial basket) . . . . . In mount, M1
    Elevation . . . . −10° to +19½°
    Traverse . . . . 360°
1 cal. .50 machine gun, M2, H.B. . . . . On ring mount
1 tripod mount, cal. .50, M3
Provision for:
5 cal. .30 carbines, M1

Ammunition, stowage
76-mm (A.P.C., M62; A.P., M79; H.E., M42A1; smoke, M88) . . . . 45 rds.
Cal. .30 carbine . . . . 450 rds.
Cal. .50 machine gun . . . . 800 rds.
Grenades, hand (smoke, WP, M8, 6; fragmentation, Mk. II, 6) 12
Smoke pots 4

76-MM GUN MOTOR CARRIAGE, M18—Continued

	Actual
Armor	
Hull	
Front, sides, and rear	
Top	½ in.
Bottom	5/16 in.
Turret	¼ in.
Front w/gunshield	
Sides and rear	¾–1 in.
	½ in.
Performance	
Sustained speed on level	
Speed on 10% grade	50 m.p.h.
Maximum grade ability	15 m.p.h.
Vertical obstacle ability	60%
Fording depth (slowest forward speed)	36 in.
Fuel capacity	48 in.
Cruising range	165 gals.
	150 miles
Vision and Fire Control	
Periscope, M6	
Periscope, M4 or M4A1, w/telescope, M47 or M47A2, and instrument light, M30 for M4A1	2
Telescope, M76C, w/instrument light, M33, or telescope, M70H, w/instrument light, M32	1
Telescope mount, M55	1
Elevation quadrant, M9, w/instrument light, M30	1
Azimuth indicator, M20 or M18	1
Communications	
Radio	SCR-610 or British No. 19
Interphone stations	5
Battery, voltage, total	24
Fire Protection and Decontamination	
Fire extinguisher, CO_2–10 lb. (fixed)	
CO_2–4 lb. (hand)	1
Decontaminating apparatus, M2, 1½ qts.	1
	1

76-MM GUN MOTOR CARRIAGE, M18

The using services felt that it would be desirable to have a gun motor carriage lighter than the 3-inch gun motor carriage, M10, one which could mount a high-powered gun. In January 1943 design was undertaken of a light gun motor carriage mounting the 76-mm high-power gun, which was later known as the 76-mm gun motor carriage, M18. This vehicle was standardized in April 1944, and a considerable number were produced and sent overseas.

This was the only track-laying vehicle ever built with a high speed of 55 miles per hour. Because of its light weight and great horsepower, it was fast and elusive. The 76-mm gun, with its tungsten carbide ammunition and a muzzle velocity of 3,400 feet per second, was able to deal with any type of German tank. Its ammunition could penetrate 7.3 inches of the best armor plate at 1,000 yards. It was a "hit-and-run" vehicle rather than one designed to stay and fight it out.

The 76-mm gun motor carriage, M18, was

M18 (tank destroyer) firing its 76-mm gun in support of Infantry attacking Wiesloch, Germany. This was a hard-hitting, speedy tank destroyer.

highly regarded by the troops and proved, when properly used, to be a valuable weapon in combat. A report by the 603rd Tank Destroyer Battalion told of an engagement in which a German Tiger tank (Mark VI) was destroyed by the 76-mm high-explosive round fuzed with the concrete-piercing shell at a range of 150 yards. The ammunition had been selected in error caused by excitement but proved deadly to the German tank. Headquarters, 1st Tank Destroyer Brigade, reported that since initial commitment in July in Normandy, its tank destroyer battalion lost seven M18 tank destroyers in enemy action against 53 German tanks and 15 self-propelled guns destroyed.

155-mm gun motor carriage, M12, in firing position.

155-MM GUN MOTOR CARRIAGE, M12

CHARACTERISTICS

Crew 6
Physical Characteristics
  Weight (gross) . . . . 58,000 lb.
  Length . . . . 22 ft., 1 in.
  Width . . . . 8 ft., 9 in.
  Height . . . . 8 ft., 10 in.
  Height of center line of bore . . . . 7 ft., 1½ in.
  Ground clearance . . . . 17⅞ in.
  Ground contact length . . . . 147 in.
  Tread (c. to c. of tracks) . . . . 83 in.
  Ground pressure . . . . 11.6 lb./sq. in.
Armament
  155-mm gun, M1918M1, M1917A1 or M1917 . . . . . On mount, M4
    Elevation . . . . −5° to +30°
    Traverse . . . . 28°
  Provision for:
    5 cal. .30 carbines . . . . Equipment of crew
    1 grenade launcher, M8 . . . . For carbine
Ammunition, stowage
  155-mm (H.E., Mk. IIIA1 or M101) . . . .
  Grenades (hand: fragmentation, Mk. II, 4; offensive, Mk. III, w/fuze, M6, 2; smoke, WP, M8, 4; thermite,
    incendiary, 2; rifle: M9A1, 10) 22

155-MM GUN MOTOR CARRIAGE, M12—Continued

		Actual	Basis
Armor			
Hull, front		1½–2 in.	3½ in.
Sides		1 in.	1 in.
Rear		¾ in.	¾ in.
Top		½ in.	½ in.
Bottom		½–1 in.	½–1 in.
Shield		¾ in.	
Performance			
Maximum speed on level			24 m.p.h.
Maximum grade ability			60%
Trench crossing ability			7 ft., 6 in.
Fording depth (slowest forward speed)			36 in.
Fuel capacity			200 gals.
Turning radius			35 ft.
Cruising range (approx.)			140 miles
Vision and Fire Control			
Panoramic telescope, M6 (with instrument light, M9, and one 14-in. extension bar)			1
Telescope, M53			1
Telescope mount, M40			1
Aiming post, M1 (with aiming post light, M14)			1
Gunner's quadrant, M1, w/case			1
Quadrant sight, M1918A1, w/cover, M1918			1
Fuze setter, M21 or M14			1
Bore sight			1
Vision slots			2
Communications			
Flag set, M113			1
Battery, voltage, total			24
Fire Protection and Decontamination			
CO₂—10 lb. (fixed)			2
Fire extinguisher, CO₂—4 lb. (hand)			2
Decontaminating apparatus, M2, 1½ qts.			2
Engine, make and model			Continental R975–C1
Type			Radial A.C.
No. of cylinders			9
Cycle			4
Fuel (gasoline)			80 octane
Max. governed speed			2,400 r.p.m.
Net hp.			353 at 2,400 r.p.m.
Max. torque			850 lb.-ft. at 1,800 r.p.m.
Transmission, type			Synchromesh
Gear ratios			
First speed			
Second Speed			7.56:1
Third speed			3.11:1
Fourth speed			1.78:1
Fifth speed			1.11:1
Reverse			.73:1
Differential, type			5.65:1
Final Drive, type			Controlled
Suspension, type			Herringbone
Idler, type			Volute spring
Track, type			Fixed
Brakes, type			Rubber block
			Mechanical

Cargo Carrier, M30, showing machine gun on mount. This ammunition and personnel transport carrier is a companion vehicle for 155-mm gun motor carriage, M12.

CARGO CARRIER, M30

CHARACTERISTICS

Physical Characteristics
Weight (gross) . . . . 47,000 lb.
Length . . . . 19 ft., 10 in.
Width . . . . 8 ft., 9 in.
Height—ring mount up, with gun . . . . 10 ft.
    ring mount, lowered, without gun . . . . 8 ft., 6 in.
Ground clearance . . . . 10 lb./sq. in.
Armament
Provision for:
5 cal. .30 carbines . . . . Equipment of crew
1 grenade launcher, M8 . . . . For carbine
1 cal. .50 machine gun, M2, H.B. (flexible) . . . . On ring mount
Ammunition, stowage
155-mm (H.E., Mk. IIIA1 or M101) . . . . 40 rounds
Cal. .50 . . . . 1,000 rounds
Grenades (hand: fragmentation, Mk. II, 4; offensive, Mk. III w/fuze, M6, 2; smoke, 4; thermite incen-
    diary, 2; rifle: M9A1, 10) 22
Vision
Protectoscopes 2
Communications
Radio SCR-610

(Other characteristics same as for 155-mm Gun Motor Carriage, M12.)

155-MM GUN MOTOR CARRIAGE, M12

Another self-propelled vehicle developed by the Ordnance Department was the 155-mm gun, which was also placed on the M4 tank chassis and designated the M12. This vehicle gave the powerful gun great mobility. Considerable numbers of these units were sent with our army to England and accompanied them across the Channel into France. Our armies immediately found that these guns were very important in breaking up German resistance. A special concrete-piercing projectile (described under "Ammunition"), had been developed for this high-powered gun, which would penetrate 7 feet of reinforced concrete. By the time our troops reached the German West Wall and encountered German pillboxes by the hundreds, this weapon was one of the decisive tools used in their destruction. Captured documents show that the Germans had

155-mm gun motor carriage, M12, sends a shell at German positions across the Moselle River in Belgium (September 8 1944). As the gunner yanks the firing lanyard, left, the soldier in foreground crouches and clamps his ears to avoid concussion. Note smoke ring flaring out of muzzle. This was the weapon which defeated the famous Siegfried Line.

considered these pillboxes immune to artillery fire, and their relatively easy destruction by the 155-mm self-propelled gun M12, came as a great surprise and disillusionment to the German troops. It had a serious effect on their declining morale.

After the break-through into Germany, the M12 battalions were for the most part attached to armored divisions to assist in the exploitation. Their performance was a revelation, both during the race across France and after the Siegfried Line had been reached.

On account of the rapid rate of advance of our armor, there was usually no medium or heavy artillery other than the M12's within a day's march of the front of an armored division. Their missions were interdiction, deep counter-battery fires, fires on medium- and long-range targets of opportunity, and covering fires during the displacements of light battalions.

As the 3rd Armored Division pushed forward from Soissons to Laon, to Mons, it moved north while the enemy's axis of retreat was due east. Enemy groups of varying strength infiltrated between the armored spearhead of the division and the unarmored general support field artillery battalion. Several infantry actions were fought by the M-12 battalion, resulting in the capture of as many as 500 prisoners in a single day. At times, the M12 was used for the close-in defense of the battery position.

The Siegfried line, an elaborate but lightly defended network of concrete fortifications, afforded an excellent opportunity to test the M12 in its best role as assault artillery.

HEAVY GUN MOTOR CARRIAGES

Because of great success of the 155-mm gun motor carriage, M12, in destroying German fortifications, the German West Wall pillboxes, and in routing German troops out of reinforced concrete buildings, the Ordnance Department went on to the construction of still heavier self-propelled gun motor carriages. The next gun to be mounted was the 155-mm gun, M1. This unit was constructed by mounting this powerful 155-mm gun on the M4 tank chassis. A number of these units were available to the American Army in the final drive across the Ruhr River, and the 155-mm gun motor carriage (M40, as it became known) was the first American gun to fire on the city of Cologne in the attack of the VII Corps, First Army.

The 8-inch howitzer was likewise mounted on the same chassis, interchangeably with the 155-mm gun, and the production of these vehicles was inaugurated in 1945. These vehicles were sent in considerable numbers to both the European and Pacific Theaters.

The largest self-propelled cannon during the war were the 8-inch gun and the 240-mm howitzer, which were mounted interchangeably on the chassis of the heavy tank, M26. Tests showed that these powerful units were ideal for the type of cave warfare encountered in the Pacific, as at Okinawa. At the close of the war, these units were being prepared for shipment to the Pacific area to be used in the invasion of Japan. The Japanese were expected to resort to cave warfare on their home islands, and it was planned to use both of these high-powered weapons, firing large projectiles with concrete-piercing fuzes into these caves to destroy enemy personnel, and minimize the expected losses of American infantrymen.

155-mm gun motor carriage, M40, firing into Germany. "Long Tom" was successfully mounted on the M4 tank chassis. This highly mobile weapon was the first to fire into Cologne, Germany.

155-MM GUN MOTOR CARRIAGE, M40

CHARACTERISTICS

Crew 8
Physical Characteristics
    Weight (gross) . . . . 82,000 lb.
    Length, hull . . . . 21 ft., 10 in.
       Overall, with armament . . . . 29 ft., 8 in.
    Width . . . . 10 ft., 4 in.
    Height (top of shield) . . . . 9 ft., 4 in.
    Ground clearance . . . . 17 in.
    Tread (c. to c. of tracks) . . . . 101 in.
    Ground contact length . . . . 173 in.
    Ground pressure . . . . 10.3 lb./sq. in.
Armament
    155-mm gun M1A1, in mount T14 1
      Elevation —5° to +55°
      Traverse 18° right and 18° left
    Cal. .50 machine gun M2 H.B. (flexible), on ring mount M49C or M66
    Provision for:
      Cal. .30 carbines 8
      Grenade launcher M8 1

155-MM GUN MOTOR CARRIAGE, M40—Continued

Ammunition, Stowage
155-mm (H.E., M101 or M101B) . . . . 20 rds.
Cal. .30 . . . . 960 rds.
Grenades, hand 12
Grenades, rifle, M9A1 10

Armor

	Actual	Basis
Hull, front, upper	½ in.	1¼ in.
Lower	4 in.–2¼ in.	4 in.
Sides, below sponson	½ in.	½ in.
Above sponson	1 in.	1 in.
Rear	½ in.	½ in.
Top	½ in.	½ in.
Bottom, first 36 inches	1 in.	1 in.
Remainder	½ in.	½ in.
Gun shield	½ in.	¾ in.

Vision and Fire Control
Periscope M6 4
Panoramic telescope M12, w/instrument light M19, on
telescope mount M18A1 1
Telescope M69E1, w/instrument light M36, on tele-
scope mount T122 1
Elbow telescope T135 (M16A1F), w/instrument light
M36, on telescope mount T124 (M71) 1
Quadrant mount M1, w/instrument light M12 1
Gunner's Quadrant M1 1

Performance
Maximum speed on level . . . . 24 m.p.h.
Maximum grade ability 60%
Trench crossing ability . . . . 8 ft.
Vertical obstacle ability . . . . 34 in.
Fording depth (slowest forward speed) . . . . 42 in.
Fuel capacity . . . . 200 gals.
Cruising Range (approx.) . . . . 100 miles
Maximum tractive effort . . . . 58,800 lb.

Communications
Radio . . . . SCR-608, 610, 628, or British No. 19
Interphone stations 4

Battery, Voltage, total 24

Fire Protection and Decontamination
Fire Extinguisher, CO$_2$–10 lb. (fixed) 2
CO$_2$–4 lb. (hand) 2

Engine, make
and model . . . . Continental R–975–C4
Type . . . . Radial, A. C.
No. of cylinders 9
Fuel (gasoline) . . . . 80 octane
Net hp. . . . . 395 at 2,400 r.p.m.
Max. net torque . . . . 944 at 1,800 r.p.m.

Transmission, type . . . . Constant mesh, synchronized
Gear ratios
First speed 7.56:1
Second speed 3.11:1
Third speed 1.78:1
Fourth speed 1.11:1
Fifth speed 0.73:1
Reverse 5.65:1

Differential, type . . . . Controlled
Steering ratio 1.515:1
Ring gear to pinion ratio 3.53:1

Final Drive, gear ratio 2.84:1
Sprocket, pitch diameter 25.04
Number of teeth 13

155-MM GUN MOTOR CARRIAGE, M40—Continued

Suspension, type	Horizontal volute spring
Wheel size	20x6¼
Track, type	Steel, single pin, center guide
Width	23 in.
Pitch	6 in.
No. of shoes per vehicle	176
Master Clutch, type	Dry, two-plate
Brakes, type	Wet, external-contracting
Operation	Manual

240-mm howitzer motor carriage. A number of these weapons were to be used to defeat the Japanese cave warfare on the Japanese home islands had the war continued.

240-MM HOWITZER MOTOR CARRIAGE, T92

CHARACTERISTICS

Crew	8
Weight (combat loaded)	125,500 lb.
Unit ground pressure	12.3 lb. per sq. in.

Armor:
 Same as 8" gun motor carriage, T93

Armament	240-mm howitzer, M1
Elevation	0° to 65°
Traverse	12° right and 12° left

Ammunition:
 6 rounds on the carriage. Additional ammunition will be carried in accompanying vehicles.
Performance:
 The same as 8-inch gun motor carriage T93
Vision and Fire Control:
 The same as for 8-inch gun motor carriage T93, except for variations in reticle in elbow telescope M16A1.
Communications:
 The same as 8-inch gun motor carriage T93

CARRIAGE, MOTOR, 8-INCH GUN, T93

CHARACTERISTICS

Crew	8
Weight (combat loaded)	131,400 lb.
Unit ground pressure	13 lb. per sq. in.

Armor:

Frontal, upper	1 in. at 55°
Frontal, lower	1 in. at 45°
Sides, lower	1 in. at 0°
Sides, upper	½ in. at 0°
Rear	½ in. at 10°
Top	⅞ in.
Gun shield	½ in.
Floor	1 in.

Armament	Gun, 8-inch, M1
Elevation	0° to plus 65°
Traverse	12° right and left

Ammunition:

6 rounds on the carriage. Additional ammunition will be carried in accompanying vehicles.

Performance	Maximum speed 15 m.p.h.
Gradeability	60%
Trench crossing ability	7 ft.
Vertical obstacle ability	46 in.
Cruising range	80 miles
Fording	55 in.
Turning radius	30 ft.

Vision and fire control equipment:

Vision cupola for driver and assistant driver
Elbow telescope M16A1E2
1 panoramic telescope M12
Elevation quadrant M1
Gunners quadrant M1

Communications:

Provision for installation of SCR 608B, SCR 610, 619 or British Set No. 19, interphone equipment with station for driver and assistant driver and two stations at the rear of the vehicle.

8-inch gun motor carriage in firing position.

Truck, ¼-ton, 4 x 4 (jeep)—Three-quarter right front view, with top lowered.

TRUCK, ¼ TON, 4 x 4 (JEEP)

CHARACTERISTICS

Crew 2
Physical Characteristics
    Weight (gross) . . . . 3,253 lb.
    Length . . . . 11 ft., ¼ in.
    Width . . . . 5 ft., 2 in.
    Height—top of cowl . . . . 3 ft., 4 in.
        top of steering wheel . . . . 4 ft., 4 in.
        with top up . . . . 5 ft., 9¾ in.
    Ground clearance . . . . 8¾ in.
    Wheelbase . . . . 80 in.
    Tread (c. to c. of tires) . . . . 49 in.
    Ground pressure . . . . 20.8 lb./sq. in.
    Tire equipment . . . . 6.00x16, 6 ply (mud and snow)
Armament
    Provision for one cal. .30 or cal. .50 machine gun
Performance
    Maximum speed on level . . . . 65 m.p.h.
        with towed load . . . . 20 m.p.h.
    Maximum grade ability 60%
        with towed load 45%
    Angle of approach . . . . 45°

TRUCK, ¼-TON, 4 x 4 (Jeep)—Continued

Angle of departure	35°
Fording depth	18 in.
Fuel capacity	15 gals.
Cruising range (approx.)	300 miles
with towed load	260 miles
Normal towed load (37-mm gun carriage or ¼-ton, 2-wheel, cargo trailer)	1,000 lb.
Payload (including driver and assistant)	800 lb.
Turning radius	17½ ft.
Communication	Radio outlet
Battery, voltage	6-12
Engine, type	"L" head
No. of cylinders	4
Cycle	4
Fuel (gasoline)	68 octane
Bore and stroke	3⅛ x 4⅜ in.
Displacement	134.2 cu. in.
Compression ratio	6.48:1
Net h.p.	54 at 4,000 r.p.m.
Max. torque	105 lb.-ft. at 2,000 r.p.m.
Crankshaft rotation	C'clockwise
Length	27 in.
Width	22½ in.
Height	26¾ in.
Ignition	Battery
Weight	355 lb.
Master clutch, type	Dry, single plate
Radiator, type	Fin and tube
Capacity of system	11 qts.
Transmission, gear ratio	
First speed	2.67:1
Second speed	1.56:1
Third speed	1.00:1
Reverse	3.55:1
Transfer case, gear ratio, low	1.97:1
High	1.00:1
Differential, gear ratio	4.88:1
Type of drive	Hypoid bevel
Steering ratio	14, 12, 14:1
Suspension, type	Semi-elliptic
Wheel construction	Divided
Brakes, type	Internal hydraulic
Brakes, Parking, type	External contracting
Front Axle, type	Full floating
Rear Axle, gear ratio	4.88:1

TRUCK, ¼ TON, 4 x 4 (Jeep)

The superiority of American military trucks and transport vehicles in this war is well known. The quarter-ton jeep with its 4 x4 drive needs no further description. The jeep was originally intended as a command and reconnaissance car, but it became a versatile, utilitarian vehicle. By the installation of an electrical generator driven off the transmission, it was changed into a highly mobile arc welder; by the use of a tandem hitch, several jeeps coupled together could be operated to tow artillery in emergencies. G.I. Joe went to the unorthodox extreme by mounting a hand-operated crane to convert the jeep into a light wrecker. It was modified in the field into an ambulance capable of carrying four patients. Its small size made it transportable by airplanes. Personnel carrier, cargo carrier, ammunition carrier—all have been functions of the jeep. The opinions of the using services can be epitomized by saying that the jeep was invaluable.

Jeeps being loaded into C-46 plane.

Truck, 1½-ton, 6 x 6, Cargo and Personnel Carrier, W/W-Dodge—Three-quarter right front view.

TRUCK, 1½-TON, 6x6 CARGO-PERSONNEL, W/W; DODGE (CHRYSLER)

CHARACTERISTICS

Gross weight	10,850 lbs.
Payload	3,000 lbs.
Wheelbase	125 in.
Tread	64¾ in.
Tire size	9.00/16
Engine	6 cylinders
Displacement	230.2 cu. in.
H.P. (max.)	92
Speed	50 m.p.h.

Truck, 2½-ton, 6 x 6, Cargo, WO/W- Reo—Three-quarter right front view.

TRUCK, 2½-TON, 6 x 6, LWB, CARGO, W/W; STUDEBAKER AND REO

CHARACTERISTICS

Gross weight	16,095 lbs.
Payload	5,000 lbs.
Wheelbase	162 in.
Tread	{ 62¼ in. F. { 67¾ in. R.
Tire size	7.50/20
Engine	6 cylinders
Displacement	320 cu. in.
H.P. (max.)	93
Speed (max.)	45 m.p.h.

Vehicle produced for International Aid. Produced with and without winch, and also as a 6 x 4 model, and as a Tractor.

Truck, 2½-ton, 6 x 6, with cargo body and ring mount, M32, as used on closed-cab vehicles.

2½-TON, 6 x 6 (4DT)

CHARACTERISTICS

Physical Characteristics
Weight (curb) . . . . 6,000 lb.
Length, long wheelbase . . . . 21 ft., 3 in.
   short wheelbase . . . . 19 ft., 2¼ in.
Width . . . . 7 ft., 4 in.
Height . . . . 7 ft., 3 3/16 in.
Ground clearance . . . . 10 in.
Tread (center to center, rear) . . . . 67¾ in.
Wheelbase, long wheelbase . . . . 164 in.
   short wheelbase . . . . 145 in.
Ground contact . . . . 406 sq. in.
Ground pressure . . . . 14.7 lb./sq. in.
Tire equipment . . . . 7.50 x 20, 8 ply
   desert . . . . 11.00 x 18, 10 ply
Armament
Truck mount, M32, M36, M37, or M37A3, for cal. .50 machine gun, M2, H.B.
(Supplied with one vehicle in four)
Performance
Maximum speed on level . . . . 45 m.p.h.
Maximum grade ability 65%
Vertical obstacle ability . . . . 10 in.
Angle of approach—w/o winch . . . . 54°
   cab-over-engine model . . . . 45°

2½-TON, 6 x 6 (4DT)—Continued

Angle of approach—with winch	31°
Angle of departure	
long wheelbase models	36°
short wheelbase models	44°
cab-over-engine model	32½°
Turning radius	32 ft.
Fuel capacity	40 gals.
Cruising range (approx.)	220 miles
with towed load	190 miles
Maximum drawbar pull	13,063 lb.
Normal towed load	4,500 lb.
Payload (including personnel)	5,350 lb.
Winch capacity	10,000 lb.
Battery, voltage, total	6
Fire Protection	Fire extinguisher
Engine, make and model	G.M.C. 270
Type	In-line, liquid-cooled
No. of cylinders	6
Cycle	4
Fuel (gasoline)	70 octane
Bore and stroke	3 25/32 x 4 in.
Displacement	269.52 cu. in.
Compression	130 lb. at C.S.
Max. governed speed	2,750 r.p.m.
Net hp.	94 at 3,000 r.p.m.
Max. torque	217 lb.-ft. at 1,600 r.p.m.
Crankshaft rotation	C'clockwise
Length	44¼ in.
Width	22½ in.
Height	32 in.
Ignition	Battery
Weight, dry (less accessories)	535 lb.
Transmission, Gear ratios	
First speed	6.06:1
Second speed	3.50:1
Third speed	1.80:1
Fourth speed	1.00:1
Fifth speed	0.799:1
Reverse	6.00:1
Transfer Case, gear ratios	
(G.M.C. model)	1.16:1; 2.63:1
(Timken model)	1.16:1; 2.61:1
Differential, type	Spiral bevel
Gear ratio	6.6:1
Steering ratio	23.6:1
Suspension, type	Semi-elliptic
Wheel size	20 x 7
Wheel construction	Disk
Master clutch, type	Dry, single plate
Radiator, type	Fin and tube
Capacity of system	19 qts.
Brakes, type	Internal hydraulic
Brakes, Parking, type	Band
Front Axle, type	Banjo or split
Rear Axle, gear ratio	6.6:1

TRUCK, 2½-TON, 6 x 6

The 2½-ton, 6 x 6 truck was typical of the many fine types of commercial trucks used by the Army. The requirement was for a truck which would have the necessary speed, stamina, and maneuverability. It was recognized that the vehicle would be required in great quantities and that extensive commercial facilities would be needed for its manufacture. The chassis consisted of militarized commercial components and was conservatively rated as 2½ tons for tactical purposes, although capable of carrying from five to six tons over improved highways. The six wheels, all power-driven, enabled the truck to negotiate mud and cross-country terrain impassible for ordinary wheeled vehicles. The 2½-ton truck was used mostly as a cargo and personnel carrier during the war. However, many other body designs were employed by the Army, including dump trucks, maintenance shop vans, and water and gasoline tankers. It functioned tactically as a prime mover for the 75-mm and 105-mm howitzers.

The 2½-ton truck became famous on the so-called "Red Ball Highway" operating between the ports of France and the armies in our push across France. Millions of tons of supplies, ammunition, and gasoline had to be transported from the coast to the armies wherever located in their high-speed drive across France into Germany. On the Ledo-Burma Road the 2½-ton truck was used literally to pour supplies into China. In our Pacific operations, cargo and

Truck, 2½-ton, 6 x 6—Short wheelbase cargo truck, shown with ring mount, M37.

dump trucks were used to build landing strips immediately after the capture of each island. As ship transportation was too slow, the trucks were modified to permit air transportation by C47 and C47A cargo airplanes. This was accomplished by splitting the frame back of the cab, and by installing brackets which permitted easy assembly. The body was split crosswise, and assembly plates were installed. The components could then be loaded into an airplane, two of which were required for the transportation of one truck.

The initial convoy of 2½-ton trucks to break the land blockade of China detours around a new causeway along the Ledo Road as the trucks move on towards Kunming, China, from the starting point at Ledo, Assam, India.

Tractor Truck, M26, used as a prime mover for Semitrailer, M15. The two vehicles in combination form the 40-ton Tank Recovery Truck-Trailer, M25.

TRACTOR TRUCK, M26

CHARACTERISTICS

Crew 7

Physical Characteristics
Weight (gross) . . . . 48,300 lb.
Length (overall) . . . . 25 ft., 4 in.
Width . . . . 10 ft., 10¾ in.
Height, to top of ring mount . . . . 10 ft., 4 in.
to top of cab . . . . ¯9 ft., 6 in.
Ground clearance . . . . 14 in.
Tread (center to center, rear) . . . . 98½ in.
Wheelbase . . . . 172 in.
Tire equipment 14.00x24, 20-ply

Armament
Ring Mount M49 1
Provision for:
Cal. .50 Machine Gun HB M2 (flexible) 1
Cal. .50 Tripod Mount M3 1
Cal. .45 submachine gun 1
Cal. .30 carbine

TRACTOR TRUCK, M26—Continued

Ammunition, Stowage
Cal. .50 . . . . 1,500 rounds
Cal. .45 . . . . 600 rounds
Grenades 24

Armor, Actual Thickness
Front . . . . ¾ in.
Sides, rear, and top . . . . ¼ in.

Performance
Maximum speed on level . . . . 26 m.p.h.
Speed on 3% grade . . . . 12 m.p.h.
Maximum grade ability 30%
Vertical obstacle ability . . . . 22 in.
Fording depth . . . . 56 in.
Angle of approach . . . . 35°
Fuel capacity . . . . 120 gal.
Cruising range (approx.) . . . . 250 miles
Maximum drawbar pull (with trailer coupled) . . . . 60,000 lb.
Payload . . . . 55,000 lb.
Normal towed load . . . . 115,000 lb.

Communications
Flag Set M238 1

Battery, Voltage, total 12

Fire Protection and Decontamination
Fire Extinguisher, CO_2—4 lb. (hand) 4
Decontaminating Apparatus M2, 1½ qt. 2

Engine, Make and model . . . . Hall Scott, 440
Type . . . . In-line, L.C.
No. of cylinders 6
Fuel (gasoline) . . . . 70-72 octane
Max. governed speed . . . . 2,100 r.p.m.
Net hp. . . . . 230 at 2,100 r.p.m.
Max. torque . . . . 810 lb.-ft. at 1,100 r.p.m.

Transmission, Type . . . . Selective sliding

Gear ratios
First speed 5.55:1
Second speed 3.27:1
Third speed 1.76:1
Fourth speed 1:1
Reverse 6.58:1

Transfer Case Gear ratios 0.75:1, 1:1, 2.62:1

Rear Axle, Gear ratio 7.69:1
Including chain reduction

Brakes, Service, Type . . . . Air
Parking, Type . . . . Drum

Semitrailer, M15, for transport of light and medium tanks.

SEMITRAILER, M15

CHARACTERISTICS

Weight (gross, without tank load)	35,000 lb.
With load	115,000 lb.
Length	38 ft., 9 in.
Length of bed	27 ft., 5 in.
Width, Normal operating	12 ft., 6½ in.
Emergency operating	10 ft., 4 in.
Width of bed	10 ft., 2 in.
Height (overall)	9 ft., 6 in.
Height of bed	3 ft., 6 in.
Ground Clearance	14 in.
Tread (center to center, rear)	131 in.
Wheelbase (center of bogie to king pin)	372 in.
Tire equipment	14.00 x 24, 20-ply
Performance, Payload	80,000 lb.
Brakes, Type	Two-shoe, fixed anchor
Operation	Internal-expanding, air

TANK TRANSPORTERS

The speed with which a mechanized army maneuvered in warfare entailed the movement of tanks over considerable distances. To accomplish this, the Ordnance Department developed the M25 tank transporter and recovery vehicle. This vehicle was composed of a six-wheel, all-driven truck tractor M26 as a prime mover for the 45-ton, rear-loading semi-trailer M15.

In order to conserve tracks, running gear, engines, and power trains, the M25 was used to transport tanks from the ports of debarkation up to where they were to go into action. Conversely, disabled tanks had to be recovered, usually under fire, and returned to the base for repair.

Although not originally intended as a cargo carrier, the M25 was frequently used in this capacity. Tank development today is continuing toward still more heavily armored vehicles. In order to keep pace, similar progress must be made in truck tractors and semi-trailers. Tractors are being developed in the 8-ton, 12-ton, 20-ton, and 25-ton classes, 6 x 6 and 8 x 8, for use with 20-ton, 45-ton, 75-ton and 100-ton semi-trailers. The addition of stakes to these trailers make them capable of hauling any kind of general cargo.

Ordnance corpsmen in France prepare to take back to a repair shop a damaged Sherman tank which will again be put into running condition. Left to right: Cpl. Michael Lazzaro, Boston, Mass., Cpl. Russell Weeks, Indianapolis, and Cpl. Almond Jellison, Portland, Maine.

Two T2 tank retrievers pull 2nd Armored Division tank out of deep snow near Les Tailles, Belgium.

18-ton High-speed tractor, M4.

18-TON HIGH-SPEED TRACTOR, M4

CHARACTERISTICS

Crew 11

Physical Characteristics
Weight (gross) . . . . 36,000 lb.
Length—Class A . . . . 17 ft., 2 in.
    Class B . . . . 16 ft., 11 in.
Width . . . . 8 ft., 1 in.
Height, to top of cab . . . . 7 ft., 10 in.
    to top of gun mount . . . . 8 ft., 3 in.
Height of pintle . . . . 29 in.
Ground clearance . . . . 20 in.
Tread (c. to c. of tracks) . . . . 80 in.
Ground contact length . . . . 124 in.
Ground pressure (with 90-mm gun) . . . . 8.75 lb./sq. in.

Armament
Ring mount, M49C, for cal. .50 machine gun
1 tripod mount, cal. .50, M3
1 carriage assembly
1 cradle assembly
Provision for:
1 cal. .50 machine gun, M2, H.B. (flexible)

18-TON HIGH-SPEED TRACTOR, M4—Continued

Ammunition
  Cal. .50 . . . . 500 rounds
  One of the following, depending on artillery towed:
  90-mm A.A. . . . . 54 rounds
  3-inch A.A. . . . . 54 rounds
  155-mm gun . . . . 30 rounds
  8-inch howitzer . . . . 20 rounds
  240-mm howitzer . . . . 12 rounds

Performance
  Maximum speed towing 90-mm A.A. gun
    On level . . . . 33 m.p.h.
    On 3% grade . . . . 20 m.p.h.
  Maximum grade ability 60%
  Trench crossing ability . . . . 5 ft.
  Vertical obstacle ability . . . . 29 in.
  Fording depth (slowest forward speed) . . . . . 41 in.
  Turning radius . . . . 18 ft., 6 in.
  Fuel capacity . . . . 125 gals.
  Cruising range (approx.) . . . . 180 miles
  Maximum drawbar pull . . . . 38,700 lb. at stall
                                  13,000 lb. at 4 m.p.h.
  Winch capacity . . . . 30,000 lb.

Battery, voltage, total 12

Fire Protection and Decontamination
  Fire extinguisher, CO_2—4 lb. (hand) 2
  Decontaminating apparatus, M2, 1½ qts. 2

Engine, make and model . . . . Waukesha 145GZ
  Type . . . . In-line
  No. of cylinders 6
  Fuel (gasoline) . . . . 70 octane
  Max. governed speed . . . . 2,100 r.p.m.
  Net hp. . . . . 210 at 2,100 r.p.m.
  Max. torque . . . . 528 lb.-ft. at 1,680 r.p.m.

Transmission, type . . . . Selective
  Gear ratios—First speed 2.166:1
    Second speed 1.555:1
    Third speed 0.437:1
    Reverse 1.822:1

Torque Converter, gear ratio 1.372:1

Differential, type . . . . Controlled
  Gear ratio 2.666:1
  Steering ratio 1.747:1

Suspension, type . . . . Horizontal volute spring
  Wheel or tire size . . . . 20 x 9

Idler, type . . . . Trailing
  Wheel or tire size . . . . 32 x 9

Track, type . . . . Steel block, rubber bushed
  Width . . . . 16 9/16 in.
  Pitch . . . . 6 in.
  No. of shoes per vehicle 130

Master Clutch, type . . . . Spring loaded, dry disk

Final Drive, type . . . . Spur gear
  Sprocket, no. of teeth 13
  Pitch diameter . . . . 25.038 in.
  Gear ratio 2.764:1

Radiator, type . . . . Fin and tube
  Capacity of system . . . . 72 qts.

Brakes, type . . . . Mechanical on controlled differential

Brakes, trailer, type . . . . Air and/or electrical

18-TON HIGH-SPEED TRACTOR, M4

Before the war, only heavy trucks and commercial-type tractors were available for towing artillery. Because of lack of cross-country mobility of trucks and the inadequate speed of commercial-type tractors, the Ordnance Department, in 1941, undertook development of full-tracked, high-speed artillery prime movers by utilizing, in their design, the suspension and other components of standard military vehicles.

To cover the range of towing requirements for artillery weapons it was considered advisable to develop three sizes of these high-speed prime movers, later standardized as High-Speed Tractors M4, M5, and M6.

Development of a prime mover for artillery loads of from 18,000 to 45,000 pounds and for transporting personnel, ammunition, and other accessories pertaining to the artillery section was undertaken in 1941. Pilot models were pro-

cured and tested; with certain modifications, these proved satisfactory and were standardized and placed in production in 1942 as the 18-ton, high-speed tractor, M4.

These tractors were produced in considerable quantity and saw service on all active battlefronts, towing the 155-mm, M1, 8-inch howitzer, M1, and 3-inch and 90-mm antiaircraft guns; they became renowned for their mechanical reliability and ruggedness. However, by flotation standards later established for military vehicles, the unit ground pressure of the M4 was found to be too high for optimum performance; and so a wider track and suspension were developed and applied, changing this tractor into the M4A1.

In the latter days of the war, M4 tractors towing ammunition trailers were used as accompanying vehicles for self-propelled artillery.

High-speed tractor, M4, towing an artillery piece.

The high-speed tractor, M4, was designed for use as prime mover for heavy artillery—155-mm guns and 8-inch howitzers. This was the unit for putting hundreds of Long Toms into position on many battlefields. The M4, and likewise the M5 and the still larger M6, met all the requirements of the war as an artillery prime mover.

The excellent performance of this vehicle, developed, produced, and dispersed throughout the world in so short a time, is a tribute to the Industry-Ordnance team whose achievements, though less spectacular than those on the fighting fronts, were nevertheless not less effective in winning the greatest victory in our military annals.

An 8-inch is towed into firing position as a field artillery unit prepares to shell the retreating Germans near Mantes Gassi-court, France, only 15 miles below Paris. August 20 1944.

Medium Tractor, M5 (PM-510) with M49, Cal. .50 Gun Mount. Three-quarter right front view.

13-TON HIGH-SPEED TRACTOR, M5

CHARACTERISTICS

Crew 9
Physical Characteristics
    Weight (gross) . . . . 28,300 lb.
    Length . . . . 15 ft., 11 in.
    Width . . . . 8 ft., 4 in.
    Height
        Top of windshield lowered . . . . 6 ft., 8 in.
        Top of canopy top . . . . 8 ft., 8 in.
    Height of pintle . . . . $28\frac{1}{4}$ in.
    Ground clearance . . . . 20 in.
    Tread (c. to c. of tracks) . . . . 83 in.
    Ground contact length . . . . $108\frac{1}{2}$ in.
    Ground pressure . . . . 11.1 lb./sq. in.
Armament
Ring mount, M49C, for cal. .50 machine gun
1 tripod mount, cal. .50, M3
1 elevator cradle, M1
Provision for:
1 cal. .50 machine gun, H.B., M2
  (flexible)

13-TON HIGH-SPEED TRACTOR, M5—Continued

9 cal. .30 rifles or 9 cal. .30 carbines }	Equipment of crew
Ammunition, Stowage	
Cal. .50	400 rounds
One of the following:	
105-mm howitzer	56 rounds
4.5-inch gun	38 rounds
155-mm howitzer	24 rounds
Performance	
Maximum speed towing 155-mm howitzer carriage, on level	35 m.p.h.
Speed on 3% grade	20 m.p.h.
Maximum grade ability, with towed load	50%
without towed load	72%
Trench crossing ability	5 ft., 6 in.
Vertical obstacle ability	18 in.
Fording depth (slowest forward speed)	53 in.
Turning radius	18 ft.
Fuel capacity	100 gals.
Cruising range (approx.)	125 miles
Maximum drawbar pull	20,300 lb.
Payload	5,000 lb.
Winch capacity	17,000 lb.
Battery, voltage, total	12
Fire Protection and Decontamination	
Fire extinguisher, CO_2—4 lb. (hand)	1
Decontaminating apparatus, M2, 1½ qts.	1
Engine, make and model	Continental, R6572
Type	In-line
No. of cylinders	6
Fuel (gasoline)	70 octane
Displacement	572 cu. in.
Max. governed speed	2,900 r.p.m.
Net hp.	235 at 2,900 r.p.m.
Max. torque	475 lb.-ft. at 1,600 r.p.m.
Transmission, type	Constant mesh
Gear ratios	
First speed	5.43:1
Second speed	3.20:1
Third speed	1.71:1
Fourth speed	1.00:1
Reverse	5.36:1
Transfer Case, gear ratios	1.00:1 and 1.71:1
Differential, type	Controlled
Gear ratio	2.60:1
Steering ratio	1.844:1
Final Drive, type	Spur gear
Sprocket, no. of teeth	14
Pitch diameter	24.56 in.
Gear ratio	2.35:1
Suspension, type	Volute spring
Wheel or tire size	20x6
Track, type	Same as Light Tank, M3
Idler, type	Trailing
Wheel or tire size	28x6

13-TON HIGH-SPEED TRACTOR, M5

At the beginning of the war many artillery-men thought that it would be unnecessary to de-velop high-speed tractors for use in artillery because it was felt that multi-drive-wheeled trucks would provide the necessary mobility for medium and heavy artillery. Many years of ex-perience, however, made the Ordnance Depart-ment sure that the trucks would be found inadequate to meet battlefield conditions, espe-cially during the spring, fall, and winter months. Consequently, the Department proceeded with the development of a series of high-speed trac-tors which would meet all requirements for light, medium and heavy artillery.

The high-speed tractor, M5, 13-ton, was de-veloped for transporting artillery, 155-mm how-itzers and 4.5-inch guns. It was also used as a prime mover for division artillery and antitank guns and other special equipment.

M5 tractors were used in great quantities in all theaters of operation and proved their worth on many battlefields.

Medium tractor, M5, towing 155-mm gun carriage on a 30 per cent side slope.

A high-speed tractor, M5, pulls a 4.5-inch gun, M1, at high speed over rough terrain.

Heavy tractor, M6. Right front view.

38-TON HIGH-SPEED TRACTOR, M6

CHARACTERISTICS

Crew 11
Physical Characteristics
  Weight (gross) . . . . 75,000 lb.
  Length . . . . 21 ft., 6 in.
  Width . . . . 10 ft., ½ in.
  Height, to top of cab . . . . 8 ft., 1 in.
    to top of gun mount . . . . 8 ft., 7 in.
  Ground clearance . . . . 20 in.
  Tread (c. to c. of tracks) . . . . 98½ in.
  Ground contact length . . . . 172 in.
  Ground pressure . . . . 9.9 lb./sq. in.
Armament
  Cal. .50 machine gun, M2, H.B. (flexible) . . . . . On ring mount, M66
    Elevation . . . . −10° to +85°
    Traverse . . . . 360°
Provision for:
1 cal. .30 rifle, M1, for driver
Ammunition, stowage
  Cal. .50 . . . . 600 rounds
  One of the following:
    4.7-in. A.A. . . . . 24 rounds
    240-mm howitzer, M1 . . . . 20 rounds
    8-in. gun, M1 . . . . 24 rounds
Performance
  Maximum speed on improved road towing 240-mm howitzer, M1, tube
    Level . . . . 20.5 m.p.h.
    2½ grade . . . . 18 m.p.h.
    5% grade . . . . 14 m.p.h.
    20% grade . . . . 3½ m.p.h.

38-TON HIGH-SPEED TRACTOR, M6—Continued

Maximum grade ability	60%
Trench crossing ability	8 ft.
Vertical obstacle ability	30 in.
Fording depth (slowest forward speed)	54 in.
Angle of approach and departure	30°
Turning radius	14 ft.
Fuel capacity	250 gals.
Cruising range (approx.)	110 miles
Winch capacity	60,000 lb.
Battery, voltage, total	12
Fire Protection and Decontamination	
Fire extinguisher, CO_2–4 lb. (hand)	2
Engine, make and model	Waukesha 145 GZ (two)
Cycle	4
No. of cylinders	12
Fuel (gasoline)	80 octane
Net hp.	191 at 2,100 r.p.m.
Max. torque	539 lb.-ft. at 1,500 r.p.m.
Transmission, type	Constant mesh with torque converters
Gear ratios	
First speed	
Second speed	2.12:1
Reverse	1.05:1
Torque Converter, gear ratio	2.76:1
Differential, type	4.5:1
Steering ratio	Controlled
Final Drive, type	1.6:1
Sprocket, no. of teeth	Herringbone
Pitch diameter	13
Gear ratios	25.04 in.
Suspension, type	3.06:1
Wheel or tire size	Horizontal volute spring
Idler, type	20 x 9
Track, type	Trailing
Width	Center guide
Pitch	21 9/16 in.
No. of shoes per vehicle	6 in.
Master Clutch, type	336
Brakes, type	Dry disk, spring-loaded
Operation	Self-energized
	Levers

38-ton high-speed tractor, M6—cross-country operation with 50,000 pounds towed load.

TRACTOR, HIGH SPEED, 38-TON, M6

The development of a very heavy mobile 8-inch gun or 240-mm howitzer required also the development of a suitable high-speed tractor for pulling these weapons cross-country. In the earlier days of the invasion of Italy, the M3 tank was used as a prime mover for these weapons. Later in the war, the high-speed, 38-ton tractor, M6, became available. This tractor was ideal, as it permitted these guns to be taken over the most difficult terrain at high speeds and put into firing position.

Heavy Tractor, M6, towing 8-inch gun, M1, load on Transport Wagon, M3A1. Three-quarter right rear view.

This is the largest ordnance high speed tractor—the M6—which was used to haul 8-inch and 240-mm guns into position on Lt. Gen. Patton's Third Army front. Two ordnance maintenance mechanics are lowering into position a huge muffler which they manufactured themselves when no new ones were available.

Truck, ¼-ton, 4 x 4, amphibian.

TRUCK, ¼-TON, 4 x 4, AMPHIBIAN

CHARACTERISTICS

Performance
Rated pay load . . . . 800 lb.
Rated towed load . . . . 1,000 lb.
Max. gradability 40%
Min. turning radius . . . . 18 ft.
Angle of approach . . . . 35°
Angle of departure . . . . 35°
Max. speed . . . . ⎰ 50 m.p.h. Land
⎱ 5½ m.p.h. Water
Cruising range . . . . ⎰ Land 250 mi.
⎱ Water 30 mi.
General Data
Crew 4
Gross weight . . . . 4,300 lb.
Height, over-all . . . . 69 in.
Length,   " . . . . 182 in.
Width,   " . . . . 64 in.
Ground clearance . . . . 8⅞ in.
Tire size . . . . 6.00 x 16, 6 ply
Tread width . . . . 48¼ in.
Electrical system . . . . 12 volts
Power train transmission . . . . Syncro-mesh
Fuel capacity . . . . 15 gals.
Winch, capacity . . . . (capstan) 3,500 lb.
H.P. per gross ton 29
Engine
Make & model . . . . Ford—GPW
Type . . . . In line 4 cyl.W.C.
Net H.P. . . . . 60 @ 3,600 r.p.m.
Governed speed . . . . Not governed

TRUCK, ¼-TON, 4 x 4, AMPHIBIAN

A requirement arose for a light amphibious truck for use in landing operations. The one-quarter-ton jeep was equipped with an amphibious body to permit operation in the water as well as on the land. A number of these vehicles were manufactured but were found to be too small to be of practical use. It was therefore replaced by the larger and more useful amphibious vehicle based on the 2½-ton truck, known as the DUKW.

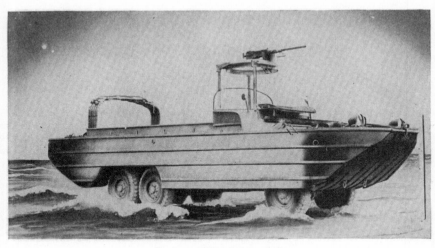

Truck, amphibian, 2½-ton, 6 x 6.

TRUCK, AMPHIBIAN, 2½-TON, 6 x 6

CHARACTERISTICS

Armament
  Mounts 1 cal. .50 M.G.
Armor
  None
Performance
  Rated pay load . . . . 5,000 lb.
  Rated towed load . . . . 4,000 lb.
  Max. gradability 60%
  Min. turning radius—
    Land . . . . 36 ft.
    Water . . . . 21 ft.
  Angle of approach . . . . 38°
  Angle of departure . . . . 26°
  Max. speed:
    Land . . . . 50 m.p.h.
    Water . . . . 6.4 m.p.h.
  Cruising range:
    Land . . . . 200 mi.
    Water . . . . 30 mi.
  Min. loaded free board . . . . 28 in.
  Max. loaded draft . . . . 51 in.
General Data
  Crew 2
  Gross weight . . . . 19,850 lb.
  Height, over-all . . . . 98 in.
  Length, " . . . . 372 in.
  Width, " . . . . 96 in.
  Ground clearance . . . . 10 in.
  Tire size . . . . 11.00x18 desert

TRUCK, AMPHIBIAN, 2½-TON, 6 x 6—Continued

Tread width	68 in.
Electrical system	6 volts
Power train	Mech. trans. 5 speed; 2 speed transfer case
Fuel capacity	40 gals.
Winch, capacity	10,000 lb.
H.P. per gross ton	9.4
Engine	
Make & model	
Type	GMC 270
Displacement	6 cyl. W. C.
Net H.P. at 2,500 r.p.m.	270 cu. in.
Governed speed	93 H.P.
	2,750 r.p.m.

The amphibian truck, 2½-ton, 6 x 6, known as the DUKW was one of the most valuable vehicles produced during the war.

It was designed by putting an amphibious body on the 2½-ton General Motors 6 x 6 truck. This truck was manufactured in large quantities and successfully used in all theaters. The DUKW was valuable in all amphibious operations for bringing men and supplies ashore from ships anchored in the harbor outside the range of land guns. This truck was very seaworthy and could maneuver in rough water. The DUKW proved itself in the invasion of France, as it did likewise in the amphibious operations of the Pacific.

Armored Car, M8.

ARMORED CAR, M8

CHARACTERISTICS

	Ammunition Stowage
Armament	
1 37-mm. gun	80 rds.
1 cal. .50 M.G.	400 rds.
1 cal. .30 M.G.	1,500 rds.
4 cal. .30 carbine	400 rds.
Grenade, frag.	6 rds.
Grenade, offensive	6 rds.
Grenade, smoke	6 rds.
Armor	**Thickness**
Average frontal	¾-⅝ in.
" side	⅜ in.
" top	¼ in.
" rear	¼ in.
" turret, front	¾ in.
" " sides	¾ in.
General Data	
Crew	4
Combat weight	16,500 lb.
Height, over-all	75½ in.
Length, "	197 in.
Width, "	100 in.
Ground clearance	11 in.
Tire size	9.00 x 20
Electrical system	12 volts
Type steering	Mechanical worm
Power train	Transmission, transfer case, inter-wheel differential
Suspension	Standard leaf spring
Fuel capacity	56 gals.
H.P. per ton (vehicle)	11.8

ARMORED CAR, M8—Continued

Performance
Max. gradability 60%
Min. turning radius . . . . 28 ft.
Max. speed . . . . 56 m.p.h.
Cruising range . . . . 350 miles
Fording depth . . . . 32 in.
Engine
Manufacturer & type . . . . Hercules Model JXD, 6 cyl. liquid cooled
Displacement . . . . 320 cu. in.
Net h.p. at 3,200 r.p.m. . . . . 110 h.p.
Governed speed . . . . None

The armored car, M8, was used in all theaters in great quantities. It was especially valuable as a cavalry weapon for reconnaissance work on roads leading to enemy positions. The 37-mm gun was very effective as an anti-tank weapon and with canister and high-explosive shell was deadly against personnel. Another highly mobile armored car developed during the war was the M38.

Light Armored Car, M38, 6 x 6.

Cargo carrier, M29C.

CARGO CARRIER, M29C

CHARACTERISTICS

Performance

Rated pay load	1,200 lb.
Max. gradability	100%
Min. turning radius	12 ft.
Angle of approach	45°
Angle of departure	30°
Max. speed	36 m.p.h.
Cruising range	150 miles
Fording depth	Amphibious

General Data

Crew	4
Gross weight	6,000 lb.
Height, over-all	71 in.
Length, "	190 in.
Width, "	68½ in.
Ground clearance	11 in.
Ground pressure	2 p.s.i.
Track width	20 in.
Electrical system	12 volts
Power train	Synchromesh transmission; controlled diff.
Fuel capacity	35 gals.
Winch, capacity	3,500 lb.
H.P. per gross ton	25

CARGO CARRIER, M29C—Continued

Engine
Make & model	Studebaker Champion
Type	6-cyl., water cooled
Displacement	169.6 cu. in.
Net h.p. at 3,800 r.p.m.	75 h.p.
Governed speed	4,200 r.p.m.

This light cargo carrier was known as the "weasel." It was originally designed for use in snow. There proved to be few requirements for a snow vehicle, but it was found to be useful in crossing mud areas. Its wide track gave it a low ground pressure (two pounds per square inch, which is less than the pressure of a man's foot). The vehicle was extensively used during the invasion of France for moving supplies forward over soft fields. It was often misused by overloading with heavy cargo, beyond its capacity. Maintenance, therefore, was often difficult. This type of vehicle has great possibilities of development to meet the future requirements of Arctic service. The M29 was made with two types of bodies, one for cargo and the other to give the carrier amphibian characteristics. The latter was known as cargo carrier, M29C.

Chapter VII

RESEARCH AND MATERIALS

Chapter VII

RESEARCH AND MATERIALS

Materials

The success of the development and production programs of the Ordnance Department during the war was due in large measure to the close cooperation of industry, technical societies, research agencies, and Government departments and services in the development and standardization of materials and processes of fabrication and treatment and the conservation of materials. The close integration of the Ordnance program with all the governmental and non-governmental agencies was accomplished by having Ordnance Department representatives on more than 150 boards, committees, and subcommittees concerned with conservation and with the research, development, and standardization of materials and processes.

In the early days of the Ordnance production program, even before Pearl Harbor, it became apparent that the supply of many essential materials was critical and that rigid conservation measures must be adopted if enough weapons and ammunition were to be furnished on time. The material requirements of all classes of ordnance items were thoroughly reviewed to determine where alternate materials could be used safely and effectively. Although practically all generally used materials were difficult to obtain at some period during the war, special attention was devoted to conservation of aluminum, chromium, copper, molybdenum, nickel, rubber, phthalic anhydride, tin, tungsten, and vanadium. Many millions of pounds of these materials were saved through substitutions. These conservation measures involved intensive study of the comparative properties and characteristics of materials, and thorough investigations and tests to determine their suitability for many special applications. The fact that the best ordnance materiel in the world was furnished in sufficient quantity to meet the needs of our own forces and our Allies is evidence of the success of the conservation program.

Specifications and Standards

Specifications and standards were an essential part of the ordnance development and production program. It was by means of such documents that the results of research, development, and standardization activities of industry, technical societies, and the Government were made effective in production and procurement. During the war, more than 600 specifications per year were prepared and coordinated by the Ordnance Department, and many more were amended to keep them in harmony with improvements and changing conditions. Many of these were the first specifications establishing limits and test methods for essential materials and treatments or results of cooperative development and standardization projects. Typical examples follow:

The first specification covering sound, high-strength, aluminum alloy die castings which could be made entirely from secondary metal was prepared and put into use by the Ordnance Department. Through the use of this specification, it was possible to make die-cast aluminum components for ammunition and fire-control instruments, even though high-grade aluminum was not allowed for these purposes.

Specifications and standards pertaining to welding and joint design were worked out in co-operation with the American Welding Society and industry. These specifications were of great value in the production and inspection of numerous ordnance items which were fabricated by welding.

A general specification covering methods of inspection and tests of paints and other organic coatings has developed in cooperation with industry, technical societies, and interested government agencies. By its adoption, test procedures were standardized with great benefit to government and industry.

A color card supplement to the general specification for paints developed by cooperative action with interested government agencies resulted in standardizing 72 colors to replace approximately 180 different shades previously used by the cooperating agencies.

A specification covering rubber and synthetic rubber for general, mechanical, aeronautical, and automotive applications (except tires) was prepared in cooperation with Joint S.A.E.-A.S.T.M. Technical Committee A and representatives of producing and using industries. This specification greatly facilitated the proper application, procurement, and inspection of all grades of natural, reclaimed, and synthetic rubbers.

In cooperation with the Technical Committee of the Society of Plastic Industries, a complete Engineering Classification of Plastics was prepared. This systematic classification and series of designations for plastic materials undoubtedly will be of great value in developing future specifications and in promoting proper application of plastics in design and production.

Development of New and Improved Materials and Processes

New and improved materials and processes were developed to meet the needs occasioned by the development of new and improved types of weapons and ammunition and the severe conditions under which materiel was transported, stored, and operated. Typical examples follow:

Experience in the testing and use of both rolled and cast homogeneous armor showed that it was essential to obtain heat-treated material having high resistance to impact at normal and sub-zero temperatures. Research and development work at the Watertown Arsenal showed that there was a definite correlation between high impact values, fibrous fracture of nicked specimens, as-quenched core hardness, and the absence of ferrite in the micro-structure of quenched and tempered steel within the hardness range normally obtained in homogeneous armor. The data developed by Watertown Arsenal and the results of various tests on armor were considered by representatives of industry and the Ordnance Department. Specifications for homogeneous rolled and cast armor were revised to require that the composition and heat treatment of the material be such that a complete fibrous (non-crystalline) fracture would be developed when specimens were notched and broken after final heat treatment. The application of this fracture test and the careful control of other factors in the production of both rolled and cast homogeneous armor resulted in great improvement in the ballistic properties.

In order to produce weapons with increased mobility, it was found necessary to use gun tubes of lighter weight with thinner walls and, consequently, of stronger steels to withstand service stresses. Experimental models of guns incorporating the stronger steels showed the need for metal which could adjust itself plastically to the high stresses occurring at the bore during firing. Furthermore, it was found necessary for the steel to maintain this toughness at sub-zero temperatures, since many cannon are required to operate under conditions of extreme cold. Research and experience showed that the basic factors affecting the toughness of homogeneous armor also affect the toughness in high-strength gun tubes. A specification for high-strength gun tubes was developed in cooperation with representatives of gun forgings manufacturers. This specification required close control of materials and manufacturing processes and specified Charpy impact values. The use of this specification and application of the metallurgical principles developed by research work at Watertown Arsenal resulted in great improvement in the properties of gun forgings.

Definite improvements were made in the performance of armor-piercing projectiles by applying the metallurgical principles found to be significant in connection with the improvement of armor and gun forgings.

An outstanding contribution of the metallurgical field of alloy steels resulted from an Ordnance-sponsored program to determine the alloying effect of additions of various special addition agents. Extremely small quantities of such addition agents have produced hardening equivalent to those gained by the common additions of nickel, chromium, manganese, or molybdenum. Data was derived from hardenability studies and other tests of several portions of a single heat of steel containing different addition agents. Furthermore, several production parts were made and given extended service tests. In this program, a good beginning was made to develop those properties which are of practical interest to the metallurgist, and the results will serve as a guide to further study. As the limitations and advantages of the special addition agents become more clearly defined, both the Ordnance Department and industry will be able to take advantage of these economical, non-critical materials.

Before the war, the armor on combat vehicles was joined by means of riveting. Until that time, there had been little or no commercial experience in the welding of high-strength alloy steels such as are used in rolled and cast armor. In cooperation with industry and research agencies, austentic electrodes were developed and used successfully in the welding of armor on tanks and other combat vehicles, providing joints superior to those obtained by riveting. Several research projects were undertaken in cooperation with N.D.R.C. to develop ferritic electrodes suitable for the welding of armor and other high-strength alloy steels. The outstanding development resulting from these projects was the NRC-2A ferritic electrode. This electrode was found to be usable in the fabrication of armor for tanks and other vehicles and for the repair of cast armor. It could be used, also, for welding high-strength, heat-treated steel plate used in the construction of other ordnance materiel.

Fuels and Lubricants

Petroleum products were of vital importance in World War II. Tremendous quantities of these materials, amounting to approximately 60 per cent of all overseas tonnage, were required for military operations. The Ordnance Department early realized the importance of fuels and lubricants to the successful performance and maintenance of materiel of all types, and initiated a research and development program to provide materials specifically designed for their military application.

The scope of military operations was such that materiel was required to perform satisfactorily under almost every conceisable condition of temperature and terrain. In developing fuels and lubricants to meet those conditions, it was necessary to go far beyond the limits established by previous commercial experience. Both equipment and supply considerations were carefully weighed and specifications were developed to provide the most suitable materials which were available in the required quantities. Specifications seldom remained in static because the demands of the aviation gasoline and rubber programs influenced the types of raw materials available.

In 1940, three types of gasoline were required for combat and transport vehicles. One tank engine required 91-octane aviation fuel and the other equipment required either 72- or 80-octane fuel. Extensive tests proved that, by modifying the one engine requiring aviation gasoline and adjusting the others for optimum performance, an 80-octane fuel would serve as a combat fuel for all Army ground equipment.

A specification was written to provide for procurement of commercial premium gasoline of 80-octane which was then available in the quantities required. It was necessary to specify three volatility grades of gasoline to coincide with the commercial practice of furnishing fuels adapted to the season of the year and the area in which they were used. As long as the bulk of our forces were in training in this country, the supply of three grades of gasoline presented no particular difficulty. However, as increasing numbers of our troops were deployed overseas for offensive operations it was apparent that distribution of three volatility grades of gasoline would present an insurmountable supply problem. It is almost impossible to determine the exact area or the season in which offensive operations will take place far enough in advance to build up stock piles of the volatility grade of gasoline required for specific operations. It was apparent that a single grade of combat fuel was desirable and that it must cover as wide a temperature range as possible.

The concept of a single-grade combat fuel was entirely new and beyond the scope of previous commercial experience. Two factors—vapor lock and cold starting—had to be investigated. Tests at the Ordnance Desert Proving Ground, Camp Seeley, California, during the summer of 1942 under extremely high temperature conditions, determined the specification limits which would afford maximum protection against vapor lock.

During the fall of 1942, cold-room tests were conducted with a group of tanks using gasolines of different volatilities to determine their cold-starting and warm-up characteristics. From the results of these tests, a fuel was formulated and furnished to the Ordnance Winter Detachment, then operating at Camp Shilo, Manitoba, Canada. Data were obtained on the cold-starting and warm-up characteristics of the fuel in the various combat and transport vehicles under test.

Data from the Camp Seeley and Camp Shilo tests were studied in the light of available materials by the Ordnance Department and representatives of Industry assisting in the problem through the Coordinating Research Council. As a result of these cooperative studies, it was concluded that a single volatility grade of fuel, providing satisfactory operation from zero degrees Fahrenheit to extreme heat, could be obtained in the quantities required without disrupting refinery operations or infringing upon the requirements of the aviation gasoline and rubber programs. Since most operations were anticipated in areas covered by this temperature range, this single grade would represent by far the greatest quantity of fuel required. Another grade, needed only in small quantities, was provided for operations below zero degrees Fahrenheit.

The development of heavy-duty engine oils for military use followed a similar pattern. Early in the war, two types of engine oils were used; straight mineral oil for gasoline engines and heavy-duty oil for Diesel engines. The straight mineral oils were covered by U. S. Navy specification. The specification for the heavy-duty oil permitted procurement of commercial products on the basis of full-scale engine tests.

As the operation of military motor vehicles increased, corrosion of alloy bearings was experienced with the straight mineral oils. This difficulty paralleled commercial experience, which indicated that the heavy-duty oils were the most suitable for engines under all operating conditions. Therefore, those oils were prescribed for use in all combat and motor transport vehicles, reducing the types of engine oil required and improving maintenance by controlling bearing corrosion and eliminating ring sticking, valve sticking, and high oil consumption.

Continued operating experience revealed several difficulties which had to be overcome. Foaming occurs when engine oils are agitated in the presence of air. Straight mineral oils form foams that break quickly. However, some additives used in the heavy-duty oils tend to stabilize foam. Oils that form stable foam present a particularly serious problem in dry sump type tank engines. With the cooperation of the Coordinating Research Council, additives were developed to control or eliminate this difficulty. Extensive service tests were conducted with foam-inhibited heavy-duty oils to determine the effectiveness of the inhibitors, and a laboratory test method was developed which closely correlated with the service tests. The specification was then amended to include an antifoam requirement.

Another difficulty encountered in the development of heavy-duty oils for military use was commonly referred to as "pour-point" reversion. Some engine oils, after exposure to fluctuating sub-zero temperature cycles, show a higher pour-point than originally indicated by laboratory determination. It was found that pour-point reversion could be controlled by careful selection of base stocks and control of the amount of pour-point depressant. With the assistance of the Coordinating Research Council, a laboratory test method was developed which properly evaluated this characteristic, and this was included in the specification.

Space does not permit more detailed discussion of the work done to develop new, or to improve existing, full-scale engine tests to evaluate engine oils more closely in terms of service conditions. The assumption of direct Ordnance responsibility for qualification of engine oils, necessitated by a critical shortage of additive and base stocks in order to provide a quick means for requalification, can only be mentioned. These developments have all been reflected in subsequent changes to U. S. Army Specifications.

Other outstanding accomplishments were: a single all-temperature recoil oil; a preservative oil for aircraft armament—for not only protection against rust but also for satisfactory performance of the weapon at all temperatures down to minus 70 degrees Fahrenheit; a preservative oil to protect engine interiors in shipment and storage—this eliminated the removal of heavy rust preventives before putting the engine in operation.

An extensive program of investigation of enemy fuels and lubricants was conducted. Close surveillance of the enemy's petroleum supplies during time of war was an essential phase of technical intelligence. Development of new equipment—particularly in the tank, motor transport, and aviation fields—proceeded hand in hand with the development of new or improved fuels and lubricants for use in that equipment. The introduction of new materiel by the enemy could be predicted on occasion by trends in the characteristics of his fuels and lubricants.

Comprehensive technical information on enemy petroleum supplies at the same time permitted maximum utilization of those captured supplies in our own equipment. This practice was highly desirable and often necessary to sustain rapid advances at the end of extended supply lines. The strategic value of technical data on enemy fuels and lubricants cannot be overemphasized. Those data revealed the source of the enemy's petroleum supplies and the method of refining. Once the source had been determined, strategic bombing denied the enemy his petroleum supplies, without which it was difficult to carry on modern mechanized warfare.

Although much has been accomplished, many problems unforeseen at present are expected to arise with the development of new equipment. The never-ending search for new and better fuels and lubricants must continue. Those products must be specifically designed for their military application and yet fit easily into a simple system of supply. The number of products specified must be kept to a minimum consistent with equipment requirements.

Technical Intelligence

This war provided a proving ground for testing in deadly combat the greatest aggregation of weapons ever contrived by the human mind. Our enemies were armed with materiel which resulted from years of research and development. It was axiomatic that, all other things being equal, the nation which led in ordnance research and development had a tremendous advantage in warfare. A long-range guided missile such as the German V-2, with an atomic warhead, a homing device, and a proximity fuze in the hands of the Germans might possibly have changed the course of the war.

To keep abreast of the enemy in ordnance development was not enough—we must remain constantly ahead of the enemy. To surpass the enemy we must know his developments. The sooner we knew his developments, the greater was our advantage. This condition applied not only with regard to radical departures in weapons designed but also to improvements on existing weapons. Weapons which killed more effectively were, for the most part, improvements on weapons which had been in existence for years. The American tank forced the Germans to increase the effectiveness of their infantry and artillery materiel. One attempted answer by the Germans was what is now commonly referred to as "hollow-charge" ammunition. As a result of this development, low-velocity weapons which were rapidly reaching obsolescence acquired new and startling deadliness. The development gave existing weapons an advantage whereby relatively heavy armor became vulnerable. Many other instances could be cited but the foregoing is particularly relevant to our discussion. It indicated that Ordnance, to keep ahead of the enemy, had to take advantage of everything we could learn which resulted from the enemy's skill in research and development.

Ordnance Technical Intelligence was organized early in the present war. It was staffed with officer and civilian personnel especially selected and trained in ordnance materiel, both foreign and domestic. The contributions of this Technical Intelligence may be summarized as follows:

It presented technical data on foreign materiel—which might be desirable for adoption in American Ordnance—to personnel charged with development of our materiel.

It kept American engineers constantly advised of the trends in foreign materiel.

It initiated and coordinated the examination and testing of enemy ordnance materiel in arsenals, laboratories, proving grounds, and in other technical agencies, both governmental and nongovernmental.

It disseminated technical information on enemy materiel from all known sources when such information pertained to the Ordnance Department's mission.

It maintained up-to-date records on enemy ordnance materiel and files for reference purposes, thus providing Ordnance engineers with extremely valuable assistance.

In view of the magnitude of the problem, the Foreign Materiel Branch was established at the Ordnance Research and Development Center, Aberdeen Proving Ground, Maryland. Enemy Equipment Intelligence Service teams in every theater of war shipped specimens of foreign materiel to Aberdeen. Here the items were photographed, catalogued, and made available for most effective examination and for development testing when appropriate.

In the early part of the war, the War Department General Staff approved the sending of special Ordnance military observers to all combat areas to analyze enemy ordnance. This was accomplished by making preliminary technical reports at the point of recovery of the materiel,

and by shipping the captured item to Aberdeen for detailed analysis when appropriate. Several shipments of captured weapons were lost at sea. Accordingly, great stress was placed upon making reports and sending them in as soon as our personnel encountered the weapon.

This work did not stop with the ending of hostilities. Tremendous benefits could accrue from the thorough exploitation of enemy research, development, and manufacturing facilities. Accordingly, the intelligence exploitation of the enemy was vigorously prosecuted. As V-E Day approached the Ordnance Department sent technical specialists from this country to Europe to provide the highest degree of skill in the investigation of German industrial and scientific facilities. Much has been written of the fine work done by Ordnance Intelligence representatives, both military and civilian, in all theaters of war. We sought the best technical talent in America for this important task. As a consequence, outstanding members of the best scientific institutions, universities, industrial research laboratories, and manufacturing firms in this country were made available and accomplished their mission against all handicaps.

Ordnance Intelligence personnel went to the front lines, worked with combat troops, advanced with them, and suffered the same hardships as frontline soldiers. They accompanied air shipments of captured Japanese rockets from Manila to Aberdeen. They took the shelter halves which form the American Army's "pup tent," rigged them as sails on landing boats, and proceeded upstream 20 miles beyond our advanced outpost in the New Guinea jungles to recover a newly developed Japanese artillery piece. They demonstrated in firings witnessed by our own troops just how effective certain enemy equipment really was. They likewise showed that certain pieces of enemy equipment, of which our troops had a psychological dread, were not what they were assumed to be. They found that many so-called technical advances of the enemy were, in reality, not advantages but industrial necessities to which they had been driven by shortages of critical materials. In many cases, enemy materiel believed to have these so-called advantages was not nearly as effective as their American counterparts.

Most of the new types of enemy materiel located were generally found in the front lines or so far forward that it was impossible, often, for long periods of time, to recover them for shipment to this country. Other types never reached the stage of a combat trial and were recovered in enemy laboratories and proving grounds after the war ended.

The information gained by the Ordnance technical investigators who went to Europe after V-E Day for the exploitation of German ordnance knowledge and technology is being made available through the Department of Commerce to American science and industry.

Ballistics

Ballistic research and instrumentation for the army is one of the functions of the Research and Development Service of the Ordnance Department. The Ballistic Research Laboratory at the Ordnance Research and Development Center was the facility which conducted the investigations in this highly technical field. Outstanding scientists and engineers were engaged at this laboratory and gave great aid in the research required for the development of new weapons used in winning the war.

The improvement of existing weapons of war and the development of new and revolutionary ones have their bases in ballistics, the science dealing broadly and fundamentally with the hurling of projectiles and missiles. Ballistics is divided into three categories: Interior, covering the phenomena surrounding setting the projectile in motion; exterior, dealing with the forces acting on the projectile in air; and terminal, involving the damaging effect of the projectile at the target—fragmentation, penetration, blast, shock. In the case of jet- and rocket-propelled projectiles, the interior and exterior ballistic phenomena occur simultaneously for a time and are not so clearly defined as those of the conventional gun-ammunition combination.

Continuous and far-reaching research in ballistics was necessary so our weapons might equal or exceed in performance those of our enemies. It entailed investigations by both empirical and theoretical methods, of the phenomena occurring in all phases of ballistics, so that new and more complete knowledge would contribute to a better understanding of the problems. It required the immediate exploitation of new developments, as they occurred, in the basic sciences underlying ballistics—physics, chemistry, mathematics—and their application to research leading to the improvement of weapons and, more important, to the development of new ones based on new and revolutionary principles.

Ballistics is a highly specialized science. The Ordnance Department had sole responsibility for this field in the Army. Likewise, the instrumentation and facilities involved in ballistic measurements and tests are peculiar to this work. Therefore, in accordance with long-established policy, the Ballistic Research Laboratory is maintained at the Ordnance Research and Development Center, Aberdeen Proving Ground. This facility, under the direction of the Ballistic Branch of the Research and Materials Division, Research and Development Service, carries out the policy stated above by maintaining a staff of trained, career scientists who conduct basic research in ballistics, carry our technical research in the application of existing knowledge to current problems, and provide a cadre of trained personnel for the expansion of activities in wartime. The location of the laboratory at Aberdeen Proving Ground was essential in order that use might be made of the extensive Ordnance test facilities which are available nowhere else in this country.

The centering of ballistic research in the Ballistic Research Laboratory did not preclude the enlistment, through contracts, of the aid of other scientific institutions on the theoretical or instrumentation problems which did not require extensive ballistic experience or facilities. This method of accomplishing research was profitable in the past and will be used in the future.

Bombing and Firing Tables

Every bomb and every gun projectile combination and every rocket required a table for its use. All ground and aircraft bombing and rocket tables for the Army Ground and Air Forces were prepared by the Ordnance Department. An average of 60 firing tables was completed each month of the war, involving approximately 1,000,000 computer man-hours per year. The tables could not have been produced without the use of computing devices in addition to the large number of people working as computers. The number of new tables reflected the ever-current changes ,in this war brought about by scientific skill and improved production facilities. Every effort was made to refine the technique used in the compilation of these tables and in the development of new, improved, and swifter methods of placing these essential tables in the hands of the using services.

ENIAC (Electronic Computing Device)

The ENIAC (Electronic Numerical Integrator and Computer), developed for the Ordnance Department by the Moore School of Electrical Engineering of the University of Pennsylvania, is a large-scale electronic computing machine, 500 times faster than any other machine in existence. It is the most intricate and complex electronic device in the world, requiring for its operation 18,000 electronic tubes (compared with 10 tubes in an average radio set, less than 1,000 in a B29 super fortress). Being a general-purpose machine, ENIAC can handle almost any mathematical problem, from the simplest to the most abtruse. It will perform more than one million additions or subtractions of ten-figure numbers in five minutes, or, if used to complete capacity, more than ten million. It automatically transfers numbers from one part of the machine to the other, so that only final results of an extensive problem need be printed. The full advantage of the high-speed electronic computation is thus gained, permitting the analysis of physical problems

An over-all view of ENIAC, showing machine in process of being prepared to solve a hychodynamical problem.

heretofore considered impractical to compute. A problem in ballistics which now requires 25 man-months of expert computers' time can be computed in two hours on this machine.

The ENIAC will be a valuable addition to the Ballistics Research Laboratory of the Army Ordnance Department at Aberdeen Proving Ground, where it is to be moved as soon as the annex to house it is completed.

Supersonic Wind Tunnel

The supersonic wind tunnel, the only one of its kind in this country, consists of a Bomb Tunnel and a Supersonic Ballistic Tunnel. The Bomb Tunnel was completed during the war and fur-

nished important areodynamic information on bombs, projectiles, and other types of missiles. This tunnel, which utilizes a number of fixed throats for control of air speed, operates at fluid velocities of from Mach numbers (the ratio of the air stream velocity to the velocity of sound) 0.1 to 0.9, and at 1.3 and 1.7. When a new throat now under construction is installed it will be possible to achieve a velocity of Mach number 4.0 in this tunnel. The gap between Mach numbers 0.9 and 1.1 cannot be investigated in wind tunnels, and the means of surmounting this gap is discussed under the text on the Aerodynamic Spark Range. The Supersonic Ballistic Tunnel, which is nearly completed, will employ a flexible throat that may be shaped by push button-con-

A view of the Bomb Tunnel Laboratory at Aberdeen Proving Ground, showing the working section of the supersonic tunnel, a part of the Schlieren photography apparatus, controls, and weighing mechanisms for measuring the forces and moments acting on the models.

trolled machinery to give any desired wind velocity between Mach numbers 0.1 and 0.9 and between Mach numbers 1.1 and 4.5. Inability during the war to install the flexible throat because of delays incident to its design and construction made the more easily and quickly built Bomb Tunnel an invaluable aid to war-time ballistic research. Schlieren photographs are taken of models tested under all conditions which may be obtained in the wind tunnels. From these photographs the pressure distribution and flow of air can be inferred. Among other valuable results, a polar coordinate graph of sighting forces versus angle of yaw is produced.

Aerodynamic Spark Range

It happens that no tunnel whatsoever can yield all necessary measurements in the vicinity of the velocity of sound, because the shock waves are reflected at unfavorable angles in this range of measurements. In view of this fact, an aerodynamic spark range 100 yards long was constructed. In addition to covering the "blind spot in the tunnel," that range also served the useful purpose of calibrating the supersonic tunnel. The areodynamics range gave very precise results. It differs from the supersonic tunnel in that, in the tunnel, the projectile is held stationary and the air ("compressible fluid") is forced past the projectile, and in the aerodynamic range the projectile is forced through the air and its behavior is recorded by extremely swift-acting electronic and photographic means. A miniature missile is fired from a gun down the darkened range in such a way that it passes 19 recording stations. As the projectile flashes by the stations,

Aerodynamic Spark Range at Aberdeen Proving Ground.

it triggers photographs of itself at each station, taking two photographs, one in the horizontal and one in the vertical planes. Illumination for

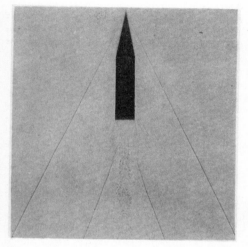

Conical-headed projectile in flight. Representative spark photo.

the photograph is supplied by a spark of high intensity which lasts about 1/100,000 second. The times of the sparks are recorded by counter chronographs which count in millionths of a second. From the recordings, the drag of the projectile, its deceleration, orientation in space, yaw, mutations, and various other associated properties are inferred. Since the range is large compared with the area of disturbance about the projectile, the projectile behaves as though it were in infinite space. The limitation imposed by the wall of the supersonic wind tunnel is overcome.

Ballistic Service Teams

It became clear in the war that there was great need for Ordnance teams in the field capable of furnishing technical service and advice to the field commanders with a minimum of delay. Ballistic teams, which were self-sufficient operating units, were trained by the Ballistic Research Laboratory. A complete team was composed of two officers and eleven enlisted men. They had their own power supply, maintenance and repair

Complete field calibration team and equipment. These teams assured the accuracy of American artillery by visiting each battery in the field and calibrating each gun or howitzer.

facilities, and transportation. The instruments used in obtaining velocities for calibration were "sky screens" and chronograph. A "sky screen" consists of a telescopic lens system and a photo-electric cell inclosed in a tube. The photoelectric cell detects the change in sky light when a projectile enters the atmospheric region intercepted by the telescope. This change in light is converted by the photoelectric cell into an electrical impulse which is amplified and used to trigger the chronograph. The chronographs are of the counter-chronograph type. They measure the time interval between the passage of the projectile over the first and second "sky screens" in units of 1/100,000 of a second. The rapidity with which this kind of behind-the-line calibration of guns was done is shown by the fact that one of the teams calibrated a full battalion (12 guns) of 155-mm guns, M1, in a single day. Two batteries of artillery were calibrated in battle position in one day while observing many precautions of camouflage, concealment, and repeated travel across the field to instruments; in this instance, no enemy counter-battery fire was received during calibration. A considerable amount of ammunition was segregated and classified, thus making possible more accurate fire by the artillerymen.

Blast Measurement and Penetration Determinations

Blast measuring instruments were developed and their use has made possible the measurement of blast and impulse of explosives. The relative blast efficiencies of explosives were swiftly and accurately determined and their relative effectiveness in warfare immediately evaluated. Continuous research and tests covering the phenomena of blast, fragmentation, and armor and concrete penetration were made. Three volumes covering Terminal Ballistics were prepared and issued to the interested services.

Ballistic Camera

The ballistic camera system was developed to determine more accurately the position of an airplane in space for data required for preparation of bombing tables. The ballistic camera became the fundamental precision device for locating points in space, especially at altitudes from 10,000 to 40,000 feet. A pair of cameras, one at each end of a fixed known baseline, and, in principle, the commonplace method of triangulation are employed. The accuracy obtainable is limited by the accuracy of plate-measurement, the accuracy of the level-corrections, the accuracy of the azimuth-setting, and, of course, the length of the baseline. In regular operation points at 35,000 feet altitude are located with total errors of only a few feet horizontally, and perhaps five times as much vertically. The residuals for individual stars on a starplate come appreciably better than this, sometimes averaging only five seconds of arc, but the precision with which the camera-orientation can be repeated, as well as other factors involved in the change from night to day, limits the operating accuracy. The mobile unit was used at Muroc Lake in the Stratosphere Bombing Program and gave valuable information on the behavior of bombs dropped from high altitudes (37,000 feet). These important data were used in design of bombs for the Air Forces.

Flash X-ray Apparatus

The ultra-high-speed X-ray equipment consists of a special X-ray tube, a surge generator, an internal timer, and a suitable high-voltage power source. With this equipment, surge potentials from 180 to 360 kilovolts are applied to the X-ray tube. The tube is a special cold cathode type made of thick glass and sealed off and made to be used in any position. The entire equipment is portable, and flash radiographs have been made in field tests of guns as large as the 105-mm, as well as in the laboratory. The surge generator, essentially a Marx circuit, functions when a 10 kilovolt surge is applied to one of the spark gaps in the circuit. The duration of the X-ray burst obtained from this equipment is approximately 1.5 microseconds. Thus, a projectile or particle moving with a velocity of 1,000 meters per second (3,300 f./s.) would move only 1.5-mm during the time the radiograph is made. The small blurring of the X-ray image obtained

A series of flash radiographs of 20-mm high-explosive-loaded shell immediately after static detonation. These remarkable radio-graphs indicate how fragments of high-explosive shell are studied in the laboratory, to insure that the maximum killing power is obtained on the battlefield. Note expansion of projectile prior to fragmentation.

from the motion of particles with velocities not greater than 1,000 meters per second is generally negligible in comparison with the effects of other factors which decrease the definition of the radiograph. These factors are the scattering of X-rays passing through blast shielding, the necessity of using X-ray intensifying screens, and the relatively large focal spot in the X-ray source. This flash X-ray apparatus was used during the war in many ways at the Ballistic Research Laboratory, Aberdeen Proving Ground. Some of these applications are: (1) Study of the motion of the projectile inside small guns; (2) study of projectiles just emerging from the muzzle of guns (37-mm to 105-mm); (3) burning rocket propellants; (4) behavior of high-explosive charges during detonation; (5) fragmentation produced by metal encased high-explosive charges; and (6) studies of fuze mechanism during functioning.

Chapter VIII

CONCLUSION

Chapter VIII

CONCLUSION

The mission of the Ordnance Department remained practically unchanged throughout the war. However, the number of weapons required in the various categories steadily increased as new weapons were needed to meet special situations—for example, jungle and cave warfare in the Pacific. The principal addition was the transfer in August 1942, from the Office of the Quartermaster General to the Ordnance Department, of the responsibility for motor transportation. This wise decision gave to Ordnance the entire army automotive problem. It will be beneficial in the postwar period, in that motor and other automotive components required for wheeled vehicles can be incorporated in the designs for track-laying vehicles, with a resulting over-all reduction in spare parts. The tasks of supplying spare parts required for automotive vehicles during the war were staggering because of the number of types of vehicles involved and our long lines of communication.

Though limited by funds, the preparations made by the Ordnance Department for the emergency between the wars were invaluable. The research and development conducted from 1920 permitted the Department in 1940 to go into immediate production of a large number of vital ordnance weapons for which the Department had drawings and specifications. This development of weapons and the organization for procurement, or "industrial mobilization," saved at least one year's time in the production of ordnance equipment. It is quite possible that if the production of ordnance weapons in the early months of the war had been delayed, serious consequences, such as the loss of the African continent might have resulted.

The policy adopted in 1940 of forming a partnership with American science and industry in the design and development of ordnance equipment was probably the only solution to this problem which could have been successful. By utilizing the vast reservoir of scientific and engineering talent, our university and commercial laboratories, and the research and engineering facilities of the country, the largest research and development program of all times was successfully achieved. Under this policy, a strong centralized control was maintained at Washington. No manufacturer aimlessly pursued research and development; on the contrary, he was informed as to what was wanted and his efforts were directed and coordinated along the lines not only desired by the Ordnance Department but approved by the combat services and the War Department.

The Ordnance Technical Committee, which was established in 1919, was successful in keeping the huge research and development program coordinated with all the agencies of the War Department, the Marine Corps, the Navy Department, and the Allied nations. This committee acted to approve each research and development project initiated, to approve new weapons for quantity production or, to use the military term, to "approve standardization" of every item manufactured.

The Ordnance system of utilizing a large number of research and engineering advisory committees to work on development programs over

309

wide fields proved sound. The members served on these advisory committees and patriotically contributed their time to this activity. The Ordnance Advisory Committee system was one of the cornerstones in the solution of research and development problems throughout the war.

The principal change made in the organization of the Ordnance Department during the war was to separate research and development from procurement functions. The Research and Development Service (then known as the Technical Division) was given full authority in June 1942 over all Ordnance Department research and development activities. This responsibility carried with it funds and the authority to make contracts and carry each item from conception through to approval by the using services and standardization by the Ordnance Technical Committee. This change accelerated the Ordnance Department's development program so greatly as nearly to double its effectiveness.

Accomplishments

The Science-Industry-Ordnance team produced results far beyond our expectations. At the peak, some 1,500 facilities were working on Ordnance research and development projects, not to count the numerous subcontractors who were called in by the prime contractors to work on some phases of their projects. During the last three years of the war, more than 1,000 major weapons and items of equipment were conceived, developed, designed, tested, standardized, and placed in quantity production. New weapons and items of equipment were approved at a rate of approximately 25 per month. By V.-J. Day, for example, not a single armored fighting vehicle of a design older than 1940 was under production. In fact, of the 1,860 major items of ordnance, not more than 350 were older in design than 1940. The speed with which new weapons were developed made the problem of introduction and effective exploitation in combat difficult.

During the last two years of the war, a system of sending a new weapon directly to the combat theater with demonstration teams was evolved. If the weapon proved to be of sufficient value compared with existing ones to warrant introduction, requisitions for the new weapons were sent back to Ordnance, and standardization and future production were then based on these requirements as generated in the field.

The following letter from Dwight D. Eisenhower, Commanding General, E.T.O., 18 January 1945, is significant:

"Battlefield reports from every front in the European Theater of Operations continue to tell of the splendid quality of our weapons and ammunition. What we need is more of both, as well as men, to finish the job.

"Last summer, the enemy was defeated in Normandy by our firepower and the team work of our splendid soldiers at their rifles, mortars, machine guns, artillery, in their tanks and tank destroyers. The enemy then retreated 500 miles, leaving behind much equipment in order to reach temporary security in his fixed defenses.

"The mobility of our Ordnance enabled us to exploit our first successes in the drive across France, into Belgium, and Germany. Moreover, throughout the war there has been a noticeable and steady improvement in the quality of many of our weapons and equipment. Such improvement is mandatory always; the alternative is stagnation and eventual disaster.

"The effectiveness of our Ordnance is partly due to simplicity in design and partly to the range of U.S. equipment which provides a weapon for every target. The enemy's battle losses have been far greater than ours. In pieces of artillery, the enemy has lost eight to our one. We have knocked out twice as many tanks as we have lost.

"We have a general superiority in quality and quantity of our Ordnance, a superiority that must always be maintained."

Postwar Plans

It would be impossible to have gone through this greatest of all programs for research and development—upon which the Ordnance Department based the expenditure of nearly 50 billion dollars for ordnance equipment for our armies and our Allies—without having gained experience and ideas as to how these activities should be conducted in the future. The plans for the future are based upon the system used during the war, geared to match the appropriations to be received from the Congress. The policy of the Department is not to build Ordnance laboratories, except for fields not ordinarily covered by other scientific and commercial agencies. For example, the Department maintains at Aberdeen Proving Ground strong personnel and facilities for research in interior and exterior ballistics. A part of this laboratory is the supersonic wind tunnel for experimentation at super velocities. Ordnance maintains at its arsenals laboratories for working on problems peculiar to weapons and equipment.

It is hoped to secure from Congress adequate funds each year to permit Ordnance research and development over its wide field. It is planned to use approximately one-third of these funds at Ordnance arsenals, laboratories, and proving grounds, and the remaining two-thirds for research and development contracts placed with qualified educational institutions, scientific laboratories, and manufacturers having strong research and development organizations and laboratory facilities. It is expected in this manner to present Ordnance problems requiring solution to selected scientific and engineering personnel of the country, and thus to maintain in peace the interest of those who will be required to produce the weapons should another emergency arise.

We were fortunate in this war that time was available to develop and produce the necessary modern weapons. It can be readily imagined that, because of new technological developments, a future emergency, if it comes, may arrive with such great suddenness that time might not be available for putting carefully laid plans into execution. It will be necessary during peace not only to formulate these plans and designs, but very largely to execute them and be prepared to strike immediately. In addition to resisting a sudden, initial attack, we must be prepared to mobilize quickly again the entire industrial capacity of the nation, with its manpower. Our plans must encompass these new and important factors which, taken together, will give a different pattern to a war emergency of the future.

INDEX

(Numbered items, such as "¼-ton," "75-mm," etc., are grouped together before alphabetical entries)

¼-ton truck, 258-260; amphibian, 280, 281
1st Army, VII Corps, 252
1st Infantry Div., 187
1st Tank Destroyer Brigade, 247
1½-ton truck, 261
2.36″ rocket, H.E.A.T., 178, 179
2½-ton truck, 262-266; amphibian, 282, 283
3″ gun, antitank, 123
3″ gun, antiaircraft, 148, 149
3″ gun, in tank, 212, 213
3″ gun motor carriage, 238, 239
3.25″ target rocket, 180, 181
3rd Armored Div., 218, 252
3rd Army, 21
4.5″ gun, 125, 126
4.5″ rocket, 182-194
4th Armored Div., 36
5th Army, Mediterranean Theater, 24
7.2″ rocket, 193
7th Air Force, 188
7th Army, Hq., E.T.O., 24
8″ gun, 134-137
8″ gun motor carriage, 252, 256, 257
8″ howitzer, 132, 133
IX Tactical Air Command, 40
12th Air Force, 188
12th Army Group, 158
13-ton tractor, 275-277
14th A.A. Command, 158
17th Airborne Div., 54
18-ton tractor, 271-274
18th F.A. Bn., 186
20-mm automatic gun, 62, 63; ammunition, 65; feed mechanism, 64
32nd Armored Reg., Co. "I," 218
37-mm gun, antiaircraft, 140-142
37-mm gun, antitank, 122
37-mm gun, automatic, 66, 67
37-mm gun, in tank, 202, 207, 228
37th Infantry Div., 171
38-ton tractor, 278-281

40-mm gun, automatic A.A. (Bofors), 146, 147
40-mm gun, twin A.A., 144, 145
57-mm recoilless rifle, 50-55
60-mm mortar, 160-163
75-mm gun, 68-70
75-mm gun, in tank, 202, 207, 229, 230
75-mm gun mount, 68
75-mm pack howitzer, 114-117
75-mm recoilless rifle, 50-55
76-mm gun, in tank, 217, 231
76-mm gun motor carriage, 244-247
81-mm mortar, 164-167
90-mm gun, A.A., 150-153
90-mm gun, in tank, 213, 217, 230
90-mm gun motor carriage, 240-243
105-mm howitzer, 118, 119, 120, 121, 194
105-mm howitzer motor carriage, 234-237
120-mm gun, A.A., 154, 155
150-mm mortar, 168-169
155-mm gun, 128-131
155-mm gun motor carriage, 248-255
155-mm howitzer, 124-127
155-mm mortar, 170-171
210-mm rocket, 195
240-mm howitzer, 136-139
240-mm howitzer motor carriage, 252, 255
443rd Sep. C.A. Bn. (A.A.), 141
507th Parachute Inf. Reg., 54
513th Parachute Inf. Reg., 54
603rd Tank Destroyer Bn., 247
702nd Tank Destroyer Bn., 242
773rd Tank Destroyer Bn., 239
776th Tank Destroyer Bn., 242, 243
803rd Tank Destroyer Bn., 239, 243
893rd Tank Destroyer Bn., Co. "B," 89, 90
914-mm mortar, 172-174

AERODYNAMIC spark range, 302, 303
Aircraft cannon, 61-70; 20-mm, 62-65; 37-mm, 66, 67; 75-mm, 68-70
Aircraft type machine gun, 38-40

American Society of Automotive Engineers, 199

American Welding Society, 294

Ammunition, 73-110; 20-mm gun, 65; 37-mm antitank gun, 122; 105-mm howitzer, 119; mortar, 159-174

Ammunition, small arms, 42-46; packaging, 45, 46; performance chart, 43

Amphibian trucks, 282-285

Antiaircraft artillery, 140-158; fire control, 155-158

Antiaircraft machine gun, 34-37; mount, 41

Antitank gun: 3″, 123; 37-mm, 122

Armor, 294, 295; body, 56; motorized, 286, 287

Armor-piercing ammunition, 81-83, 88-90, 295

Arsenals, manufacturing, 8

Artillery, antiaircraft, 140-158; heavy, 128-139; light, 113-123; medium, 124-127; transportation of, 267-280

Artillery fire control, 139; antiaircraft, 155-158

BABY Long Tom, 152

Ballistic camera, 304

Ballistic Service Teams, 303, 304

Ballistic tunnel, 301, 302

Ballistics, 299-306

BAR (rifle), 32

Bastogne, 36

Battle of the Bulge, 36, 139

Bazooka, 47-49, 178, 179

Blast measurement, 304

Bofors gun, 146, 147

Bomb tunnel, 301, 302

Bombing tables, 299, 300

Bombs, 102-105; antiricochet attachments, 107; chemical, 108; cluster adapters, 103, 105, 106; fragmentation, 105; fuzes, 108-110; parachute, 106, 107; rocket-propelled, 194; semi-armor-piercing, 108

Browning automatic rifle, cal. .30 (BAR), 32

Browning machine gun: cal. .30, 27, 33; cal. .50, 34-40; cal. .50, aircraft type, 38-40; cal. .50, ground type, 34-37; water-cooled, 33, 34, 36

CALIBRATION of guns, 303, 304

Camera, ballistic, 304

Cannon, antiaircraft, 61-70; 20-mm, 62-65; 37-mm, 66, 67; 75-mm, 68-70

Carbine, 22-24

Cargo carrier, 250, 288, 289

Carriages, gun, 124-126, 128-131, 134, 135; antiaircraft, 140; antitank, 123

Carriage, gun motor, 144, 145, 234-257; heavy, 253-257

Carriage, howitzer, 118-121, 124-126, 132, 133, 138, 139

Carriage, howitzer motor, 234-237, 252, 255

Carriage, howitzer, pack, 114-117

Cartridges, 42; armor-piercing and incendiary, 44, 45

Center Task Forces, 21

Chronograph, 304

Colt automatic pistol, cal. .45, 26

Concrete-piercing projectile, 81-83, 251

DEMOLITION rocket, 193

DUKW, 284, 285

ENIAC, 300, 301

Eisenhower, Gen. Dwight D., 21; quoted, 310

Electrode, ferritic, 295

Electronic computing device, 300, 301

Electronic power control, 140, 143, 155

Explosives, 73-76

FEED mechanism, 20-mm gun, 64

Fire control: A.A. artillery, 140, 155-158; artillery, 139, 140

Firing tables, 299, 300

Flares, 100-102

Flash reducers, 79-81

Flashless-smokeless propellants, 78, 79

Fuels and lubricants, 295-297

Fuzes: artillery, 83-85; bomb, 108-110; concrete-piercing, 130; radio proximity (V.T.), 85-88; rocket, 189, 190

GAGES, 12

Garand rifle, 16-18; with grenade launcher, 19-21

General Grant tank, 200-202, 207

General Pershing tank, 214-218

General Sherman tank, 203-209, 212, 213, 218; with swimming device, 232, 233

Giles, Major Gen. Barney, quoted, 40

Grenades, 90, 91; hand, 91, 92; launcher, 19-21; rifle, 92, 93

Ground type machine gun, 34-37

Gun, 3″ antiaircraft, 148, 149

Gun, 3″ antitank, 123

Gun, 3", in tank, 212, 213
Gun, 3", motor carriage, 238, 239
Gun, 4.5", 125, 126
Gun, 8", 134-137
Gun, 8", motor carriage, 252, 256, 257
Gun, 20-mm automatic, 62, 63; ammunition, 65; feed mechanism, 64
Gun, 37-mm antiaircraft, 140-142
Gun, 37-mm antitank, 122
Gun, 37-mm automatic, 66, 67
Gun, 37-mm, in tank, 202, 207, 228
Gun, 40-mm automatic antiaircraft (Bofors), 146, 147
Gun, 40-mm twin antiaircraft, 144, 145
Gun, 75-mm, 68-70; mount, 68
Gun, 75-mm, in tank, 202, 207, 229, 230
Gun, 76-mm, in tank, 217, 231
Gun, 76-mm, motor carriage, 244-247
Gun, 90-mm antiaircraft, 150-153
Gun, 90-mm, in tank, 213, 217, 230
Gun, 90-mm, motor carriage, 240-243
Gun, 120-mm antiaircraft, 154, 155
Gun, 155-mm antiaircraft, 128-131
Gun, 155-mm, motor carriage, 248-255
Gun calibration, 303, 304
Gun motor carriage, 144, 145, 234-257
Gun mount, see Mount.

HEAVY artillery, 128-139
Helmet, 56
High-speed tractor, 271-281
Honey (tank), 228
Howitzer, 8", 132, 133
Howitzer, 75-mm pack, 114-117
Howitzer, 105-mm, 118-121, 194; motor carriage, 234-237
Howitzer, 155-mm, 124-127
Howitzer, 240-mm, 136-139; development, 11, 12; motor carriage, 252, 255

ILLUMINATING projectiles, 90
Integration Committees, see Ordnance Engineering Advisory Committee.
Intelligence, technical, 297-299

JEEP, 258-260

LAUNCHER, grenade, 19-21

Launcher, rocket, 47-49, 177-195; 4.5" H.E., 184-191; clustered, 185, 186; multiple 7.2", 192, 193; multiple-tube, 187, 188; zero-rail, 188
Lewis, Major Gen., quoted, 137
Light artillery, 113-123
Little David, 172-174
Long Tom, 130, 272
Lubricants, 295-297

M1 CARBINE, 22-24
M1 carriage, 8" howitzer, 132, 133
M1 carriage, 75-mm pack howitzer, 114
M1 carriage, 155-mm gun, 128-131
M1 carriage, 155-mm howitzer and 4.5" gun, 124-126
M1 carriage, 240-mm howitzer, 138, 139
M1 gun, 4.5", 125, 126
M1 gun, 8", 134-137
M1 gun, 40-mm, 144-147
M1 howitzer, 8", 132, 133
M1 howitzer, 155-mm, 124-127
M1 howitzer, 240-mm, 136-139
M1 mortar, 81-mm, 164-167
M1 mount, 120-mm A.A. gun, 154, 155
M1 rifle, 16-18; with grenade launcher, 19-21
M1A1 gun, 155-mm, 128-131
M1A1 howitzer, 75-mm pack, 114-117
M1A1 mount, 90-mm A.A. gun, 150-153
M1A2 gun, 37-mm, 140-142
M1E4 gun, tank, 76-mm, 231
M2 automatic gun, 20-mm, 63
M2 Browning machine gun, 34-40
M2 carbine, 24
M2 carriage, 8" gun, 134, 135
M2 carriage, 105-mm howitzer, 118, 119
M2 rocket, 3.25", target, 180, 181
M2A1 howitzer, 105-mm, 118, 119
M2A2 mount, 3" A.A. gun, 148, 149
M3 automatic gun, 20-mm, 62, 63
M3 Browning machine gun, 40
M3 gun, 3" antiaircraft, 148, 149
M3 howitzer, 105-mm, 120, 121
M3 submachine gun, 30, 31
M3 tank, light, 219-221, 228
M3 tank, medium (Gen. Grant), 200-202, 207
M3A1 carriage, 37-mm gun, 140
M3A1 carriage, 105-mm howitzer, 120, 121
M3A1 gun, 37-mm antitank, 122
M4 automatic gun, 37-mm, 66, 67

M4 automatic gun, 75-mm, 68-70
M4 tank, medium (Gen. Sherman), 186, 203-209, 212, 213, 218; with swimming device, 232, 233
M4 tractor, 18-ton high-speed, 271-274
M5 gun, 3″ antitank, 123
M5 tank, light, 222-224, 229
M5 tractor, 13-ton high-speed, 275-277
M6 carriage, 3″ gun, 123
M6 mount, 75-mm gun, 68
M6 tank, heavy, 210-213, 217
M6 tractor, 38-ton high-speed, 278-281
M6A3 rocket, 2.36″ H.E.A.T., 178, 179
M7 grenade launcher, 19-21
M7 motor carriage, 105-mm howitzer, 234-237
M8 armored car, 286, 287
M8 carriage, 75-mm pack howitzer, 115-117
M8 rocket, 182, 185, 186, 188, 190
M9 automatic gun, 37-mm, 67
M10 motor carriage, 3″ gun, 238, 239
M10 rocket launcher, 185
M12 motor carriage, 155-mm gun, 248-252
M15 mount, 37-mm A.A. gun, 141
M15 semitrailer, 269
M16 rocket, 183, 186, 190
M17 rocket launcher, multiple 7.2″, 192, 193
M18 motor carriage, 76-mm gun, 244-247
M18 recoilless rifle, 57-mm, 50-55
M19 mortar, 60-mm, 160-162
M19 motor carriage, twin 40-mm gun, 144, 145
M20 recoilless rifle, 75-mm, 50-55
M24 tank, light, 69, 225-227, 229
M25 (T21) rocket, 7.2″, 193
M25 tank transporter, 269
M26 motor carriage: 8″ gun, 252; 240-mm howitzer, 252
M26 tank, heavy (Gen. Pershing), 214-218
M26 tractor truck, 267, 268
M29 cargo carrier, 288, 289
M30 cargo carrier, 250
M36 motor carriage, 90-mm gun, 240-243
M40 motor carriage, 155-mm gun, 252-255
M45 mount, multiple cal. .50 machine gun, 143
M63 mount, 41
M1903A4 rifle, 25
M1911A1 pistol, 26
M1919A6 Browning machine gun, 27
M1928A1 Thompson submachine gun, 29
MacArthur, Gen. Douglas, quoted, 18

Machine gun: aircraft type, 38-40, 61, 70; antiaircraft, 34-37, mount, 41; Browning, 27, 33-40; cal. .30, 27, 33; cal. .50, 34-40, 141, 142, 143, with 37-mm A.A. gun, 141; ground type, 34-37; heavy barrel, 35-37; water-cooled, 33, 34, 36
Machine gun mounts: M63, 41; tree, 28
Materials and processes, 293-295
Maxson turret, 143
Medium artillery, 124-127
Miley, Major Gen., 54
Mine exploder, 96, 97
Mines: antipersonnel, 94, 95; antitank, 93, 94
Mortars, 159-174; 60-mm, 160-163; 81-mm, 164-167; 150-mm, 168-169; 155-mm, 170, 171; 914-mm (Little David), 172-174
Motor transport, 258-289, 309
Mount: 3″ A.A. gun, 148, 149; 37-mm A.A. gun, 141; 75-mm gun, 68; 90-mm A.A. gun, 150-153; 105-mm mortar, 168; 120-mm A.A. gun, 154, 155; antiaircraft machine gun, 41; multiple cal. .50 machine gun, 143; see also Carriage.
Multiple cal. .50 machine gun mount, 143
Multiple-tube rocket launcher, 187, 188

NATIONAL Defense Research Committee, 11, 295

OFFICE of Scientific Research and Development, 11, 295
Oils, see Fuels and Lubricants.
Ordnance Dept., 3-13; cooperation with industry, 8-12, 293-296, 309-311; organization, 6, 310; organization chart, 5; postwar plans, 310, 311; weapon development and testing, 293-306, 310
Ordnance Engineering Advisory Committees, 9, 10
Ordnance Research Advisory Committee, 10-12
Ordnance Technical Committee, 6, 8, 13, 309, 310
Ordnance Technical Intelligence, 297-299

PATTON, Gen. George S., quoted, 21, 209
Photoflash munitions, 100, 101
Pistol, automatic, cal. .45, 26
Priest (howitzer carriage), 237
Primers, 76-78, 79

Projectiles, illuminating, 90
Propellants, 76-78; flashless-smokeless, 78, 79
Pyrotechnics, 98-102

RADAR, 157
Recoilless rifles, 50-55; mount, 52
Research and development, 293-306, 309-311
Research and Development Service, 6, 7, 11, 310
Rifle: Browning automatic, 32; Garand, 16-18, with grenade launcher, 19-21; recoilless, 50-55; sniper's, 25; Springfield, 17
Rockets, 177-195; 2.36″, 178, 179; 4.5″, 182-191, 194; 7.2″, 193; 210-mm, 195; demolition, 193; fuzes, 189, 190; H.E., 182, 183, 185, 186, 188, 190; H.E.A.T., 178, 179; target, 3.25″, 180, 181
Rocket launchers, 47-49, 177-195; 4.5″ H.E. rocket, 184-191; clustered, 185, 186; multiple 4.5″, 184; multiple 7.2″, 192, 193; multiple-tube, 187, 188; zero-rail, 188
Rocket propulsion units, 194, 195

SEMITRAILER, 269
Shaped charges, 81-83
Signal and flare ammunition, 98-102
Sky screen, 304
Small-arms ammunition, 42-46; performance chart, 43
Sniper gun, 152
Sniper's rifle, 25
Specifications and standards, 293, 294
Springfield rifle, 17, 25
Standardization procedures, 12, 13
Stratosphere bombing program, 304
Submachine gun, cal. .45, 30, 31; Thompson, cal. .45, 29
Supersonic wind tunnel, 301, 302
Swimming devices, tank, 232, 233

T12 MOUNT, 105-mm mortar, 168
T13 mortar, 150-mm, 168-169
T22 rocket, 4.5″, 190, 194
T25 mortar, 155-mm, 170, 171

T26 tank, 217, 218
T27 rocket launcher, 185, 186
T34 rocket launcher, 186
T36 rocket launcher, 210-mm, 195
T47 rocket launcher, 189
T54 rocket, 4.5″, 189
T66 rocket launcher, 184
T92 motor carriage, 240-mm howitzer, 255
T93 motor carriage, 8″ gun, 256, 257
T100E3 tree mount, 28
Tank guns, 231
Tank transporters, 269, 270
Tanks, 199-233; and rockets, 192, 193; German, 218; heavy, 210-218; light, 199, 219-229; medium, 186, 199-209, 212, 213, 218; swimming devices, 232, 233
Target identification munitions, 101
Target rocket, 180, 181
Telescopic sight, 25
Testing, 293-306, 310
Thompson submachine gun, 29
Tractor truck, 267, 268
Tractors, 271-281
Tree mount, 28
Triple threat gun, 152
Trucks: ¼-ton, 258-260; 1½-ton, 261; 2½-ton, 262-266; amphibian, 282-285; tractor, 267, 268
Tunisian campaign, 39
Twin 40-mm A.A. gun motor carriage, 144, 145

V.T. FUZE, 85-88; on rockets, 190

WATER-COOLED machine gun, 33, 34, 36
Weapons; captured enemy, 297-299; development and testing, 11, 140, 293-306, 310
Weasel, 288, 289
Welding, 294, 295
Wind tunnel, supersonic, 301, 302

X-RAYS, ultra-high-speed, 304-306

ZERO-RAIL rocket launcher, 188